THE
PACKAGE DESIGN
BOOK
3

pentawards

THE PACKAGE DESIGN BOOK 3

TASCHEN

diamond

14

beverages

22

food

132

body

232

luxury

278

other markets

340

FOREWORD

Jean Jacques & Brigitte Evrard
Founders of Pentawards

For many of the world's packaging design professionals, the Pentawards are now seen as the most prestigious competition in the field, and a key event on any packaging designer's calendar. The success of the awards can be attributed not only to the competition itself, but above all to the remarkable quality of the designs presented each year.

The Pentawards international jury is composed of leading packaging design professionals as well as design managers from a number of large commercial brands: Suntory (Japan), BIC (USA), Procter & Gamble (Europe), GSK (Singapore), Kimberly-Clark (USA) and Aekyung (South Korea). Each year, over 1,500 packaging designs from around the globe are judged for their creativity, innovation and branding, and the most outstanding designs in each category are awarded Bronze, Silver, Gold and Platinum Pentawards. The design that manages to win over the entire jury and secure the most overall votes is awarded the highly coveted Diamond Pentaward.

This book features all the winning designs from 2013 and 2014, bringing you the best of what's going on in the global packaging design industry today. It is intended to be a valuable resource and a source of inspiration for anyone with an interest in packaging creation: students, designers, manufacturers, engineers, brands and consumers.

Aside from awarding prizes, the Pentawards' mission is the worldwide promotion of packaging design among companies, media, economic and political bodies, and the general public.

We hope you enjoy reading this guide to contemporary packaging design, and that it helps you to see the everyday products you buy in a brand new light of quality, creativity and innovation—the driving forces of our civilization.

Have fun exploring the world of packaging!

VORWORT

Jean Jacques & Brigitte Evrard
Gründer von Pentawards

Für Verpackungsdesign-Profis aus aller Welt sind die Pentawards mittlerweile der prestigeträchtigste Wettbewerb der Branche und somit ein zentrales Event im Kalender aller Verpackungsdesigner. Dass diese Preisverleihung derart erfolgreich ist, muss man nicht nur dem Wettbewerb selbst zuschreiben, sondern vor allem der bemerkenswerten Qualität der Designs, die jedes Jahr präsentiert werden.

Die internationale Jury der Pentawards setzt sich aus führenden Profis im Verpackungsdesign sowie Designmanagern verschiedener großer kommerzieller Marken zusammen: Suntory (Japan), BIC (USA), Procter & Gamble (Europa), GSK (Singapur), Kimberly-Clark (USA), Aekyung (Südkorea). In jedem Fahr werden 1.500 Verpackungsdesigns aus der ganzen Welt hinsichtlich Kreativität, Innovation und Branding beurteilt. Für jede Kategorie werden besonders herausragende Designs mit Pentawards in Bronze, Silber, Gold und Platin gewürdigt. Gelingt es einem Design, die gesamte Jury für sich einzunehmen und sich in der Schlussabstimmung die meisten Stimmen zu sichern, bekommt es den heiß begehrten Diamond Pentaward verliehen.

In diesem Buch werden alle Preisträger der Jahre 2013 und 2014 vorgestellt. So bekommen Sie das Beste dessen, was aktuell in der Branche des globalen Verpackungsdesigns passiert. Gedacht ist dieses Werk als wertvolle Ressource und Inspirationsquelle für alle, die sich für Schöpfungen des Verpackungsdesigns interessieren: für Studierende, Designer, Hersteller, Ingenieure, Marken und Verbraucher.

Neben der Verleihung der Preise betrachten es die Pentawards als ihre Mission, weltweit bei Firmen, Medien, ökonomischen und politischen Institutionen sowie der allgemeinen Öffentlichkeit auf das Verpackungsdesign aufmerksam zu machen und es zu fördern.

Wir hoffen, dass Sie diesen Leitfaden des zeitgenössischen Verpackungsdesigns gerne studieren und dass er Ihnen hilft, die alltäglich von Ihnen gekauften Produkte im neuen Licht der Qualität, Kreativität und Innovation zu sehen – den treibenden Kräften unserer Zivilisation!

Viel Spaß beim Erkunden der Welt der Verpackungen!

PRÉFACE

Jean Jacques & Brigitte Evrard
Fondateurs des Pentawards

Pour beaucoup de professionnels du design de packaging, les Pentawards sont devenus la référence mondiale, la compétition à laquelle il faut participer. Ce succès n'est pas seulement dû à la compétition elle-même, mais surtout à la qualité remarquable des créations qui y sont présentées chaque année.

Le jury international des Pentawards est composé pour moitié de noms réputés du design de packaging et pour l'autre de responsables design de grandes marques : Suntory (Japon), BIC (États-Unis), Procter & Gamble (Europe), GSK (Singapour), Kimberly-Clark (États-Unis), Aekyung (Corée du Sud). Chaque année, plus de 1 500 emballages, provenant des quatre coins du monde, sont jugés pour leur créativité, leur innovation, leur pertinence marketing ; les plus remarquables sont récompensés de Bronze, Silver, Gold et Platinum Pentawards. L'emballage qui a su séduire l'ensemble du jury et qui a remporté le plus de suffrages reçoit l'unique et prestigieux Diamond Pentaward.

Ce livre regroupe toutes les créations récompensées en 2013 et 2014. Il s'agit donc de ce qui se fait aujourd'hui de mieux dans le monde en matière de design de packaging, une référence et source d'inspiration pour tous les passionnés d'emballages, étudiants, designers, fabricants, ingénieurs, responsables de marques, consommateurs...

Outre la remise de récompenses, Pentawards a pour mission la promotion du design de packaging auprès des sociétés, de la presse, des autorités économiques et politiques et du grand public en général, partout dans le monde.

Nous vous souhaitons beaucoup de plaisir à parcourir ce livre référence et espérons qu'il vous fera découvrir les produits que vous achetez quotidiennement sous un autre angle, celui de la créativité, de la qualité et de l'innovation qui sont les moteurs de notre civilisation.

Bon voyage au pays des emballages.

SO MUCH CREATIVITY!

Gérard Caron
Founder of Carré Noir
Designer of the website www.admirabledesign.com
Chair of the Pentawards jury since 2007

When reading this book—the Pentawards' third publication—I am struck by the incredible ingenuity of packaging designers. Because what does this job come down to, after all? Designing packaging for typically standardized, mass-produced products. Nothing spectacular can come of that. And yet...

Emerging markets in design...

And yet all nations are taking part in this worldwide contest; even countries that don't immediately spring to mind when it comes to design—El Salvador, Armenia, Ukraine, Vietnam, Romania and Ecuador, to name but a few—have competed for and won Pentawards.

Looking down the list of nations that have participated since the launch of the competition, the arrival of these emerging or developing nations is striking. Countries just emerging on to the design scene are typically overflowing with creativity, snapping up awards with innovative designs that often fly in the face of market conventions. It is worth considering the possible reasons for this phenomenon. While it is difficult to generalize, I would like to propose two principal explanations.

The first relates to the design process in large countries whose design market is already well established, such as the USA, Japan, France or the UK. In these countries, the marketing sector is highly developed and has a strong influence on decision-making regarding ideas presented by designers. These ideas must then undergo rigorous testing before they can be approved and put on the market. As a result, it is fairly common to see the most interesting ideas slip through the net in favor of designs upon which there is broader consensus. By contrast, in countries that are just emerging on to the design scene, the designer's opinion carries considerably more weight; the decision-making process is often shorter, thereby encouraging more daring design choices. I am inclined to say that, in these countries, marketing is kept in its rightful place and more in balance with the role of design.

The second factor that could explain the creative drive in emerging countries is, I believe, the consumer. In such countries, consumerism is a fairly recent phenomenon that still holds a sense of discovery, of shared enjoyment, even leisure. After years of economic austerity, the shackles are finally coming off. Russia is an interesting case in point. The country has long been a nation of incredibly talented graphic designers with only limited outlets for creative expression. Consumers were confronted with stores that had no real competition, or had little to no stock.

A "Chinese school" of design?

The same can be said for another of the world's largest nations: China. The number of Chinese submissions has increased eightfold in only three years. The winning designs reveal a particularly important phenomenon: the emergence of a distinctly Chinese style. These are no mere imitations of standard Western designs—which, incidentally, has never been the case—but expressions of a Chinese cultural and economic vision that still manage to integrate Western marketing norms. The case of China is fascinating, and given the vastness of its market and its increasing international clout, we can only imagine what creative shock waves it will cause over the next few decades. There may be interesting days ahead in the design industry, whether in packaging, or in the fashion, commercial architecture or engineering sectors.

The "screen generation" is here!

Glancing through this book, another interesting observation can be made: the arrival on the market of the "screen generation"—consumers who have been staring at a screen and tapping on a keyboard on a daily basis since early childhood. It was always clear that this generation, brought up on TV series, manga and video-games, would have a different vision of design than those that came before it, so it was only a matter of time.

Have we reached the tipping point? It is a question we may ask ourselves when studying the designs in this year's Pentawards. The jury noticed a striking number of streamlined designs with little or no embellishment, often composed of bold typographical elements revealing the nature of the product without showing its appearance. No enticing image, no idyllic landscapes, no beaming children. Just a strong text and a 2D graphic.

Flat packaging?

Flat Design, a style influenced by new everyday technologies, has arrived on the scene with its fair share of commercial giants. Samsung, Apple, Google and Facebook have given birth to a new web-inspired graphic style that prioritizes readability. Flat Design strips away 3D effects from digital media and apps, including drop shadows, gradients, textures and all other superfluous stylistic features. We might not yet have reached the age of "flat packaging," but the way has certainly been paved.

We may ask whether the concept doesn't represent a regression in graphic design—an impoverishment of the creative component. I would tend to disagree as long as the role of packaging design is primarily to influence purchasing decisions. Branding is essential, hence the choice of bold typefaces.

An outright rejection of Flat Design would be to ignore the concept of "upstream design," which involves asking the right questions, accurately targeting a market, finding the right typographic hierarchy, as well as selecting a color that's geared towards the market. Everything becomes a matter of the utmost precision, of pixel-level details. Everything counts: symbols, pictograms, text boxes and all other icons.

I prefer to see it as the appearance of a style that is more rational against a style that is more emotional. This confrontation of styles is exciting to witness and will not end with the victory of one over the other, but rather in a balance between the two forms that mirrors the balance between the two sides of the brain: one is rational, the other emotional. And recent studies indicate that the side that has the last word in our decision-making is... the right side, the side of emotion.

Whether it be "flat" or imaginative, the Pentawards will continue to showcase human creativity for many years to come.

UNGLAUBLICH VIEL KREATIVITÄT!

Gérard Caron
Gründer von Carré Noir
Designer der Website www.admirabledesign.com
Seit 2007 Vorsitzender der Pentawards-Jury

Beim Lesen dieser dritten Pentawards-Veröffentlichung war ich verblüfft vom unbeschreiblichen Einfallsreichtum der Verpackungsdesigner. Denn worauf läuft es bei ihrem Job letzten Endes hinaus? Auf die Gestaltung von typischen, standardisierten Massenprodukten. Was kann daraus schon Spektakuläres entstehen? Und doch…

Neu entstehende Märkte für Designs…
Und doch nehmen alle Nationen an diesem weltweiten Wettbewerb teil – sogar Länder, die einem nicht als Erstes in den Sinn kommen, wenn man an Design denkt: El Salvador, Armenien, die Ukraine, Vietnam, Rumänien und Ecuador, um nur einige zu nennen, sind in den Wettbewerb eingestiegen und haben Pentawards gewonnen.

Überfliegt man die Liste der Länder, die seit Beginn dieses Wettbewerbs teilgenommen haben, erstaunt einen die Ankunft dieser aufstrebenden oder sich entwickelnden Nationen. Länder, die sich gerade in der Designszene entfalten, platzen üblicherweise beinahe vor Kreativität und ergattern Auszeichnungen mit ihren innovativen Designs, die den üblichen Konventionen des Markts oft diametral entgegenstehen. Es lohnt sich, einen Blick auf die möglichen Gründe für dieses Phänomen zu werfen. Zwar sind verallgemeinernde Aussagen schwierig, aber zwei wesentliche Erklärungen will ich ins Spiel bringen.

Die erste hängt mit dem Designprozess in großen Ländern wie den USA oder Japan, Frankreich und Großbritannien zusammen, deren Designmarkt bereits gut etabliert ist. In diesen Ländern ist der Marketingsektor in hohem Maße ausgebaut und beeinflusst die Entscheidungen wesentlich, die hinsichtlich der von den Designern präsentierten Konzepte und Ideen getroffen werden. Diese Ideen müssen sich anschließend rigorosen Tests unterziehen, bevor sie akzeptiert und auf den Markt gebracht werden. Als Folge davon kommt es relativ häufig vor, dass die interessantesten Ideen durchs Raster fallen zugunsten von Designs, bei denen der Konsens breiter ist. Im Kontrast dazu wird in Ländern, die sich gerade in der Designszene etablieren, der Meinung des Designers ein weitaus größeres Gewicht beigemessen; Entscheidungsfindungen sind oft kürzer und ermöglichen mutigere Designentwürfe. Ich neige also zu der Feststellung, dass das Marketing in solchen Ländern seinen angemessenen Platz bekommt und gegenüber dem Design viel ausgewogener ist.

Der zweite Faktor, der den kreativen Drive aufstrebender Länder erklären könnte, ist meines Erachtens der Konsument. In diesen Ländern ist Konsumverhalten ein recht neues Phänomen, dem noch die Aura des Entdeckens, der gemeinsame Genuss oder gar Muße anhaftet. Nach Jahren des ökonomischen Mangels kann man schließlich seine Fesseln abschütteln. Ein solch interessanter Fall ist Russland. Dieses Land beheimatet schon lange unglaublich talentierte Grafikdesigner, die sich aber nur sehr begrenzt kreativ ausdrücken konnten. Als Verbraucher kam man in Geschäfte, die weder im echten Wettbewerb standen noch einen ausreichenden Warenbestand aufwiesen.

Eine „chinesische Schule" des Designs?
Das Gleiche lässt man auch über eine andere der weltweit größten Nationen sagen, nämlich China. In nur drei Jahren haben sich die chinesischen Beiträge verachtfacht. Die preisgekrönten Designs präsentieren ein ganz besonders wichtiges Phänomen: Nun erscheint ein charakteristisch chinesischer Stil. Dabei handelt es sich nicht bloß um Imitationen westlicher Standarddesigns (was im Übrigen nie der Fall war), sondern um den Ausdruck einer typisch chinesischen kulturellen und ökonomischen Vision, der es trotzdem gelingt, westliche Marketingnormen zu integrieren. China ist hier ein ganz besonders faszinierendes Beispiel. Angesichts des riesigen chinesischen Markts und seines enorm wachsenden internationalen Einflusses können wir uns kaum ausmalen, welch kreative Schockwellen von dort in den nächsten Jahrzehnten zu erwarten sind. In der Designbranche liegen interessante Zeiten vor uns, sei es beim Packaging oder im Fashion-Bereich, bei kommerzieller Architektur oder dem Ingenieurswesen.

Die „Screen Generation" ist da!
Beim Durchblättern dieses Buches stellen wir eine weitere interessante Tatsache fest: Die „Screen Generation" ist am Markt angekommen, also jene Verbraucher, die von Kindesbeinen an von Bildschirmen lesen und mit Tastaturen tippen. Es war immer klar, dass diese Generation, aufgewachsen mit Fernsehserien, Mangas und Videospielen, eine ganz andere Designvision haben würde als die davor – alles also nur eine Frage der Zeit.

Haben wir hier nun eine Schwelle überschritten? Diese Frage sollten wir uns stellen, wenn wir die Designs bei den diesjährigen Pentawards begutachten. Die Jury bemerkte, dass eine bemerkenswerte Zahl stromlinienförmiger

10

Designs mit wenig oder gar keinen Verzierungen eingereicht wurde, die oft nur aus kraftvollen typografischen Elementen bestanden, aus denen man auf die Natur des Produkts schließen konnte, ohne dass es zu sehen war. Keine verlockenden Bilder, keine idyllischen Landschaften, keine strahlend lächelnden Kinder. Nur ein prägnanter Text und eine zweidimensionale Grafik.

Flat Packaging?

Flat Design ist als Designstil von den neuen alltäglichen Technologien beeinflusst und wird bereits von einer ansehnlichen Gruppe kommerzieller Giganten eingesetzt. Samsung, Apple, Google und Facebook sorgen für einen neuen, vom Web inspirierten Grafikstil, der die Lesbarkeit in den Vordergrund stellt. Beim Flat Design fallen die 3D-Effekte der digitalen Medien und Apps weg, z.B. Schlagschatten, Farbverläufe, Texturen und alle überflüssigen stilistischen Features. Wir sind wohl noch nicht im Zeitalter des „Flat Packaging" angekommen, aber der Weg dorthin ist gewiss geebnet.

Wir sollten uns fragen, ob dieses Konzept nicht einen Rückschritt im Grafikdesign repräsentiert – eine Verarmung der kreativen Komponente. Einer solchen Aussage würde ich eher nicht zustimmen, solange die Rolle des Verpackungsdesigns primär darin liegt, Kaufentscheidungen zu beeinflussen. Branding ist essenziell und so auch die Entscheidung für kraftvolle Typografien.

Ein grundsätzlicher Verzicht auf Flat Design wäre, das Konzept des „Upstream Design" zu ignorieren, bei dem es darum geht, die richtigen Fragen zu stellen, einen Markt zielgenau zu bedienen, die richtige typografische Hierarchie zu finden und ebenso die passende Farbe, die genau auf den Markt zugeschnitten ist. Alles wird zu einer Sache größtmöglicher Präzision und pixelgenauer Details. Alles zählt und wird berücksichtigt: Symbole, Piktogramme, Textkästen und alle anderen Icons.

Ich ziehe es vor, dies als Erscheinen eines Stils zu betrachten, der rationaler ist im Vergleich zu einem eher emotionalen Stil. Diese Konfrontation der Stile ist außerordentlich spannend zu beobachten und wird nicht mit dem Sieg einer Seite enden, sondern vielmehr zu einer Balance zwischen beiden Formen führen, die die Balance zwischen unseren Gehirnhälften widerspiegelt: Eine ist rational, die andere emotional. Und aktuelle Untersuchungen weisen darauf hin, dass jene Hälfte, die bei unserer Entscheidungsfindung das letzte Wort hat, immer die rechte Gehirnhälfte ist ... also die gefühlsbetonte.

Aber egal ob „flat" oder fantasievoll – die Pentawards schenken uns noch viele weitere Jahre ein grandioses Forum menschlicher Kreativität!

QUE DE CRÉATIVITÉ !

Gérard Caron
Fondateur de Carré Noir
Editeur de www.admirabledesign.com
Président du jury Pentawards depuis 2007

En feuilletant ce livre, le troisième consacré aux Pentawards, on est saisi par l'esprit d'inventivité des designers de packagings. Car en réalité en quoi consiste ce métier ? Décorer un emballage de produits la plupart du temps normalisés, fabriqués en série. Rien de très exaltant en sorte ! Et pourtant...

Les pays émergents du design...

Et pourtant tous les pays s'y mettent, tous les pays participent à ce grand match mondial ; même des pays auxquels on ne pense pas à priori quand on parle de design. Salvador, Arménie, Ukraine, Vietnam, Roumanie, Équateur, entre autres, concourent et remportent des Pentawards.

À regarder la liste des pays participants depuis la création de ce concours, on est frappé par l'arrivée de ces pays émergents ou en voie de développement. Ces nations qui s'ouvrent au design sont souvent d'une créativité débordante et raflent des prix grâce à cet esprit d'innovation qui va souvent jusqu'à casser les codes du marché. Il est intéressant de se demander quelle est la raison de ce phénomène. Il est bien entendu difficile de généraliser mais pour autant, je vois deux raisons principales.

La première tient au processus de création vis-à-vis de grands pays où le design est bien établi comme les États-Unis, le Japon, la France et la Grande-Bretagne, pays où le marketing est développé et puissant dans les prises de décision sur les projets présentés par les designers. Projets qui sont ensuite soumis à des tests avant leur acceptation et la mise sur le marché. Il n'est pas rare alors de voir les projets les plus remarquables passer à la trappe au bénéfice de créations plus consensuelles. En revanche dans ces pays qui s'ouvrent au design, le poids d'influence du designer est plus important ; il a en face de lui une chaîne de décision souvent beaucoup plus courte, ce qui pousse à des choix plus courageux. J'aurais envie de dire que le marketing est alors à sa juste place et en équilibre avec le rôle du design.

La seconde raison qui pourrait expliquer cet élan de créativité dans ces nouveaux pays est, à mes yeux, le consommateur lui-même. La consommation est un phénomène récent chargé encore d'esprit de découverte, de plaisir partagé en famille, voire de loisir. Après tant d'années de sévérité économique la bride se relâche. Le cas de la Russie est particulièrement révélateur. De tous temps ce pays a été une terre de graphistes de grand talent qui n'avaient que

peu de moyens d'expression, les consommateurs trouvaient des commerces sans réelle concurrence, peu ou pas approvisionnés.

Un design chinois ?

Je pourrais dire la même chose d'un autre grand pays : la Chine. Le nombre de dossiers soumis au jugement du jury a été multiplié par huit en trois ans ! Et les créations primées révèlent un point particulièrement important : l'émergence d'un style de design typiquement chinois. Il ne s'agit plus de copier les codes du design occidental, ce qui a été le cas au départ, mais bien de manifester une vision culturelle et économique chinoise... tout en intégrant les codes marketing de l'Occident. C'est tout à fait intéressant car compte tenu de l'étendue de ce marché et de son poids grandissant dans le monde, on ne peut que prévoir des bouleversements créatifs dans les décennies à venir. Cela nous annonce des jours animés dans les métiers du design qu'ils soient dans le domaine du packaging ou de l'architecture commerciale, de la mode ou de l'industrie.

Quand la « screen generation » débarque !

En feuilletant cet ouvrage un autre constat s'impose : l'arrivée sur le marché des « screen generations », ces consommateurs qui ont toujours eu un écran devant leurs yeux, un clavier à manipuler depuis leur enfance. À force de dire qu'ils vont avoir une autre vision du design que leurs aînés, eux qui sont gavés de séries, de manga, de jeux vidéo, cela devait arriver un jour.

Sommes-nous arrivés à ce point de basculement ? C'est véritablement la question qu'on est en droit de se poser en analysant les créations de cette édition Pentawards, où le jury a eu à noter un nombre impressionnant de créations au design efficace, sans fioritures, souvent composées de typographies fortes qui annoncent la nature du produit sans en montrer l'apparence ; pas de belle photo appétissante, pas de paysages idylliques. Pas de sourires d'enfants, mais un texte puissant et un graphisme en deux dimensions.

Le flat packaging ?

Sous l'influence des nouvelles technologies, le « flat design » débarque dans notre quotidien avec son lot de marques puissantes : Samsung, Apple, Google, Facebook... Elles ont donné naissance à un nouveau style graphique directement inspiré du Web qui met en avant la lisibilité. Dans les médias numériques et les applications, le flat design retire les effets en profondeur sous Photoshop, les volumes, les ombres portées, les dégradés, les textures, la 3D...tout élément décoratif et superflu. Nous n'en sommes pas encore au « flat packaging », mais la voie se trace...

On peut alors se demander s'il ne s'agit pas d'une régression graphique, d'un appauvrissement du facteur créatif. Pour ma part, je ne le pense pas dans la mesure où le packaging est avant tout là pour démontrer son efficacité dans l'acte d'achat. L'impact et la reconnaissance de la marque sont essentiels, d'où des choix typographiques forts.

Ce serait oublier le « design en amont » qui consiste à se poser les bonnes questions, cibler juste, trouver la bonne hiérarchie des textes...et la sélection de la couleur adaptée au marché. Tout devient affaire de précision, de détails jusqu'aux pixels car tout compte : les symboles, les pictogrammes, les cartouches et les icônes.

Je parlerais plutôt de l'apparition d'un design plus rationnel versus un design émotionnel. Tout cela est passionnant à suivre et ne conclura pas par la victoire de l'un ou de l'autre. Ce sera plutôt un équilibre des deux formes de design à l'image des deux hémisphères de notre cerveau : l'un est rationnel l'autre est émotionnel. Et les études récentes tendent à démontrer que celui qui a le dernier mot dans nos prises de décision est...le cerveau droit, celui de l'émotion.

Pentawards sera encore pour longtemps une belle démonstration de la créativité humaine qu'elle soit « flat » ou imaginative...

diamond

Best of the show

PENTAWARD'S DIAMOND

Jean Jacques & Brigitte Evrard
Founders of Pentawards

A single crowning jewel

The international jury of 11 packaging design experts and marketing managers from large global brands represent the 11 principal cultures of the commercial world. The deep-rooted culture of the Japanese is, of course, vastly different from that of the French or the Swedish, or even the Koreans. The same goes for British and American cultures.

Even if product marketing processes, production techniques and retailing systems follow international norms, culture in its truest sense—that which characterizes a civilization—gives each person a unique perspective that is informed by his or her education and cultural background.

In this beautifully presented book you will discover designs that are distinctively Japanese, altogether English, 100 percent American. Each one is outstanding, of course, and creative, and will inspire and amaze you, but not all of these designs are intended for the global commercial market.

Amongst those designs which are produced for general distribution, each year the nationally and culturally diverse Pentawards jury unites to designate certain entries as being "universally designed." These designs are effective in the global market regardless of their geographical provenance. Indeed,

it is impossible to guess where they are from or which culture produced them. They are truly universal, the product of all cultures. These designs are born classics.

From among them, one is singled out as being the most extraordinary. In 2013, the Diamond Pentaward was claimed by the four million individually designed bottles of Absolut Vodka Unique, and in 2014 by a small transparent bottle bearing the Evian logo in the form of a water droplet—the universal symbol for water—proving that less is often more.

Ein einziges Kronjuwel

Die internationale Jury aus elf Experten des Verpackungsdesigns und Marketingmanagern großer globaler Marken repräsentiert die elf wesentlichen Kulturen der kommerziellen Welt. Die tief verwurzelte Kultur des Japanischen ist natürlich völlig anders als die der Franzosen oder Schweden oder sogar der Koreaner. Das Gleiche gilt für die britische und die amerikanische Kultur.

Obwohl die Prozesse im Produktmarketing, die Produktionstechniken und Einzelhandelssysteme internationale Normen befolgen, verleiht Kultur in wahrsten Sinne des Wortes (als das, was eine Zivilisation charakterisiert) jeder Person eine einmalige und unverwechselbare Perspektive, die durch ihre Bildung und ihren kulturellen Hintergrund geprägt ist.

In diesem wunderbaren Buch entdecken Sie Designs, die ganz typisch japanisch, insgesamt absolut britisch oder hundertprozentig amerikanisch sind. Jedes von ihnen ist natürlich hervorragend und kreativ, jedes Design wird Sie inspirieren und verblüffen, aber nicht alle sind für den globalen kommerziellen Markt gedacht.

Jedes Jahr kommt die national und kulturell vielfältig zusammengesetzte Pentawards-Jury zusammen, um einige dieser Einreichungen, die für den internationalen Verkauf produziert werden, als „universelle Designs" zu nominieren. Diese Designs sind ungeachtet ihrer geografischen Herkunft auf dem globalen Markt wirksam. Es ist unmöglich zu erraten, woher sie stammen oder in welcher Kultur sie produziert wurden. Sie sind wirklich universell, ein Produkt aller Kulturen. Diese Designs sind geborene Klassiker.

Aus dieser Runde wird schließlich ein Design herausgegriffen, das wirklich das außergewöhnlichste überhaupt ist. Für das Jahr 2013 wurde der Diamond Pentaward den vier Millionen individuell gestalteten Flaschen Absolut Vodka Unique verliehen, und 2014 wurde damit ein kleines, transparentes Fläschchen mit dem Evian-Logo in Form eines Wassertröpfchens geehrt, dem universellen Symbol für Wasser (ein Beweis dafür, dass weniger oft mehr ist).

PENTAWARD'S DIAMOND

Un seul et unique diamant

Un jury international composé de spécialistes en design de packaging et de responsables marketing de grandes marques mondiales est, par essence, une représentation des principales cultures du monde industrialisé. Le jury Pentawards regroupe onze nationalités, onze cultures donc. Bien sûr, la culture profonde d'un Japonais est très différente de celle d'un Français ou d'un Suédois, même d'un Coréen. Idem entre un Anglais et un Américain.

Si les processus marketing, les techniques de production, les systèmes de commercialisation des produits répondent à des normes internationales, la culture au sens propre, celle qui caractérise les différentes civilisations, donne à chaque individu un regard personnel, fruit de son éducation et de son milieu culturel.

Vous découvrirez dans ce beau livre des emballages purement japonais, tout à fait anglais, 100 % américains... ils sont superbes sans aucun doute, créatifs aussi et ils seront pour vous source d'inspiration, d'étonnement. Ces emballages n'ont toutefois pas vocation à être commercialisés mondialement.

Il n'en est pas de même pour certains. Chaque année, le jury Pentawards, toutes cultures et nationalités confondues, s'accorde à désigner unanimement certains emballages comme étant universellement conçus. Ces créations, qu'importe leur origine nationale, ont vocation globale. Nul ne peut dire leur origine, nul ne peut trouver la culture qui les a produites. Ce sont des emballages universels, fruits de toutes les cultures de l'humanité mélangées, des classiques dès leur naissance.

Et parmi ceux-là, un seul est désigné comme étant le plus marquant. En 2013, ce sont les quatre millions de bouteilles d'Absolut Vodka Unique, toutes différentes, qui ont remporté le Pentawards Diamant, et en 2014 une petite bouteille transparente en forme de goutte signée Évian, symbole parfait de l'eau... Less is more.

ABSOLUT VODKA
ABSOLUT UNIQUE

Creative Direction: John Lagerqvist, Marten Knutsson
Account Direction: Cecilia Steenberg Forsberg
Art Direction: Fredrik Lindquist
Copywriting: Tove Norstrom
Account Management: Anna Andrén
Final Art: Andy Chong, Anna Jarl
Client: The Absolut Company, Jonas Thalin, Mattias
Westphal, Louise Arén, Anna Bergfeldt, Erik Naf
Company: Family Business
Country: Sweden

DIAMOND PENTAWARD 2013
ESKO PRIZE

For years **Absolut Vodka** has led the way with innovation in vodka packaging, with limited-edition series such as Absolut Disco, Absolut Rock and Absolut Illusion. For 2012, it was time to redefine the limited edition itself. The idea was to make four million unique bottles, so that each and every one became a limited edition on its own. This meant the production line had to be completely rebuilt, and every possible aspect of glass decoration be re-employed in a new way. Nearly every bottle sold out before the campaign period was over, without any price-offs, which in general is a must when retailing during the busy end-of-year season.

Schon seit Jahren führt **Absolut Vodka** bei der innovativen Verpackung von Wodkaflaschen und brachte in Sonderauflagen Absolut Disco, Absolut Rock und Absolut Illusion heraus. 2012 war die Zeit gekommen, die Limited Edition selbst neu zu definieren. Die Idee war, vier Millionen Flaschen als Unikate herzustellen, sodass jede eine eigene Limited Edition darstellte. Das bedeutete, die Fertigungsstraße vollständig neu zu organisieren, damit alles, was bei der Glasverzierung möglich ist, auf neuartige Weise eingesetzt werden konnte. Noch vor Ablauf der Kampagne war praktisch jede Flasche verkauft, und das ohne Rabatte, was bei Angeboten in der Hauptsaison Ende des Jahres ansonsten unverzichtbar ist.

Pendant des années, **Absolut Vodka** a été le pionnier des emballages innovants de vodka, avec des éditions limitées comme Absolut Disco, Absolut Rock et Absolut Illusion. En 2012, la révision du concept même d'édition limitée s'est imposée : l'idée était de fabriquer quatre millions de bouteilles, chacune unique en son genre. La ligne de production a donc dû être entièrement repensée et chaque touche décorative réutilisée différemment. Presque toutes les bouteilles se sont vendues avant la fin de la campagne sans appliquer de réductions, tout un luxe au moment des fêtes de fin d'année.

From the outset, **Evian Drop** was conceived as a project putting consumers' needs at its heart and to locate the bottles in outlets where they wouldn't typically be found. The new design emphasizes purity and presents a bottle which can be drunk in one go, like a glass of water, and which has no cap but a lid, no label but a sticker on the top. By retailing the bottles in places like premium non-food stores, hairdressers and pharmacies, and most radically from mobile units selling them in heavy traffic in Paris, this changes the rules of the game: water now comes to the consumer, instead of them having to go and look for it in a shop.

Von Anfang an konzipiert sich **Evian Drop** als Produkt, das den Bedarf der Verbraucher ins Zentrum stellt und Flaschen dort anbietet, wo man sie normalerweise nicht vermutete. Das neue Design betont Reinheit und präsentiert eine Flasche, die auf einmal weggetrunken werden kann wie ein Glas Wasser. Sie ist nicht mit Kronkorken, sondern Folie verschlossen und weist kein Etikett, sondern einen Aufkleber oben auf. Durch den Verkauf der Flaschen z.B. in Premium-Nonfood-Läden, Friseurgeschäften und Apotheken und am radikalsten durch mobile Units im dichten Pariser Straßenverkehr änderte Evian die Spielregeln: Der Kunde braucht sich keinen Laden mehr zu suchen, sondern lässt das Wasser zu sich kommen.

Le projet **Evian Drop** a d'emblée été pensé pour cibler les besoins des consommateurs et distribuer les bouteilles via un réseau atypique. Le nouveau design rime avec pureté et la bouteille peut être bue d'un trait, comme un verre d'eau. Le bouchon a été remplacé par un opercule qui fait office d'étiquette. La vente des bouteilles dans des magasins non alimentaires haut de gamme, des salons de coiffure, et même à des stands mobiles au milieu des embouteillages parisiens, change radicalement les règles du jeu : l'eau vient au consommateur, au lieu que ce dernier doive chercher où se la procurer.

EVIAN
PURE DROP

Design: Frédéric Brasse, Grand Angle Design
Company: Evian, Group Danone
Country: France

DIAMOND PENTAWARD 2014
ESKO PRIZE

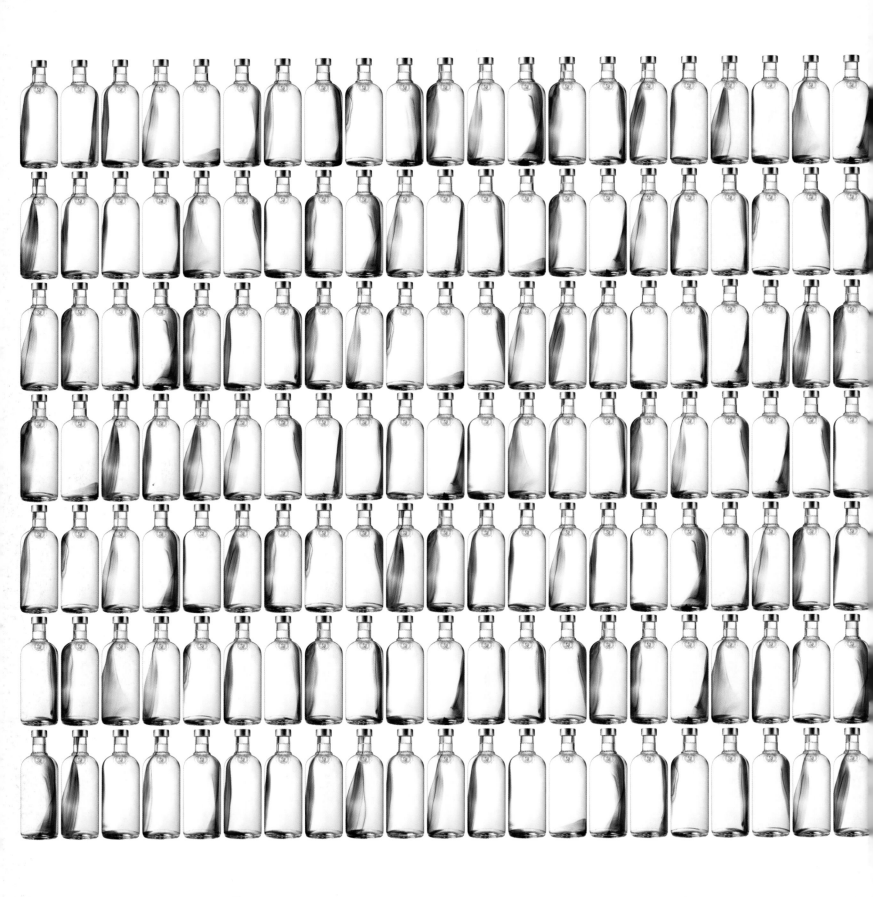

Best of the category

Water

Soft drinks, juices

Coffee & tea

Functional beverages

Beer

Ciders and low-alcohol drinks

Wines

beverages

Wine as bag-in-box

Spirits

Limited editions, limited series, event creation

Distributors' / Retailers' own brands

Casks, cases, gift boxes, ice buckets

Packaging concept

If a brand stands out from other brands chiefly because of its color, name and shape, in the world of beer, mainly sold in cans, it is not easy to break out. So when Metaphase Design Group came up with a can shaped like a bow-tie this was something quite new, while overcoming the technical difficulties of producing large quantities of such cans at speed makes the result even more impressive. The primary aim was to create a more attractive can, both visually and functionally, in order to attract new customers to this American classic. Holding this **Budweiser** can in your hand is enough to understand the added value to the brand, thanks to the distinctive shape in perfect harmony with the logo. You could not do better!

In einer Welt hauptsächlich in Dosen verkaufter Biere ist es nicht einfach, sich durch Farbe, Namen und Form deutlich von Rest abzuheben. Als Metaphase Design Group ihre Dose in Form einer Fliege für Frack oder Smoking vorstellte, war dies etwas völlig Neues. Das Resultat beeindruckt noch mehr, wenn man berücksichtigt, welche technischen Schwierigkeiten zu bewältigen sind, um Dosen in solch großen Mengen schnell zu produzieren. Das Hauptziel war, eine visuell und funktional noch attraktivere Dose zu schaffen und so dem amerikanischen Klassiker neue Kunden zu erschließen. Man braucht die **Budweiser**-Dose nur in die Hand zu nehmen, um zu verstehen, welchen Mehrwert die Marke der charakteristischen Form, die perfekt mit dem Logo harmoniert, verdankt. Das kann man nicht verbessern!

Si une marque se distingue des autres principalement par sa couleur, son nom et sa forme, il est difficile de se réinventer dans le monde de la bière où les canettes dominent le marché. Metaphase Design Group a créé l'événement en inventant une canette en forme de nœud papillon. Les difficultés techniques ont su être maîtrisées, ce qui a permis la production rapide de grandes quantités. L'objectif premier était de créer une canette plus attrayante et plus pratique afin de capter de nouveaux clients. La prise en mains de cette canette **Budweiser** suffit à comprendre la valeur ajoutée de la marque, grâce à sa forme en parfaite harmonie avec le logo : difficile de faire mieux !

ANHEUSER-BUSCH INBEV BUDWEISER

Design: Metaphase Design Group (Bryce Rutter, Jonathan Sundy, David Kusch)
AB InBev: Pat McGauley, Lori Shambro, Thuy Vi Quach-Braig, Mark Viox, Danielle Miller, Tim Buening, Lee Crossley
DCA: Peter Kay
Company: Metaphase Design Group
Country: USA
Category: Best of the category beverages

PLATINUM PENTAWARD 2013

ABSOLUT VODKA
ABSOLUT ORIGINALITY

Creative Direction: Magnus Skogsberg Tear (Happytear)
Account Direction: Joakim Pettersson (Happytear)
Production Management: Susan Norrgards (Happytear)
Art Direction: Ola Johansson (Destrito)
Photography: Magnus Torsne (Hall & Lundgren)
Retouch: Andreas Lindstrom (Bildinstitutet)
Client: Elin Berg (The Absolut Company)
Company: Happytear
Country: Sweden
Category: Best of the category beverages

PLATINUM PENTAWARD 2014

Through inventive engineering, a drop of blue cobalt may be added to molten glass at an exact moment during bottle production, resulting in beautiful blue streaks, each different from one another. Four million such bottles were produced for **Absolut Vodka**, elegantly drawing attention to the brand and at the same time representing its spirit of originality. The packaging and its promotion also champion craft values and communicate the distilled essence of the drink, while making the shade of Nova blue into a symbol of its premium quality. In-store visibility is also enhanced with this association between brand and a particular color.

Infolge erfindungsreicher Ingenieurskunst wird während der Flaschenproduktion in einem exakt kalkulierten Moment dem Schmelzglas ein kobaltblauer Tropfen hinzugesetzt. Das führt zu wunderschönen blauen, einzigartigen Schlieren. Vier Millionen solcher Flaschen wurden für **Absolut Vodka** produziert und machen elegant auf diese Marke aufmerksam. Gleichzeitig repräsentiert jede einzelne den Geist der Originalität. Verpackung und Werbung verweisen auf die Handwerkskunst und kommunizieren die destillierte Essenz des Getränks. Als Symbol für die Premiumqualität steht der Farbton Nova-Blau. Dass die Marke mit einer bestimmten Farbe assoziiert wird, sorgt für erhöhte Sichtbarkeit im Laden.

Une prouesse d'ingénierie permet d'ajouter une goutte de cobalt bleu à du verre fondu au cours de la production de la bouteille, ce qui donne de superbes traînées azurées. Quatre millions d'unités ont été fabriquées pour **Absolut Vodka**, une façon élégante de promouvoir la marque et de démontrer un esprit d'originalité. L'emballage et sa promotion sont aussi la preuve d'un talent artisanal et expriment l'essence distillée de la boisson. La teinte bleu Nova incarne la qualité exceptionnelle, et la visibilité en magasins est assurée par l'association de la marque à une couleur spécifique.

UNI-PRESIDENT
BAMA MINERAL WATER

Brand/Graphic Design: Brandimage
Creative Direction: Sofan Man
Art Direction: Liem Cheung, Eric Goh
Shape Design: In Spirit Design
Creative Direction: Christophe Blin
Company: Uni-President Enterprises
Country: China
Category: Water

GOLD PENTAWARD 2013

The village of Bama in southern China is home to more centenarians than any other place in the world, owing to special geological characteristics which yield a uniquely mineralized water. The simple bottle shape and graphics here, using celestial blue with metallic silver hot-stamping, reflect the purity of the place, whilst the glass embossing, based on an infinity pattern, creates a radiant energy that plays with light and symbolizes the longevity properties of the water. The overall effect is a mineral water that appeals to the emerging middle class of Chinese consumers who are concerned about their health, and who value premium products that support their wellbeing.

Im südchinesischen Dorf Bama leben mehr Hundertjährige als irgendwo sonst in der Welt. Das verdanken sie besonderen geologischen Gegebenheiten, die zu einem einmaligen Mineralwasser führen. Die einfache, heißgeprägte Form der Flasche und die Grafiken mit ihrem leuchtenden Blau und dem metallischem Silber spiegeln die Reinheit des Ortes. Zugleich bricht sich in der auf einem unendlichen Muster beruhenden Prägung das Licht in energetischem Strahlen und symbolisiert, welch langes Leben der Inhalt dieser Flasche erwirkt. Dieses Mineralwasser spricht die gesundheitsbewusste aufstrebende chinesische Mittelklasse wirksam an, welche Premiumprodukte schätzt, die ihr Wohlbefinden unterstützen.

Dans le village de Bama, au sud de la Chine, vivent plus de centenaires que nulle part ailleurs dans le monde, grâce à la géologie du lieu qui procure une eau minéralisée unique en son genre. La forme simple et l'étiquette, un transfert à chaud mariant bleu céleste et argent, sont à l'image de la pureté de l'endroit. Le verre gaufré selon un motif infini transmet une énergie rayonnante, jouant avec la lumière et symbolisant les propriétés de longévité de l'eau. Le résultat est une eau minérale qu'achète la classe moyenne émergente des consommateurs chinois soucieux de leur santé et valorisant les produits sains de qualité.

Aqua maintains that through design all goods can have a soul and so connect with consumers at an emotional level. The design here breaks with the usual category codes and instead features rounded vertical ribs and a subtle green to suggest the refraction and tones more often found with glass bottles. Soft and elegant, the form also captures the essence and light of the Mediterranean, while the packaging does its bit for sustainability, using natural polypropylene with no color additives, and a label printed in just two colors. In addition, the manufacturing has been tailored to achieve a significant reduction in the carbon footprint.

Aqua achtet speziell darauf, dass Design allen Waren eine Seele verleihen kann, um die Kunden auf emotionaler Ebene anzusprechen. Dieses Design durchbricht die üblichen Codes seiner Kategorie. Die abgerundete vertikale Rippung und die dezente Grüntönung greifen das Spiel von Farbe und Licht auf, wie man es sonst bei Glasflaschen findet. Sanft und elegant fängt die Form Essenz und Licht des Mittelmeeres ein. Die Packung steht für Nachhaltigkeit, da sie aus Naturfaser-Polypropylen ohne Farbzusätze produziert ist und ein nur zweifarbig bedrucktes Etikett trägt. Außerdem hat man den Herstellungsprozess zugunsten einer signifikant reduzierten Klimabelastung angepasst.

Aqua a pour philosophie que le design confère une âme au produit et lui permet de connecter sur le plan émotionnel avec les consommateurs. Ici, le design rompt avec les codes habituels : des nervures verticales et un vert subtil imitent la réfraction et les tons plus souvent propres aux bouteilles en verre. Légère et élégante, la forme capte l'essence et la lumière de la Méditerranée, alors que l'emballage prouve être durable, fait de polypropylène naturel sans colorants artificiels. L'étiquette ne compte que deux couleurs et la fabrication a été personnalisée pour réduire de façon notable l'empreinte carbone.

AQUA
NATURAL MINERAL WATER

Design: Series Nemo team
Company: Series Nemo
Country: Spain
Category: Water

GOLD PENTAWARD 2014

NY2O AMERICAN PREMIUM WATER

Design: Esther Slubski (bottle/label) with the support
of Soma Creative Group
Company: NY2O LLC
Country: USA
Category: Water

SILVER PENTAWARD 2014

PERRIER

Global Creative Direction: Patrick Veyssière
Creative Direction: Matthieu Bourlon
Company: Dragon Rouge
Country: France
Category: Water

SILVER PENTAWARD 2014

EVIAN
ESSENCE

Design: Frédéric Brasse, Grand Angle Design
Company: Evian, Group Danone
Country: France
Category: Water

SILVER PENTAWARD 2013

ICELANDIC GLACIAL

Design: Team One
Executive Direction: Julie Michael
Management Supervision: Heather Hogan
Production: Sleever
Country: USA
Category: Water

SILVER PENTAWARD 2013

KIRIN
NATURAL MINERAL WATER

Design: Tatsuya Hamajima, Satoshi Umeda,
Kota Sagae, Masayuki Inoue, Megumi Shimada,
Miko Sakamoto, Kotaro Miyatake, Keigo Muto,
Hoshino Hidenobu, Motofumi Osumi,
Yuna Kayukawa, Atsushi Otaki
Company: Dentsu
Country: Japan
Category: Water

BRONZE PENTAWARD 2014

AIX LES BAINS
LES MOUSQUETAIRES
INTERMARCHÉ

Design: Damien Bourne,
Wilfried Hermel,
Laurent Lepoitevin
Company: Sidel
Country: France
Category: Water
BRONZE PENTAWARD 2013

BEPPU SAKURA ONSENSUI

Creative/Art Direction: Kota Sagae
Production: Mizue Matsumoto
Design: Aki Tsuzuki
Company: Saga Inc.
Country: Japan
Category: Water
BRONZE PENTAWARD 2014

BE TRUE

Design: Pavla Chuykina, Katya Teterkina, Arthur Schreiber, Galima Ahmetzyanova
Company: StudioIn
Country: Russia
Category: Soft drinks, juices

SILVER PENTAWARD 2014

CHIOS GARDENS NFC JUICES

Managing Direction: Emmanouela Bitsaxaki
Creative Direction: George Karayiannis
Graphic Design: Eleni Pavlaki
Studio Management: Alexandra Papaloudi
Photography: Stelios Tzetzias
Company: 2Yolk
Country: Greece
Category: Soft drinks, juices

GOLD PENTAWARD 2014

Without departing from the usual type of packaging for fruit drinks, this new juice line still had to stand out amongst others in the **Chios Gardens** range, not to mention the rest of the competition. When it becomes apparent just how much fruit needs to be pressed to fill a carton, such a simple fact provides a ready source for the ideal imagery to use. For example, here is a carton of five oranges, four apples and a peach, delivered to your door by your neighborhood grocer — as communicated by other details in the design, such as the tied string, hand-written text and the stamp saying, "Registered Mail from Chios".

Ohne den Rahmen der für Fruchtdrinks üblichen Verpackung zu sprengen, sollte diese neue Saftlinie sich von anderen aus dem Sortiment von **Chios Gardens** und vor allem auch denen der Konkurrenz abheben. Wenn deutlich wird, wie viele Früchte für einen solchen Karton auszupressen sind – dieser Fakt lässt sich ideal als Bildquelle nutzen. Hier z. B. ist ein Karton mit fünf Orangen, vier Äpfeln und einem Pfirsich, der Ihnen vom Supermarkt ums Eck geliefert wird – kommuniziert auch in weiteren gestalterischen Details wie dem geknoteten Bindfaden, dem handgeschriebenen Text und der Briefmarke mit der Aufschrift „Registered Mail from Chios".

Partant pas de l'habituel emballage pour jus de fruits, cette nouvelle gamme devait se démarquer des autres produits de la marque **Chios Gardens** et bien entendu de ses concurrents. En montrant la quantité de fruits à presser pour remplir un carton, l'imagerie idéale est toute trouvée. Par exemple, un carton contenant cinq oranges, quatre pommes et 1 pêche vous est livré à domicile par l'épicier du quartier, comme l'illustrent le design avec l'attache en ficelle, le texte dans une police manuscrite et le tampon « Courrier recommandé de Chios ».

JUPÍK
AQUA & SPORT AQUA

Art Direction: Juraj Demovič, Juraj Vontorčík
Design / Illustration: Juraj Demovič, Juraj Vontorčík,
Lívia Lörinczová, Riordan Ruskin-Tompkins
Photography: Jakub Dvořák
Company: Pergamen Trnava
Country: Slovakia
Category: Soft drinks, juices

GOLD PENTAWARD 2013

ZEROH!

Creative Direction: Morten Throndsen
Design: Eia Grødal
Artwork: Jarle Paulsen
Company: Strømme Throndsen Design
Country: Norway
Category: Soft drinks, juices

SILVER PENTAWARD 2013

RIDNA MARKA

Art Direction/Design: Yurko Gutsulyak
Project Management: Zoryana Gutsulyak
Company: Yurko Gutsulyak Studio
Country: Ukraine
Category: Soft drinks, juices

SILVER PENTAWARD 2014

+MORE

Art Direction: Kayhan Bashpinar
Strategy Direction: Yunus Baran
Distribution Management: Aygun Islamzade
Key Account Management: Araz Salimov
Company: Genna'Baku
Country: Azerbaijan
Category: Soft drinks, juices

SILVER PENTAWARD 2013

LIMO

Creative Direction: Bjørn Rybakken
Design: Alexandra Kloster
Managing Direction: Line Støtvig
Account Management: May Britt Lunde Baumann
Production Management: Henning Arnesen
Company: Tangram Design
Country: Norway
Category: Soft drinks, juices
BRONZE PENTAWARD 2014

EPLESLANG

Graphic Design: Ida Ekroll, Kristine Five Melvær
Account Management: Turid Rønningen,
Ragnhild Schei
Illustration: Peter-John de Villiers
Company: Dinamo Design
Country: Norway
Category: Soft drinks, juices
BRONZE PENTAWARD 2014

SUNTORY GOKURI BANANA

Creative Direction: Yoji Minakuchi (Suntory),
Hiroyuki Ishiura (Suntory)
Art Direction: Kiyono Morita (Suntory)
Design: Kotobuki Seihan Printing
Illustration: Shoji Waki
Company: Kotobuki Seihan Printing
Country: Japan
Category: Soft drinks, juices

BRONZE PENTAWARD 2013

PEPSI CO.

Chief Creative Officer: Stanley Hainsworth
Creative Direction: Steve Barrett
Design Direction: Sean Horita
Design Lead: Dave Schlesinger
Design: Jay Ostby, Ryan Maloney
Client: Pepsi R&D / Design
Company: Tether
Country: USA
Category: Soft drinks, juices

BRONZE PENTAWARD 2013

**PARIS BAGUETTE
KOFFY**

Design: Karim Rashid
Company: Karim Rashid
Country: USA
Category: Coffee & tea (ready-to-drink)

GOLD PENTAWARD 2013

To promote these two new products, a black tea with milk and a premium type of matcha tea, amongst young, busy, everyday consumers in China who want a well-made, healthy tea that is also quick and easy to drink, an appropriate new packaging design was needed. Since both drinks are best whisked first, with the aid of a special Japanese bamboo tool, the shape of this implement was incorporated into the bottle's structure producing a completely distinctive yet natural-looking new form. Meanwhile, the graphics combined the Chinese and English words for tea around a T-shape, giving a smart, contemporary look to appeal to the target group.

Als Werbung für zwei neue Produkte – einem Schwarztee mit Milch und einem Matcha-Premiumtee – für junge, vielbeschäftigte chinesische Verbraucher, die einen gut zubereiteten, gesunden Tee wünschen, der schnell und einfach getrunken wird, brauchte es ein neues, passendes Verpackungsdesign. Weil beide Getränke am besten zuerst schaumig gerührt werden, griff man für die Struktur der Flasche die Gestalt dieses speziellen japanischen Rührbesens aus Bambus auf. Das ergab eine absolut charakteristische und doch natürlich wirkende neue Form. Außerdem wurden die chinesischen und englischen Zeichen für Tee in T-Form grafisch kombiniert, was einen smarten, aktuellen Look für die Zielgruppe ergibt.

Un nouveau design bien pensé s'imposait pour le lancement d'un thé noir au lait et d'un thé matcha raffiné auprès d'une clientèle jeune et active en Chine, demandeuse de thés sains et de qualité, mais aussi faciles et rapides à déguster. Les deux boissons étant meilleures si elles sont d'abord fouettées à l'aide d'un outil japonais spécial en bambou, la forme de cet accessoire a été intégrée à celle de la bouteille pour donner un objet original mais non pas moins naturel. Le graphisme mélange le mot thé en Mandarin et en Anglais autour d'une forme de T, ce qui confère une image contemporaine pertinente pour le public ciblé.

MATCHA MILK TEA

Creative Direction / Design: Gregory Tsaknakis
Illustration: Ioanna Papaioannou
Company: Mousegraphics
Country: Greece
Category: Coffee & tea (ready-to-drink)

SILVER PENTAWARD 2014

TINE
ISTE

Design: Siv Beate Farstad
Creative Direction: Bjørn Rybakken
Production Management Direction: Klaus Dalseth
Production Management: Henning Arnesen,
Mette Nerhagen
Account Management: Stine Wergeland,
May Britt Lunde Baumann
Company: Tangram Design
Country: Norway
Category: Coffee & tea (ready-to-drink)

SILVER PENTAWARD 2013

IYEMON CHA
REDESIGN

Creative Direction: Yoji Minakuchi
Art Direction/Design: Keiko Genkaku
Company: Suntory Business Expert
Country: Japan
Category: Coffee & tea (ready-to-drink)

SILVER PENTAWARD 2013

LIPTON ICE TEA

Creative Direction: Claire Robertshaw
Design Direction: David Robinson
Design: Adam Hunt (senior), Ian Robertshaw
3D Branding Direction: Phil Bordet-Stead
3D Creative Direction: Laurent Robin-Prevallee
3D Design: Ben Davey
Direction of Realization: Ed Mitchell
Creative Direction Brand Language: Holly Kielty
Client Direction: Bryony Moodie
Client Services Direction: Birgitte Woehlk
Client Management: Charlotte Robson
Business Direction: John Morris
Print Consulting: David Benjamin
Client: Andy Jordan, Emmanuelle Chivot
(Pepsi Lipton International)
Company: Design Bridge
Country: UK
Category: Coffee & tea (ready-to-drink)

GOLD PENTAWARD 2014

ISKAFFE BARISTA

Creative Direction: Bjørn Rybakken
Design: Kiki Plesner
Managing Direction: Line Støtvig
Account Management: Stine Wergeland
Production Management: Mette Nerhagen
Company: Tangram Design
Country: Norway
Category: Coffee & tea (ready-to-drink)

BRONZE PENTAWARD 2014

SUNTORY TEA+

Creative Direction: Yoji Minakuchi (Suntory),
Barry Deutsch (DDW)
Art Direction/Design: Satoshi Abe (Suntory),
Harumi Kubo, Jess Giambroni (DDW)
Logo: Ryuichi Tateno
Company: Suntory Business Expert
Country: Japan
Category: Coffee & tea (ready-to-drink)

BRONZE PENTAWARD 2014

MING MING SHI CHA

3D Design: In Spirit Design
Creative Direction: Christophe Blin
Brand/Graphic Design: Bravis International
Creative Direction: Yoshito Watanabe
Companies: In Spirit Design, Bravis International
Country: Spain, Japan
Category: Coffee & tea (ready-to-drink)

SILVER PENTAWARD 2014

In order to stand out in a crowded retail sector, often using similar palettes or visual cues, coffee packaging needs to represent the style and strength of each blend, as well as the premium quality of brand and product. Based on a clean minimalist scheme, each of these **Rio** blends is represented with crisp, isolated imagery against a white background to achieve clarity and visual strength on the shelf. The design for each bag projects the coffee-drinking experience of the blend it contains, from the powerful kick of a stallion to the smooth comfort of an armchair, with the imagery being gauged to intrigue the consumer and invite them to pick this bag of their preferred blend and engage with its story.

Um sich in einem Einzelhandelsbereich abzuheben, in dem sich oft ähnliche Sortimente oder visuelle Anreize zusammendrängen, muss eine Kaffeeverpackung Stil und Stärken jeder Mischung sowie die Premiumqualität von Marke und Produkt verkörpern. Ein aufgeräumtes und minimalistisches Schema repräsentiert jede **Rio**-Mischung, und mit der knackigen, freigestellten Bildgestaltung vor weißem Hintergrund entfaltet sie im Regal optische Kraft und Klarheit. Jede Tüte projiziert mit ihrem Design den Genuss der enthaltenen Kaffeemischung – vom kraftvollen Tritt eines Hengsts bis zum lässigen Komfort des Lehnstuhls. Die Bildgestaltung macht den Käufer kalkuliert neugierig und lädt ihn ein, seine Tüte mit der Lieblingsmischung zu wählen und sich mit deren Story zu beschäftigen.

Pour se démarquer dans un secteur surchargé où palettes de couleurs et repères visuels se répètent, les emballages de café doivent évoquer le style et la force de chaque mélange, ainsi que l'excellente qualité de la marque et du produit. Suivant une approche minimaliste, chaque mélange **Rio** est associé à des images sur un fond blanc pour un plus grand impact. Le design des sacs renvoie à l'expérience de dégustation du café qu'ils renferment, qu'elle qu'en soit l'intensité. Le visuel est pensé pour intriguer le consommateur et l'inviter à plonger dans l'histoire du mélange choisi.

RIO COFFEE

Creative Direction: Anthony De Leo, Scott Carslake, Tom Crosby
Design: Tom Crosby
Company: Voice
Country: Australia
Category: Coffee & tea (dry and capsules)

GOLD PENTAWARD 2013

THOMPSON'S FAMILY TEA

Creative Direction: John Wynne
Design: Adam Wilford
Company: BrandMe
Country: UK
Category: Coffee & tea (dry and capsules)

SILVER PENTAWARD 2013

Punjana has been in the hands of the Thompson family since its first appearance in 1896, but to develop its appeal based on expert blending and to shed any possible associations with budget teas a simple rebranding was made. The new **Thompson's Family Teas** emphasize this heritage, while Punjana, still the hero of the range, has become one of the core blends, each with its individual back-of-pack story. To retain loyal consumers, the existing pack design was kept but re-imagined following a visit to London's Transport Museum and its collection of 1930s posters. This distinctive graphic illustration style, which chimes with the brand's own industrial history, was then redeployed, coupled with a charming and modernistic feel.

Der Thompson-Familie gehört Punjana bereits seit Gründung im Jahre 1896. Nun sollte dessen Appeal weiterentwickelt werden. Um ausgehend von der Expertenmischung jede mögliche gedankliche Verknüpfung mit preisgünstigen Teesorten abzuschütteln, wurde ein einfaches Rebranding vorgenommen. Die neuen **Thompson's Family Teas** betonen dieses Erbe, während Punjana, weiterhin Held in diesem Bereich, zur zentralen Mischung wurde und jeweils eine individuelle Story auf der Rückseite der Verpackung erhielt. Um loyale Konsumenten zu binden, bewahrte man das vorhandene Verpackungsdesign, bereitete es aber nach einem Besuch im Londoner Transport Museum und dessen Sammlung von Plakaten der 1930er Jahre neu auf. Dieser charakteristische Illustrationsstil passt sehr gut zur Geschichte der Marke selbst und wurde gemeinsam mit einem ansprechenden und modernistischen Look neu umgesetzt.

Punjana appartient à la famille Thompson depuis son lancement en 1896. L'image de la marque a toutefois été repensée afin de conquérir le marché avec des mélanges de qualité, ainsi que de gommer toute association à des thés bas de gamme. Les nouveaux thés de la famille **Thompson** mettent l'accent sur cet héritage; Punjana reste le héros de la gamme et est devenu l'un des mélanges de base, qui ont tous leur histoire au dos de l'emballage. Pour plaire aux clients existants, le design a été conservé mais réinventé, après la visite du musée des transports de Londres et de sa collection d'affiches des années 30. Ce style d'illustration graphique bien reconnaissable est en phase avec l'évolution de la marque; il a été réinterprété et doté d'une touche moderniste élégante.

RIO COFFEE

Creative Direction: Tom Crosby
Art Direction: Anthony De Leo, Scott Carslake
Design: Tom Crosby
Illustration: Nate Williams
Copywriting: David Mackrell
Company: Voice
Country: Australia
Category: Coffee & tea (dry and capsules)

SILVER PENTAWARD 2014

TEA BAR

Creative Direction: Steven de Cleen
Design: Gertjan Muishout
Company: PROUDdesign
Country: Netherlands
Category: Coffee & tea (dry and capsules)

BRONZE PENTAWARD 2014

QUEENSLEY

Creative Direction: Alexey Fadeev
Design: Vera Zvereva
Account Management: Ksenia Parkhomenko
Company: Depot WPF
Country: Russia
Category: Coffee & tea (dry and capsules)

SILVER PENTAWARD 2013

SUNRISE RE POT
TAIWAN ALISHAN TEA SERIES

Design: Victor Branding Design
Company: Victor Branding Design
Country: Taiwan
Category: Coffee & tea (dry and capsules)

BRONZE PENTAWARD 2013

GUIDING

Design: Shen Haijun
Company: Oracle Creativity Agencies
Country: China
Category: Coffee & tea (dry and capsules)
SILVER PENTAWARD 2014

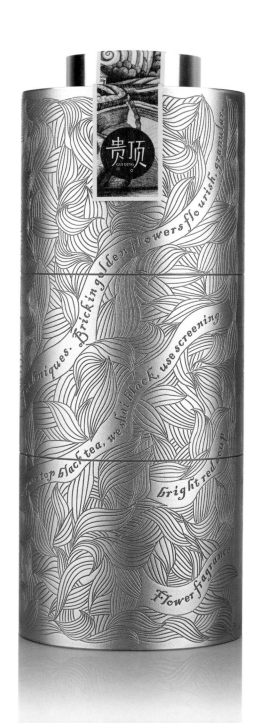

This range of teas and infusions, sold only by **The Library Gyms**, is made from the best ingredients and blended for detox, relaxation and to refresh mind and body. The package design turns an object at hand into something newly functional: the jars are recycled wine bottles, simply cut and polished by hand. The individual lids, hand-lathed from carefully chosen local woods, are made by artisans in Central Africa, thus helping them to be self-sufficient. The environmentally and socially responsible design aims to raise the profile of locally made products worldwide and help alleviate poverty and raise self-esteem through talented crafted trade.

Dieses Tee- und Aufguss-Sortiment, exklusiv von **The Library Gyms**, besteht aus besten Zutaten, die je nach Mischung zum Entgiften, zur Entspannung oder zur Erfrischung von Körper und Geist gedacht sind. Das Packungsdesign verwandelt ein Alltagsobjekt in etwas funktionell Neues: Recycelte Weinflaschen wurden einfach abgeschnitten und von Hand poliert. Die individuellen Verschlüsse aus sorgfältig ausgewählten heimischen Hölzern sind von Kunsthandwerkern in Zentralafrika gedrechselt, die dadurch autark bleiben können. Das nachhaltige und umweltbewusste Design zielt darauf, weltweit das Profil lokal produzierter Waren zu fördern, soll Armut lindern und durch talentiertes Kunsthandwerk das Selbstbewusstsein stärken.

Cette gamme de thés et d'infusions, uniquement vendus par **The Library Gyms**, est faite à partir des meilleurs ingrédients ; les mélanges se veulent détoxifiants, relaxants et rafraîchissants pour le corps et l'esprit. Le design de l'emballage donne de nouvelles fonctions à des objets : les pots sont ainsi des bouteilles de vin recyclées, taillées et polies à la main. Des artisans d'Afrique centrale travaillent les couvercles dans du bois local choisi avec soin, et peuvent ainsi être autosuffisants. Le design responsable en matière d'environnement, par la promotion de produits locaux à l'échelle mondiale, mais aussi sur le plan social, vise à sortir des artisans de la pauvreté et à augmenter leur estime de soi.

LIBRARY LEAVES

Design: Karen Welman, Andrew Lyons, Peter Horridge, Zana Morris, Corinne Spurrier, People of the Sun
Company: Pearlfisher
Country: UK
Category: Coffee & tea (dry and capsules)

GOLD PENTAWARD 2014

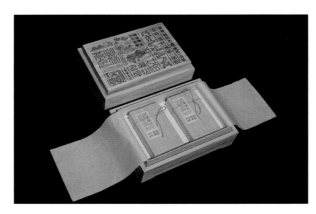

XINLIN TEA
1793 CHAOSHAN OLD PORT GONGFU TEA CULTURE

Design: Lin Shaobin
Company: Lin Shaobin Design
Country: China
Category: Coffee & tea (dry and capsules)

SILVER PENTAWARD 2014

TWININGS
NEW KNIGHT ERRANTRY

Design: Vike Chan
Company: KHT Brand Consulting & Management
Country: China
Category: Coffee & tea (dry and capsules)

BRONZE PENTAWARD 2013

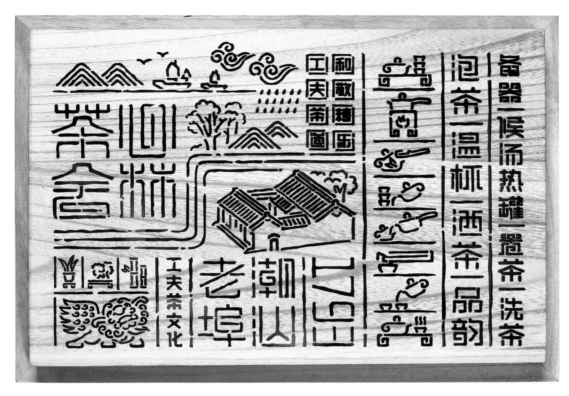

ALMA DE CUBA

Creative Direction: Perry Haydn Taylor
Company: Big Fish
Country: UK
Category: Coffee & tea (dry and capsules)

GOLD PENTAWARD 2014

In the 1940s, Cuba was the world's biggest coffee exporter, shipping 20,000 tons of beans every year. But after the Revolution a steady decline in production set in, until by 2012 it looked as though the last cup had been drunk. Then along came Phillip Oppenheim, a former member of parliament and card-carrying Cubaphile, who got together with some old pals to restore Cuban coffee to its rightful place. By introducing the brand name **Alma de Cuba** (soul of Cuba) and channeling the spirit of local folk art to create an evocative design scheme, the hope is that these bold packs have just as much soul as the coffee itself.

In den 1940er Jahren exportierte Kuba als weltweit größter Kaffeeproduzent jährlich 20.000 Tonnen Bohnen. Doch nach der Revolution sank die Produktion stetig, bis es 2012 so schien, als sei die letzte Tasse Kaffee getrunken. Da machte sich Phillip Oppenheim, ein ehemaliges Mitglied des britischen Parlaments und ausgewiesener Kuba-Fan, mit einigen alten Kumpels daran, den kubanischen Kaffee wieder auf sein verdientes Podest zu setzen. Die Einführung des Markennamens **Alma de Cuba** (Seele von Kuba) und das von der heimischen Volkskunst inspirierte, lebendige Designschema lässt hoffen, dass diese Packungen genauso viel Seele enthalten wie der Kaffee selbst.

Dans les années 40, Cuba était le plus grand exportateur de café au monde, avec 20 000 tonnes de grains expédiés par an. La production a accusé après la Révolution un déclin continu, pour connaître son minimum en 2012. Jusqu'au jour où Phillip Oppenheim, ancien membre du Parlement britannique et cubaphile affirmé, s'est associé à de bons amis pour rendre au café cubain la place qui lui revenait. La marque **Alma de Cuba** (l'âme de Cuba) a été lancée en transmettant par son design évocateur tout l'esprit de l'art populaire de l'île, et l'espoir que le café soit aussi intense que son emballage est audacieux.

BLACK SHEEP COFFEE

Design: Cartils creative team
Company: Cartils
Country: Netherlands
Category: Coffee & tea (dry and capsules)

SILVER PENTAWARD 2014

LA PLACE KOFFIE

Creative Direction: Carole van Bekkum
Creative Team: Leonie van Dorssen, Sanne Angenent
Company: DreamCatch
Country: Netherlands
Category: Coffee & tea (dry and capsules)

BRONZE PENTAWARD 2014

PISTOL & BURNES

Creative Direction: Matthew Clark, Roy White
Design: Roy White, Liz Wurzinger, Steph Gibson
Illustration: Matthew Clark
Company: Subplot Design
Country: Canada
Category: Coffee & tea (dry and capsules)

BRONZE PENTAWARD 2014

TASTEFUL TEA

Design: Victor Branding Design
Company: Victor Branding Design
Country: Taiwan
Category: Coffee & tea (dry and capsules)

BRONZE PENTAWARD 2014

SCHULP VRUCHTENSAPPEN

Art Direction/Design: Arthur van Hamersveld
Creative Direction: Steven de Cleen
Company: PROUDdesign
Country: Netherlands
Category: Functional beverages

GOLD PENTAWARD 2014

INK

Creative Direction: Bjørn Rybakken
Design: Alexandra Kloster
Managing Direction: Line Støtvig
Account Management: Bente Hauge
Production: Henning Arnesen
Company: Tangram Design
Country: Norway
Category: Functional beverages

SILVER PENTAWARD 2014

POLA BURNING PLUS

Art Direction: Yushi Watanabe
Design: Hiromi Kobayashi
Company: Pola
Country: Japan
Category: Functional beverages

SILVER PENTAWARD 2013

SILK
SAKURA AND KOUJI

Art Direction: Koichi Sugiyama
Design: Minako Endo
Production: Yasutomo Ishii
Company: Maru
Country: Japan
Category: Functional beverages

BRONZE PENTAWARD 2014

CALIFIA FARMS

Creative Direction: Margo Chase
Design: Paula Hansanugrum
Company: Chase Design Group
Country: USA
Category: Functional beverages

SILVER PENTAWARD 2013

SUJA
ESSENTIALS

Design: Becky Nelson, Jeremy Dahl
Company: Bex Brands
Country: USA
Category: Functional beverages

BRONZE PENTAWARD 2014

BIOLA

Design: Emelie Spjuth, Alexandra Kloster
Creative Direction: Bjørn Rybakken
Managing Direction: Line Støtvig
Account Management: Bente Hauge
Production Lead: Klaus Dalseth
Company: Tangram Design
Country: Norway
Category: Functional beverages

BRONZE PENTAWARD 2013

OTE

Design Direction: Jon Stubley
Design: Simon Morrow
Creative Services Management: Lee Forster
Company: Elmwood
Country: UK
Category: Functional beverages

SILVER PENTAWARD 2014

SPRUCE TIP STOUT

Creative Direction: Andrew Samuel, David Walker
Art Direction/Design: Rory O'Sullivan
Company: Saint Bernadine Mission Communications
Country: Canada
Category: Beer

BRONZE PENTAWARD 2014

ST STEFANUS

Design: Hamish Shand, Chris Noakes, David Beard
Company: Brandhouse
Country: UK
Category: Beer

GOLD PENTAWARD 2013

Two gay farmers, Phil Palmer and Michael Butcher, established a small farm and brewery on the site of a Civil War Roundhead encampment for the first Battle of Newbury, Berkshire (UK), which took place on September 20, 1643. This premium beer is hand-crafted and aimed at a unisex market, designed to appeal to women but without alienating men. Different feathers from the farm's chicken breeds identify the individual beers, with the feathers being steam-cleaned, then hand-applied in the labeling process, making the bottles attractive, tactile and each one completely unique. The beer names themselves come from the soldiers who fought on the land.

Die beiden schwulen Farmer Phil Palmer und Michael Butcher gründeten einen kleinen Hof mit Brauerei, dort, wo sich während der ersten Schlacht des Englischen Bürgerkriegs im britischen Berkshire am 20. September 1643 nahe Newbury das Militärlager der Roundheads befand. Dieses handgebraute Premiumbier bedient einen Unisexmarkt: Es spricht in seiner Art Frauen an, verprellt aber auch keine Männer. Verschiedene Federn der auf der Farm gezüchteten Hühnerrassen kennzeichnen die einzelnen Biere. Die Federn werden dampfgereinigt und dann per Hand aufs Etikett aufgebracht. Das macht die Flaschen attraktiv, taktil und völlig einzigartig. Die Namen der Biere selbst stammen von den Soldatengruppen, die auf dem Gebiet gekämpft haben.

Deux agriculteurs homosexuels, Phil Palmer et Michael Butcher, ont établi une petite ferme et une brasserie sur le site d'un cantonnement des Roundheads pendant la guerre civile, lors de la première Bataille de Newbury au Berkshire (Royaume-Uni) qui s'est déroulée le 20 septembre 1643. Cette bière artisanale de qualité s'adresse à un marché unisexe et est pensée pour plaire aux femmes sans pour autant exclure le public masculin. Les plumes des différentes races de poulets élevés à la ferme identifient chaque bière : elles sont nettoyées à la vapeur et appliquées à la main lors du processus d'étiquetage pour rendre les bouteilles attirantes, texturées et absolument uniques. Les bières sont nommées d'après les soldats ayant combattu au front.

TWO COCKS

Design: Bronwen Edwards, David Beard
Company: Brandhouse
Country: UK
Category: Beer

SILVER PENTAWARD 2013

GOLD MINE BEER

Creative Direction: Andrey Kugaevskikh
Design: Sergey Gerasimenko
Company: Svoe Mnenie
Country: Russia
Category: Beer

GOLD PENTAWARD 2014

KIRIN SUMIKIRI

Design: Bravis International team
Company: Bravis International
Country: Japan
Category: Beer

SILVER PENTAWARD 2013

BEERS OF LA BRASSERIE DU CHÂTEAU

Art Direction: Priscilla Balmer, Yvo Hählen
Graphic Design: Yvo Hählen
Illustration: Priscilla Balmer, Yvo Hählen
Company: A3 Studio
Country: Switzerland
Category: Beer

BRONZE PENTAWARD 2014

HEINEKEN
THE CLUB BOTTLE

Art Direction: Ramses Dingenouts
Design: Peter Eisen, Stéphane Castets
Illustration: Matt W. Moore
Company: dBOD
Country: Netherlands
Category: Beer

SILVER PENTAWARD 2014

DOLINA

Design: Daniel Morales, Javier Euba
Company: Moruba
Country: Spain
Category: Beer

SILVER PENTAWARD 2014

Dolina, the first artisanal beer from Burgos (Spain), is named after Gran Dolina, one of Europe's foremost archeological sites. Taking this as the design's leitmotif, together with searching and discovery, an interesting experimental result came about in which the consumers themselves are able to make a find. The beer-drinker's reflex scratching at a bottle label resembles the work of archeologists at a dig, but here as the label is scratched away the skull of *Homo heidelbergensis* is revealed. Scratching off the back label reveals this to be the world's most intact fossilized human skull, whose discovery at Dolina proved revolutionary.

Dolina, das erste hausgemachte Bier aus dem spanischen Burgos hat seinen Namen von Gran Dolina, einer der wichtigsten archäologischen Grabungsstätten Europas. Darauf bezieht sich auch das Designleitmotiv: Der Kunde gelangt durch Suchen und Entdecken zu einem interessanten experimentellen Resultat. Das reflexhafte Kratzen vieler Biertrinker am Flaschenetikett ähnelt der Arbeit eines Archäologen bei Ausgrabungen: Wenn man das Etikett abkratzt, stößt man auf den Schädel des *Homo heidelbergensis*. Rubbelt man dann noch die Rückseite frei, erfährt man, dass es sich hier um den am besten erhaltenen fossilen Menschenschädel handelt, dessen Entdeckung in Dolina eine Sensation war.

Dolina, la première bière artisanale fabriquée à Burgos (Espagne), tire son nom de Gran Dolina, l'un des sites archéologiques les plus célèbres d'Europe. Tel est le leitmotiv du design, qui joue avec les notions de fouilles et de découvertes et permet aux consommateurs de faire eux-aussi une trouvaille. Le réflexe qu'un buveur de bière a de gratter l'étiquette de la bouteille s'apparente au travail des archéologues : ici toutefois, c'est le crâne d'un *Homo heidelbergensis* qui apparaît petit à petit. Il s'agit du fossile humain le plus intact au monde qui a été exhumé lors d'une découverte exceptionnelle sur le site de Dolina.

HAMOVNIKI BEER

Design: DDH creative team
Company: Dutch Design House
Country: Russia
Category: Beer

BRONZE PENTAWARD 2013

SOL

Brand Direction: Eugene Bay
Creative Direction: John Comitis, Pieter Jelle
Braaksma, Gerwin Scholing, Martijn Doolaard
Account Management: Susanne Leydes
Global Management Sol: Vicente Cortina (Heineken)
Company: VBAT
Country: Netherlands
Category: Beer

BRONZE PENTAWARD 2013

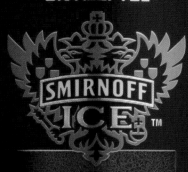

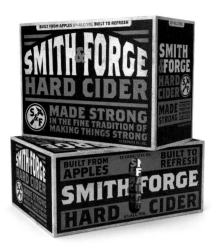

SMITH & FORGE HARD CIDER

Design: George Argyros, James Pietruszynski,
Adam Ferguson, Justin Berglund
Company: Soulsight
Country: USA
Category: Ciders & low-alcohol drinks

SILVER PENTAWARD 2014

SMIRNOFF ICE
BLACK

Creative Direction: Lee Arters
Associate Design Direction: David Parsons
Senior Design: Clara Chang
Client Direction: Fiona Atzler
Senior Client Management: Trae Watlington
Company: Landor Associates
Country: USA
Category: Ciders & low-alcohol drinks

GOLD PENTAWARD 2013

HANSA BORG BREWERIES
GREVENS CIDER

Managing Direction: Line Støtvig
Creative Direction: Bjørn Rybakken
Design: Kiki Plesner-Löfroth
Production Lead: Mette Nerhagen
Account Management: Stine Wergeland
Client: Hansa Borg Bryggerier
Client Product Management: Marvel Stigen Skreien
Client Design Management: Eirik Abelsen
Company: Tangram Design
Country: Norway
Category: Ciders & low-alcohol drinks

BRONZE PENTAWARD 2013

Air (Alcohol Inspired Refresher), a new sparkling alcohol beverage in the ready-to-drink category, employs a graphic treatment based on the periodic table to create a strong visual identity and communicate key product attributes. Three flavors were released in slim cans and their corresponding four-packs, with the overall can design keeping to the sophisticated simplicity of the color-coded label element. The clean design and bright color palette directly convey the drink's promise of refreshment, and this is further emphasized by the tagline "Come up for Air". The system also utilizes the core brand color blue to communicate the water ingredient as well as providing a neutral backdrop for the graphic elements.

Air (*Alcohol Inspired Refresher*) ist das neue spritzige alkoholische Getränk aus der Kategorie der trinkfertigen Produkte. Seine grafische Gestaltung setzt auf das Periodensystem, um eine kraftvolle visuelle Identität zu schaffen und die zentralen Produktattribute zu vermitteln. Die drei Geschmacksrichtungen sind in schlanken Dosen und den entsprechenden Viererpacks erhältlich. Das Dosendesign richtet sich insgesamt nach der anspruchsvollen Einfachheit des farbkodierten Elements auf dem Etikett. Schon mit dem aufgeräumten Design und seiner leuchtenden Farbpalette verspricht das Getränk Erfrischung, was zusätzlich durch den Slogan „Come up for Air" betont wird. Das System nutzt Blau als zentrale Markenfarbe. Das vermittelt die wesentliche Zutat Wasser und schafft auch einen neutralen Hintergrund für die grafischen Elemente.

Air (*Alcohol Inspired Refresher*) est une nouvelle boisson gazeuse dans la catégorie des prêts à boire. Le traitement graphique part du tableau périodique pour créer une forte identité visuelle et transmettre les attributs clés du produit. Trois parfums ont été lancés dans des canettes élancées et des packs de quatre assortis, le design d'ensemble respectant la simplicité sophistiquée des éléments classés par couleur. Le design impeccable et les tons vifs évoquent la promesse de rafraîchissement de la boisson, ce qui est également souligné par le slogan « Come up for Air ». Le concept se sert également du bleu propre à la marque pour matérialiser l'ingrédient eau et offrir un fond neutre pour les éléments graphiques.

AIR

Creative Direction: David Turner, Bruce Duckworth, Sarah Moffat
Design: Georgiana Ng, Matt Lurcock
Design Direction: Rebecca Au Williams
Company: Turner Duckworth: London & San Francisco
Country: UK, USA
Category: Ciders & low-alcohol drinks

SILVER PENTAWARD 2013

XIDE

Creative Direction: Isabelle Dahlborg Lidström
Design Direction: Andreas Linnell
Industrial Design: Jonas Lundin, Lisa Burman
Production Management: Judith Socha
Client Service Direction / Brand Strategist:
Linn Eklund
Final Art: James Wright
Company: Nine
Country: Sweden
Category: Ciders & low-alcohol drinks

SILVER PENTAWARD 2013

MOLSON COORS CANADIAN CIDER

Art Direction: Ron Wong
Design: Ryan Irven, Brian Stafflinger
Company: Spring Design Partners
Country: USA
Category: Ciders & low-alcohol drinks

BRONZE PENTAWARD 2014

HARRY BROMPTON'S

Design: Cartils creative team
Company: Cartils
Country: Netherlands
Category: Ciders & low-alcohol drinks

GOLD PENTAWARD 2014

SHICHIHONYARI

Design: Yoshiki Uchida, Shohei Onodera
Creative/Art Direction: Yoshiki Uchida
Company: Cosmos
Country: Japan
Category: Ciders & low-alcohol drinks

SILVER PENTAWARD 2014

WILD TURKEY
AMERICAN HONEY

Creative Direction: Christopher Reay
Design: Andy Audsley, Lara Ashworth
Company: Cowan Design, London
Country: UK
Category: Ciders & low-alcohol drinks

BRONZE PENTAWARD 2013

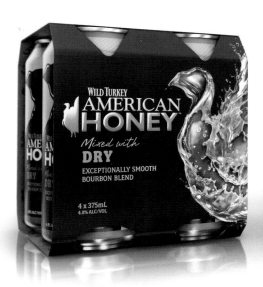

Paperboy is about as green as it's possible to make a wine bottle. Each one is made from compressed recycled paper, printed with natural inks and with a recyclable sleeve inside just as you find in a wine-box. The bottles are nevertheless rigid and strong, even ice bucket-safe for three hours, and require only 15% of the energy normal bottles take to produce. They weigh only an ounce when empty and so save a considerable amount of energy in shipping. In aiming to be the most environmentally friendly wine around, the bottle's form targets those who are already aware while the brand name and retro graphics are directed to early adopters.

Die Weinflasche **Paperboy** wird so grün wie nur irgend möglich produziert. Jede Flasche besteht aus gepresstem Recyclingpapier, bedruckt mit natur-belassener Tinte, darin eine recycelbaren Hülle wie in einem normalen Weinkarton. Die Flaschen sind dennoch stabil und widerstandsfähig. Man kann sie sogar bis zu drei Stunden ins Eisfach stellen. Die Herstellung benötigt nur 15% der für normale Flaschen verbrauchten Energie. Leer wiegen sie gerade 30 Gramm und sparen damit bei der Auslieferung beträchtlich Energie. Die Zielsetzung lautete, der umweltfreundlichste Wein überhaupt zu sein. Dafür richtet sich die Form der Flasche an jene, die bereits umweltbewusst sind, während Markenname und Retro-Grafik sich an die Early Adopters wenden.

Paperboy est aussi écologique que peut l'être une bouteille de vin. Chacune est fabriquée en papier recyclé, imprimée avec des encres naturelles et accompagnée d'un manchon recyclable comme ceux présents dans les coffrets de vins. Les bouteilles sont toutefois rigides et résistantes, peuvent rester plongées dans un seau à glace pendant trois heures et ne demandent que 15% de l'énergie habituellement nécessaire pour fabriquer des bouteilles standard. Leur poids à vide est de 30 grammes, ce qui réduit l'énergie dépensée en transport. Visant à être le vin le plus respectueux de l'environnement, la forme de la bouteille convainc ceux déjà responsables, alors que le nom et le graphisme rétro parlent aux acheteurs qui veulent s'aventurer.

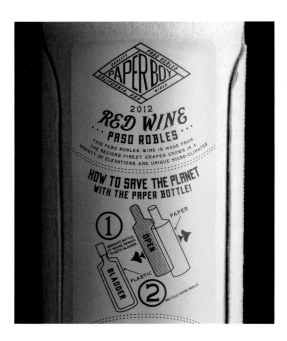

SQUARE MILE
CRANBERRY HOLIDAY CIDER

Design/Illustration: Kristin Casaletto
Creative Direction/Copywriting: Ben Jenkins
Company: Sasquatch
Country: USA
Category: Ciders & low-alcohol drinks
BRONZE PENTAWARD 2014

TRUETT HURST
PAPERBOY WINE

Art Direction: Kevin Shaw
Design: Cosimo Surace
Company: Stranger & Stranger
Country: UK
Category: Wines

GOLD PENTAWARD 2014

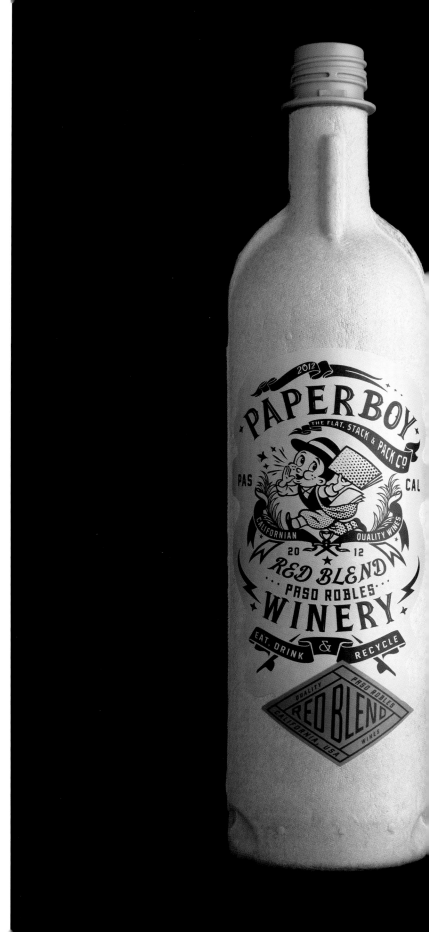

PURE DROPS

Design: Bob Studio design team
Company: Bob Studio
Country: Greece
Category: Wines

SILVER PENTAWARD 2014

DRY RED
P.G.I. PELOPONNESE
2012

DRY WHITE
P.G.I. PELOPONNESE
2013

DRY ROSE
P.G.I. KORINTHIA
2013

RASURADO

Creative Direction/Design:
Daniel Morales, Javier Euba
Copywriting: Albert Martinez
Lopez-Amor
Company: Moruba
Country: Spain
Category: Wines

GOLD PENTAWARD 2013

LUMOS SELECCION

Design: Roman Ruska, Francisca Martín
Company: Ruska, Martín, Associates
Country: Germany
Category: Wines

SILVER PENTAWARD 2013

Why does a wine taste the way it does? To answer that, **Lumos** printed every contributory factor on the label, discarding the usual florid description for a scientific and immediately intelligible system using diagrams, icons and color coding. Every wine can thus be identified individually by its own optical flavor chart, developed in conjunction with wine experts. This indicates not only the detailed flavors, but also which flavor complexes are dominant. Each bottle is labeled with a number, inspired by Chanel No. 5 and deliberately echoing the world of fragrances. The rest of the label is designed in the spirit of the DIN Standard typeface, as developed by Siemens engineer Ludwig Goller in 1925 — the Chairman of the German DIN committee.

Warum schmeckt ein Wein genau so und nicht anders? Als Antwort schreibt **Lumos** alle wesentlichen Faktoren aufs Etikett. Die üblichen blumigen Beschreibungen werden zugunsten eines wissenschaftlichen und sofort verständlichen Systems von Diagrammen, Symbolen und Farbkodierungen verworfen. So lässt sich jeder Wein anhand individueller optischer Geschmackskarten identifizieren, die zusammen mit Weinexperten entwickelt wurden. Darin werden nicht nur detaillierte Geschmacksnoten aufgeführt, sondern auch, welcher geschmackliche Komplex vorherrscht. Jede Flasche bekommt, inspiriert von Chanel No. 5, seine eigene Zahl, was mit Bedacht auf die Welt der Düfte anspielt. Ansonsten ist das Etikett im Geiste der DIN-Standardschrift designt, wie sie 1925 der Siemens-Ingenieur Ludwig Goller als Vorsitzender des deutschen DIN-Ausschusses entwickelt hat.

Pourquoi chaque vin possède-t-il un goût propre? Pour répondre à cette question, **Lumos** a imprimé sur l'étiquette tous les facteurs jouant un rôle. Au lieu de l'habituelle description travaillée, des diagrammes, des icônes et un code de couleurs offrent une représentation très intelligible. Chaque vin peut donc être identifié par son propre graphique d'arômes mis au point avec des experts en vins. Le consommateur découvre ainsi le détail des saveurs et sait quel bouquet est dominant. Chaque bouteille est marquée d'un numéro, telle un flacon de Chanel N°5, faisant délibérément écho au monde des parfums. Le reste de l'étiquette est conçu dans l'esprit de la police DIN Standard développée en 1925 par Ludwig Goller, ingénieur chez Siemens et directeur du comité allemand DIN.

With vineyards scattered across one particular celebrated wine region, winemakers search high and low for the finest grapes to produce this new range of wines – hence the name **Hither & Yon**, an archaic way of saying "here and there". The ampersands derived from the brand name give the range a strong visual consistency whilst allowing for abundant variations in pictorial expression. Each one reflects the style of its wine, its color, aroma and palette, with lettering placed in different positions on each label to echo the idea of here and there. Only the best of each vintage is bottled and each ampersand is unique to a certain vintage. They will never be repeated so the range will continue to expand with new designs for each new release.

Wenn Weingärten sich breitgefächert über eine besonders gefeierte Weinregion verteilen, suchen Winzer allerorten nach den besten Trauben, um das neue Weinsortiment zu produzieren. Daher rührt auch der Name **Hither & Yon**: Dieser sehr altmodische Ausdruck steht für „hier und dort". Das aus dem Markennamen abgeleitete kaufmännische Und-Zeichen verleiht dem Sortiment seine starke visuelle Konsistenz und ermöglicht zugleich auch zahlreiche Varianten im bildlichen Ausdruck. Jede einzelne reflektiert den Stil des Weines, seine Farbe, das Aroma und seine Bandbreite. Die auf dem Etikett verteilte Beschriftung greift das Konzept eines „Hier und Dort" wieder auf. Nur die besten Trauben eines Jahrgangs werden auf Flaschen gezogen, und jedes Und-Zeichen wird für einen bestimmten Jahrgang einmalig gestaltet. Dieses wiederholt sich nie, und darum erweitert sich das Sortiment ständig um neue Designs.

Avec des vignes disséminées dans une région viticole de renom, les viticulteurs recherchent les cépages les plus fins pour produire cette nouvelle gamme de vins, d'où le nom **Hither & Yon**, une façon démodée pour dire « here and there » (ici et là). Les esperluettes assurent une bonne cohérence visuelle et de riches variantes illustratives. Chacune reflète le style du vin, sa couleur, son arôme et sa palette, et le texte est agencé différemment sur les étiquettes pour renvoyer à l'idée d'ici et là. Seul le meilleur de chaque cru est mis en bouteilles et chaque esperluette est unique à un certain millésime. Jamais répétées, elles permettent d'étendre la gamme avec de nouveaux designs à chaque lancement.

HITHER & YON

Design: Anthony De Leo,
Scott Carslake, Tom Crosby,
David Mackrell
Company: Voice
Country: Australia
Category: Wines

SILVER PENTAWARD 2013

CRIANZAS Y VIOEDOS R. REVERTE

Creative Direction: Alexey Fadeev
Art Direction: Alexandr Zagorskiy
Illustration: Vadim Bryksin
Calligraphy: Julia Zhdanova
Design: Alexandr Kishchenko
Copywriting: Ekaterina Lavrova
Company: Depot WPF
Country: Russia
Category: Wines

BRONZE PENTAWARD 2014

GLOVELY

Creative Direction: Alexey Fadeev
Art Direction: Alexandr Zagorskiy
Copywriting: Ekaterina Lavrova
Company: Depot WPF
Country: Russia
Category: Wines

BRONZE PENTAWARD 2014

COMON SAVA

Design: Arthur Schreiber, Pavla Chuykina,
Roman Inkeles, Maxim Kadashov
Company: StudioIn
Country: Russia
Category: Wines

BRONZE PENTAWARD 2013

GARNACHA
CENTENARIA

D. O. Navarra

2010

TERRA ANDINA

Creative Direction: Mariano Gioia
Executive YG Design:
Sebastian Yañez
Company: YG Design
Country: Argentina
Category: Wines
BRONZE PENTAWARD 2013

UPROOT WINE

Creative Direction: David Turner,
Bruce Duckworth, Sarah Moffat
Design Direction: Robert Williams,
Rebecca Au Williams
Design: Mike Gertz, Georgiana Ng
Production Direction: Craig Snelgrove
Company: Turner Duckworth: London & San Francisco
Country: UK, USA
Category: Wines
SILVER PENTAWARD 2014

90

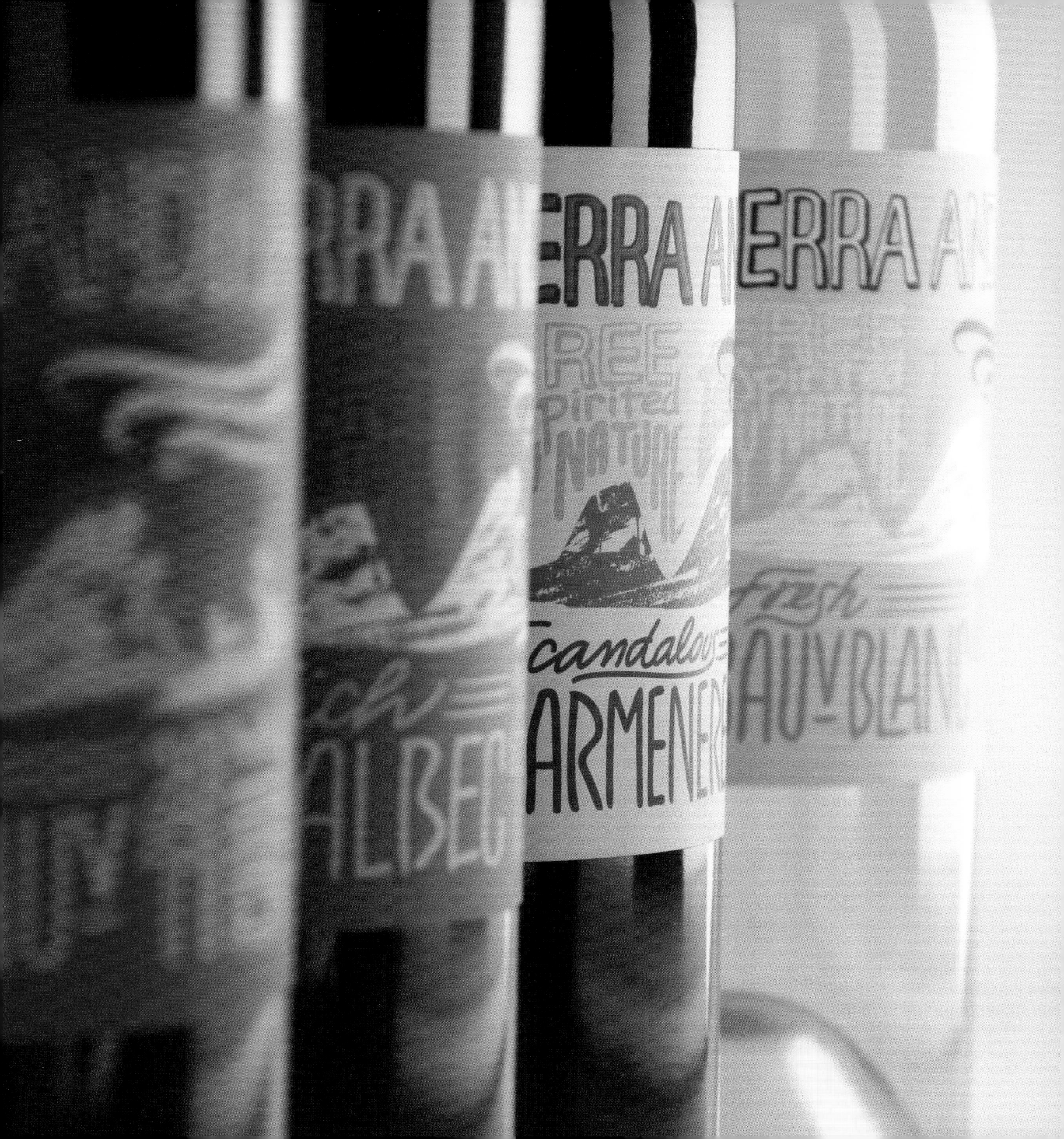
NATURE
Fresh

Winemaker's Selection is a range of wines picked by world-renowned winemakers to represent the industry's "state-of-the-art", beginning with Alberto Fenocchio from Italy. To involve the winemakers as closely as possible, making every wine unique but linked to the others by a common theme, they were asked to select a decorated ceramic plate from their home and tell a little story about it. Each plate gives a sense of place, and associations with food and culture, whilst their ordinary domestic usage is transformed as the story reveals facets of the winemaker's personality and thus of the wine as well. The personal touch is supported by a handwritten dedication and information about the winemaker, along with the grape and the terroir.

Winemaker's Selection ist ein von weltbekannten Winzern ausgewähltes Sortiment, um die aktuellen Erzeugnisse der Branche vorzustellen, beginnend mit Alberto Fenocchio aus Italien. Damit jeder Wein einzigartig bleibt, aber gleichzeitig mit den anderen über ein gemeinsames Thema verbunden ist, wurden die Winzer so eng wie möglich eingebunden: Sie sollten aus ihrem Zuhause eine dekorierte Keramikplatte wählen und dazu eine kleine Geschichte erzählen. Jedes Keramikstück lässt ein Gespür für den Ort wach werden. Es schafft Assoziationen mit Essen und Kultur und transformiert gleichzeitig seine gewöhnliche Nutzung im Haushalt, während die Story Aspekte der Winzerpersönlichkeit und damit auch des Weines enthüllt. Die persönliche Note wird durch eine handgeschriebene Widmung sowie durch Infos über Winzer neben denen über Traube und Terroir unterstützt.

Winemaker's Selection est une gamme de vins choisis par des viticulteurs de renommée mondiale pour représenter la « crème » du secteur, en commençant par l'Italien Alberto Fenocchio. L'idée était de faire des vins uniques partageant un thème commun et d'impliquer le plus possible les viticulteurs : ces derniers ont dû prendre chez eux une assiette en céramique et expliquer une anecdote la concernant. Chaque assiette évoque un lieu et les relations avec la nourriture et la culture ; son usage domestique s'efface pour révéler des facettes de la personnalité du viticulteur et donc du vin en soi. La touche personnelle est ajoutée par la dédicace à la main et des informations personnelles, sur le cépage et sur le terroir.

WINEMAKER'S SELECTION ALBERTO FENOCCHIO

Design: Henrik Olssøn, Erika Barbieri
Company: Olssøn Barbieri
Country: Norway
Category: Wine as bag-in-box
GOLD PENTAWARD 2013

Winemaker's Selection ®

WINEMAKER'S SELECTION IS A SERIES
OF WINES SELECTED BY SOME OF THE MOST
RECOGNIZED WINEMAKERS IN THE WORLD.
THEY WISH TO SHARE THEIR PASSION AND
DEDICATION FOR WINE MAKING, AND HAVE
CAREFULLY CHOSEN SOME OF THEIR
FAVORITE BLENDS FOR YOU TO ENJOY.
WITH THIS SELECTION OF DIFFERENT WINES
FROM DIFFERENT ORIGINS, WE HOPE TO
BRING THESE GENEROUS WINE REGIONS AROUND
THE WORLD CLOSER TO YOUR HOME.
A WINE FROM WINEMAKER'S SELECTION AIMS
TO ENRICH YOUR MEAL AND CREATE MEMORABLE
MOMENTS FOR YOU AND YOUR FRIENDS.

PLATE BY RICHARD GINORI
COURTESY OF FONDAZIONE MUSEO DELLA
CERAMICA DI MONDOVÌ · ITALY

BARBERA
D'ALBA DOC

PRODUCT OF ITALY

Winemaker's Selection ®
ALBERTO FENOCCHIO *Alberto fenocchio*
BARBERA D'ALBA
PRODUCT OF ITALY

FENOCCHIO ®

CORNISH ORCHARDS

Design: Mark Girvan, David Jones
Company: Buddy Creative
Country: UK
Category: Wine as bag-in-box

SILVER PENTAWARD 2013

IPL WINE POUCH RANGE

Design: Simon Tame, Debbie Seal
Company: Dare!
Country: UK
Category: Wine as bag-in-box

SILVER PENTAWARD 2013

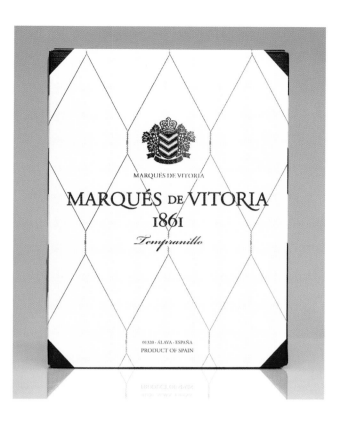

MARQUÉS DE VITORIA 1861

Design: Henrik Olssøn, Erika Barbieri
Company: Olssøn Barbieri
Country: Norway
Category: Wine as bag-in-box

BRONZE PENTAWARD 2013

RENÉ BARBIER ROSÉ BAG-IN-BOX
LIMITED EDITION BY CAMILLA THULIN

Design: Camilla Thulin, Robin Grann
Company: Freixenet Nordic
Country: Sweden
Category: Wine as bag-in-box

BRONZE PENTAWARD 2013

When **Absolut** wanted to raise its profile amongst bartenders around the world, and to promote itself as an inspiration for creating cocktails, an elegant design was settled on which reflected the focus and craftsmanship of the mixologist Nick Strangeway. The strong silhouette of the bottle recalls the brand's heritage and expertise in distillation, as is also stated by the alchemical symbol positioned at the neck. The color coating on the glass is inspired by 17th-century apothecary jars and also serves to protect the natural ingredients. The design clearly differentiates this range as something new and distinct from Absolut.

Absolut schickte sich an, unter den Barkeepern weltweit sein Profil zu schärfen und sich als Inspiration für die Kreation von Cocktails ins Spiel zu bringen. Dazu entschied man sich für ein elegantes Design, das die Kunst des Mixologen Nick Strangeway reflektieren und fokussieren sollte. Die kraftvolle Silhouette der Flasche ruft Erinnerungen an das Erbe der Marke und deren Expertise im Destillieren hervor. Das wird außerdem im alchemistischen Symbol am Flaschenhals aufgegriffen. Der Farbüberzug des Glases ist von den Apothekergefäßen des 17. Jahrhunderts inspiriert und dient ebenfalls dem Schutz der natürlichen Zutaten. Das Design hebt sich eindeutig als etwas Neues und im Sortiment von Absolut Einzigartiges ab.

Quand **Absolut** a décidé de se faire valoir auprès des barmans de la planète et de s'afficher comme une inspiration à l'élaboration de cocktails, la marque a misé sur un design élégant reflétant l'approche et le savoir-faire du mixologue Nick Strangeway. La silhouette franche de la bouteille rappelle l'héritage et l'expertise en matière de distillation, comme l'indique aussi le symbole alchimique sur le goulot. Le verre teinté rappelle les flacons d'apothicaire du XVIIᵉ siècle, tout en protégeant les ingrédients naturels de la lumière. Le design crée la nouveauté avec cette offre inédite signée Absolut.

SMIRNOFF WHITE

Executive Creative Direction: Graham Shearsby
Creative Direction: Asa Cook
Design Direction: Sam Cutler
3D Creative Direction: Laurent Robin-Prevallee
3D Design: Ben Davey
Realization: Ed Mitchell
Client Business Direction: Kasia Bannon
Client Direction: Susanne Wild
Client: Steve Honour, Steve White (Diageo)
Company: Design Bridge
Country: UK
Category: Spirits

BRONZE PENTAWARD 2014

Inspired by the brand's glamorous past, **Smirnoff White** is a new premium product specially designed for the global retail travel market, freeze-filtered and chilled to -6 °C to produce exceptional smoothness. The marriage of glass with the white porcelain-effect finish is beautiful and jarring, suggesting both modern techniques and historic extravagance. To create a rich sense of layering, the bottle's facets reflect the baccarat crystal of the Tsar's court while the angular forms and diffracted light mimic shards of Arctic ice. The bottle is thus sure to stand out sharply and capture the attention and imagination of travelers worldwide.

Inspiriert von der glamourösen Vergangenheit der Marke, positioniert sich **Smirnoff White** als neues Premiumprodukt speziell für den globalen Reisenden-Markt. Ein Filterprozess mit Eis und die Kühlung auf -6 °C sorgen für außergewöhnliche Samtheit. Schön und gleichzeitig irritierend wirkt es, wie das Glas mit dem Finish aus weißem Porzellan verschmilzt und somit neben moderner Technik auch die historische Extravaganz herausstellt. Die Flaschenfacette greift den Bakkarat-Kristall vom Hofe des Zaren auf, während das in den eckigen Formen gebrochene Licht arktische Eissplitter nachbildet – so entsteht ein vielschichtiges Design. Die Flasche hebt sich scharf vom üblichen Sortiment ab und zieht sofort die Aufmerksamkeit und Fantasie von Reisenden in aller Welt auf sich.

Inspiré du passé glamour de la marque, **Smirnoff White** est un produit haut de gamme pensé pour la clientèle habituée des « Duty Free Shops ». Filtrée à froid, cette vodka est réfrigérée à -6 °C pour lui conférer une exceptionnelle douceur. Le mariage du verre et d'une finition de porcelaine blanche est somptueux et impactant, marque de modernité et d'extravagance. Pour donner l'impression de couches, les facettes de la bouteille reflètent le cristal de Baccarat de la cour du tsar, alors que les formes angulaires et la lumière diffractée imitent les éclats de glace arctique. La bouteille a tout pour s'imposer et plaire aux voyageurs.

QIAN'S GIFT MAOTAI-FLAVOR STYLES

Design: Peng Chong
Company: Pesign Design
Country: China
Category: Spirits

BRONZE PENTAWARD 2013

SVEDKA VODKA

Executive Creative Direction: Sam O'Donahue
Creative Direction/Design: Pierre Jeand'Heur
Design: Daniela Sbarbati
Vice-President Marketing: Diana M. Pawlik
Direction/Marketing Services: Andi Carey
Company: Established
Country: USA
Category: Spirits

SILVER PENTAWARD 2013

Slamseys Fruit Gin is made in small batches using traditional methods but those on the family farm were keen for it to reach a wider audience. Steeped in history, yet avoiding the image of the country bumpkin, the brand would need to be desirable and at home in the most stylish of bars. The resulting design follows the discovery that one of Britain's greatest naturalists, John Ray, was born not far from the farm in 1627. In tribute to his meticulous cataloguing of the local flora and fauna, each flavor (blackberry, raspberry and sloe) sports its own set of insects, in a production run limited to 1,000 labels for each. The detailed illustrations and classic typography echo the adherence to craft, while the sturdy bottle shape and vibrant gin colors lend a fresh, modern feel.

Slamseys Fruit Gin wird mittels traditioneller Methoden in kleinen Mengen hergestellt, aber die Farm in Familienbesitz legt es darauf an, ein größeres Publikum zu erreichen. Die Marke ist sehr geschichtsträchtig, will aber vermeiden, hinterwäldlerisch zu wirken. Man will begehrenswert und selbst in den topgestylten Bars zuhause sein. Nachdem man entdeckt hatte, dass John Ray, einer der größten britischen Naturforscher, im Jahre 1627 nicht weit von der Farm entfernt geboren wurde, richtete man darauf das Design aus. In Anerkennung seiner akribischen Katalogisierung der lokalen Flora und Fauna zeigt jede Geschmacksrichtung (Brombeere, Himbeere und Schlehe) eine eigene Insektenart und wird in einer auf jeweils 1.000 Label begrenzten Edition produziert. In den detaillierten Illustrationen und der klassischen Typografie klingt das Bewahren der Handwerkskunst an, während eine robuste Flaschenform und leuchtende Gin-Farben für die frische, moderne Anmutung sorgen.

Slamseys Fruit Gins est produit en petites quantités et selon des méthodes traditionnelles. Cette exploitation familiale cherchait cependant à capter un public plus large. Empreinte d'histoire mais en évitant toute connotation rurale, la marque devait être prisée et trouver sa place dans les bars les plus sophistiqués. Le design s'inspire de la découverte que John Ray, l'un des plus grands naturalistes britanniques, est né tout près de la ferme en 1627. En hommage à sa méticuleuse classification de la flore et de la faune locales, chaque saveur (mûre, framboise et prune) possède son propre lot d'insectes et une production limitée à 1 000 étiquettes. Les illustrations détaillées et la typographie classique évoquent le goût du métier, alors que la forme robuste de la bouteille et les couleurs vives du gin transmettent fraîcheur et modernité.

SLAMSEYS FRUIT GINS

Creative Direction: Shaun Bowen
Design: George Hartley
Account Direction: Kerry Plummer
Company: B&B Studio
Country: UK
Category: Spirits

SILVER PENTAWARD 2013

TANQUERAY NO. TEN

Executive Creative Direction: Graham Shearsby
Creative Direction: Emma Follett
3D Creative Direction: Laurent Robin-Prevallee
3D Design: Ben Davey (senior), Jiah Lee
Realization: Ed Mitchell
Creative Direction Brand Language: Holly Kielty
Client Direction: Claire Riley (senior), Debbie Barber
Client: Jeremy Lindley, Montserrat De Rojas (Diageo)
Company: Design Bridge
Country: UK
Category: Spirits

GOLD PENTAWARD 2014

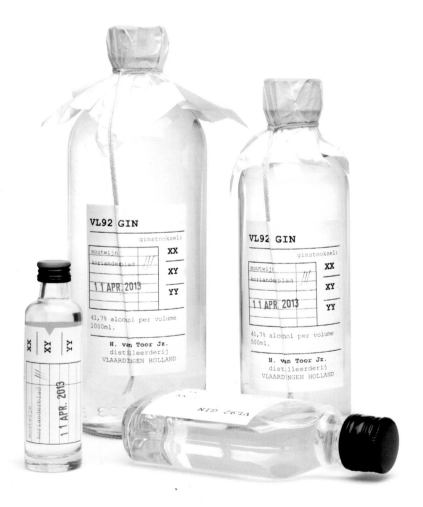

VL92 GIN

Design: Sietze Kalkwijk, Rick de Zwart
Company: Rare Fruits Council
Country: Netherlands
Category: Spirits

BRONZE PENTAWARD 2013

J&B Rare Scotch blend whisky was born in London in the mid-19th century, about the same time that tattoos began to spread through the city, from sailors to the upper classes and even Edward VII. To mark the spirit's London origins in a memorable way J&B commissioned 25 bottles to be tattooed for real. Firstly, they were covered with a latex skin, like that used in tattoo practice and the color of human skin to highlight the illusion. Paris-based tattooist Sébastien Mathieu then set to work, little knowing how hard it would be: each bottle took around 20 hours to be completed. A single basic design was used, but each bottle is unique.

J&B Rare Scotch Blend Whisky kam Mitte des 19. Jahrhunderts in London zur Welt, etwa zur gleichen Zeit, als in der Stadt Tätowierungen bei Bewohnern aller Schichten in Mode kamen – von Seeleuten bis in die oberen Klassen , selbst bei König Edward VII. Um die Londoner Wurzeln dieses geistreichen Getränks zu würdigen, ließ J&B tatsächlich 25 Flaschen tätowieren. Um die Illusion noch mehr zu vervollkommnen, wurden sie zuerst in eine hautfarbene Latexhülle eingewickelt – ähnlich jener, die man bei der Ausbildung von Tätowierern nutzt. Der Pariser Tätowierkünstler Sébastien Mathieu ging dann an die Arbeit, ohne zu ahnen, wie schwer seine Aufgabe war: Denn an jeder Flasche saß er etwa 20 Stunden. Hier wurde ein einfaches Grunddesign eingesetzt, doch jede Flasche ist ein Unikat.

Au milieu du XIXᵉ siècle, le whisky **J&B Rare Scotch** a vu le jour à Londres ; à cette époque, les tatouages ont commencé à devenir célèbres en ville, des marins aux classes supérieures, y compris le propre Edward VII. Pour célébrer les origines londoniennes du spiritueux, J&B a recommandé que 25 bouteilles soient véritablement tatouées. Elles ont d'abord été recouvertes d'un film en latex, comme celui utilisé par les tatoueurs, de couleur chair pour parfaire l'illusion. Le tatoueur parisien Sébastien Mathieu s'est ensuite attelé à la tâche, loin d'imaginer la difficulté de l'ouvrage : chaque bouteille a demandé environ 20 heures de travail. Le design choisi est simple, mais chaque bouteille est unique.

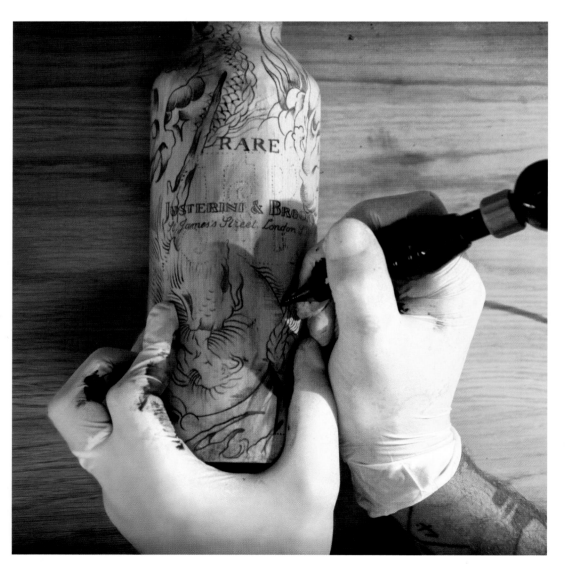

J&B
REAL TATTOOED BOTTLES

Chief Creative Officer: Kay Hes
Chief Salientist Officer: William Black
Tattoo: Sébastien Mathieu
Company: Button Button
Country: France
Category: Limited editions, limited series, event creations

GOLD PENTAWARD 2014
SLEEVER PRIZE

JEKER LIMITED EDITION

Design: Rodrigo Córdova
Company: Factor Tres Branding
Country: Mexico
Category: Limited editions,
limited series, event creations

SILVER PENTAWARD 2013

JOHNNIE WALKER BLACK

Creative Direction: Simon Adamson
Company: Bloom London
Country: UK
Category: Limited editions,
limited series, event creations

SILVER PENTAWARD 2014

BIRDS EYE ESTATE

Creative Direction: Tony Ibbotson
Design: Tim Heyer
Company: The Creative Method
Country: Australia
Category: Limited editions,
limited series, event creations

SILVER PENTAWARD 2014

VELKOPOPOVICKY KOZEL

Art Direction / Design: Yurko Gutsulyak
Company: Yurko Gutsulyak Studio
Country: Ukraine
Category: Limited editions, limited series, event creations

BRONZE PENTAWARD 2013

20°C

0°C

HEINEKEN

Art Direction: Jeremy Vince
Strategic Direction: Yan Chiabai
Deputy Direction General: Franck D'Andrea
Company: Raison Pure Paris
Country: France
Category: Limited editions,
limited series, event creations

BRONZE PENTAWARD 2014

COKE SOCHI 2014

Creative Direction: David Turner, Bruce Duckworth, Sarah Moffat
Design Direction: Brian Steele
Production Direction: Craig Snelgrove
Design Management: Josh Michels
Design: Melissa Chavez
Illustration: Thomas Hennessy
Production Artist: Jeff Ensslen
Client: Pio Schunker (senior vice-president), Frederic Kahn (design management), Coca-Cola North America
Company: Turner Duckworth: London & San Francisco
Country: UK, USA
Category: Limited editions, limited series, event creations

BRONZE PENTAWARD 2014

BEYONCÉ FUTURE POP
PEPSICO 2013 MUSIC CAMPAIGN

Creative Direction: Christopher Stern
Associate Creative Direction: Adam Walko
Art Direction: JP Elliot, Grace Kao
Account Direction: Cynthia Davies
Account Management: Colleen Drake
Photography: Patrick Demarchelier
Company: Safari Sundays
Country: USA
Category: Limited editions, limited series, event creations

SILVER PENTAWARD 2013

WILLIAMSON TEA

Creative Direction: Moyra Casey
Design: Sue Bicknell
Company: Springetts Brand Design Consultants
Country: UK
Category: Limited editions, limited series,
event creations

GOLD PENTAWARD 2013

POUR MOI
THE ART OF COFFEE

Design: Nicola Johnston
Studio Management: Shaun Green
Company: SMR Creative
Country: UK
Category: Limited editions,
limited series, event creations

BRONZE PENTAWARD 2013

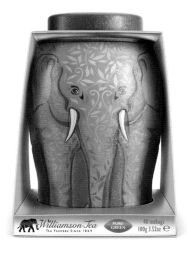

TRUETT HURST
SAFEWAY BOTTLE SLEEVES

Creative Direction: Kevin Shaw
Design: Cosimo Surace, Ewa Oliver
Company: Stranger & Stranger
Country: UK
Category: Distributors'/Retailers' own brands

GOLD PENTAWARD 2013

These eye-catching bottle sleeves were launched with the specific aim of spicing up the appearance of the wine shelves. The patented design features everything from quotes and recipes to retro imagery and even different ties at the top. Amongst rows of glass bottles the sleeves really stand out, adding interest for shoppers and making these bottles ideal gifts. The increased sleeve area offers possibilities to engage with customers in a way a tiny back label never could — everyone just wants to pick them up and read them. Feedback from both the retailer and customers has been incredible and has resulted in plans to extend the range.

Diese auffälligen Flaschenhüllen sollten speziell dem Ziel dienen, die Wirkung im Weinregal zu optimieren. Das patentierte Design zeigt alles Mögliche: Zitate und Rezepte bis hin zu Retrobildern und sogar unterschiedliche Krawatten oder Bänder am Flaschenhals. Stehen die Flaschen im Regal, fallen ihre Hüllen wirklich sehr auf und wecken das Interesse der Käufer, was sie zum idealen Geschenk macht. Durch die großzügige Gestaltung bietet die Hülle weitere Möglichkeiten, die Kundschaft auf eine Weise einzubeziehen, die mit winzigen Etiketten auf der Rückseite nie möglich wäre — man fühlt sich förmlich genötigt, die Flasche in die Hand zu nehmen und lesen. Die begeisterten Rückmeldungen von Händlern und Kunden gleichermaßen führten zu Planungen für ein erweitertes Sortiment.

Ces manchons de bouteilles pleins d'originalité ont été lancés dans le but d'égayer les rayonnages de vins. Le design breveté inclut des citations, des recettes, une imagerie rétro et différentes fermetures au col. Au milieu des rangées de bouteilles, les manchons se distinguent clairement et se présentent comme un cadeau idéal. L'espace qui leur est dédié a été augmenté : les clients sont intéressés à les toucher et à les observer, ce qui n'est pas le cas avec une étiquette standard. Les avis des magasins comme des clients ont été très positifs, au point d'envisager d'étendre la gamme.

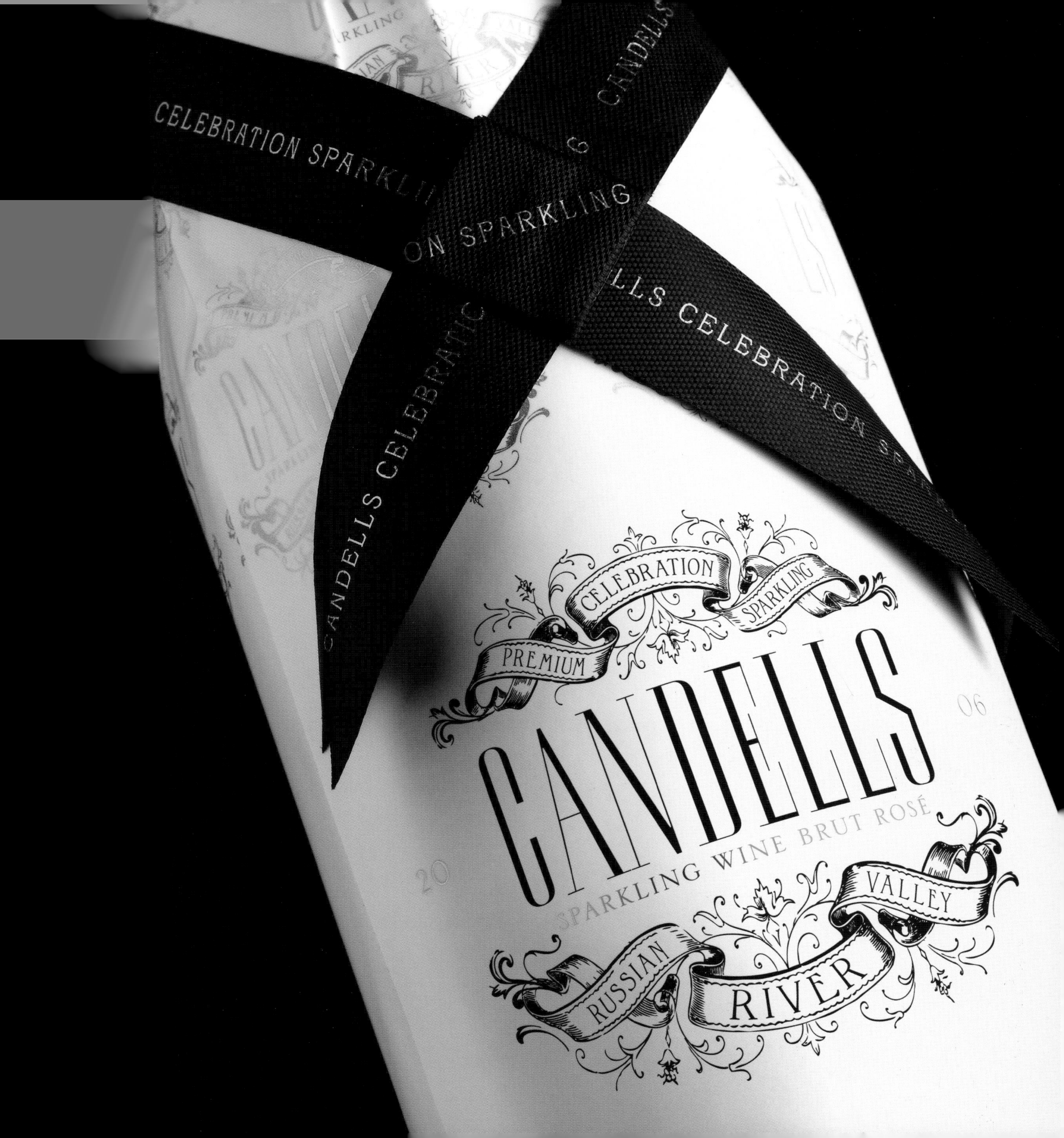

CELEBRATION SPARKLING

CANDELLS CELEBRATION

ON SPARKLING

CANDELLS CELEBRATION SPARKLING

CANDELLS CELEBRATIC

CELEBRATION SPARKLING

PREMIUM

CANDELLS

SPARKLING WINE BRUT ROSÉ

20   06

RUSSIAN   RIVER   VALLEY

DELHAIZE – ICED TEA

Creative Direction: Jürgen Hûughe
Design: Marloes Zwaenepoel
Photography: Quatre Etoiles
Company: Quatre Mains
Country: Belgium
Category: Distributors'/
Retailers' own brands

SILVER PENTAWARD 2014

TESCO FINEST
ROAST AND GROUND COFFEE

Design: Jon Sleeman, Simon Pemberton
Company: Pemberton & Whitefoord
Country: UK
Category: Distributors'/Retailers' own brands

SILVER PENTAWARD 2013

BRIGADERIA
TEA TIME COLLECTION

Creative Direction: Gustavo Piqueira
Design: Gustavo Piqueira, Samia Jacintho
Assistant Design: Marianne Meni,
Caroline Vapsys, Marcela Souza
Company: Casa Rex
Country: Brazil
Category: Distributors'/Retailers' own brands
BRONZE PENTAWARD 2013

CONTINENTE COFFEE CAPSULES
ORIGENS

Design: Sonae design team
Company: Sonae MC
Country: Portugal
Category: Distributors'/Retailers' own brands
SILVER PENTAWARD 2014

ICA TEA

Concept Direction: Jacob Bergström
Art Direction: Malin Mortensen
Production Management: Ida Stagles
Production Design: Monica Holm
Company: Designkontoret Silver
Country: Sweden
Category: Distributors'/Retailers' own brands

BRONZE PENTAWARD 2014

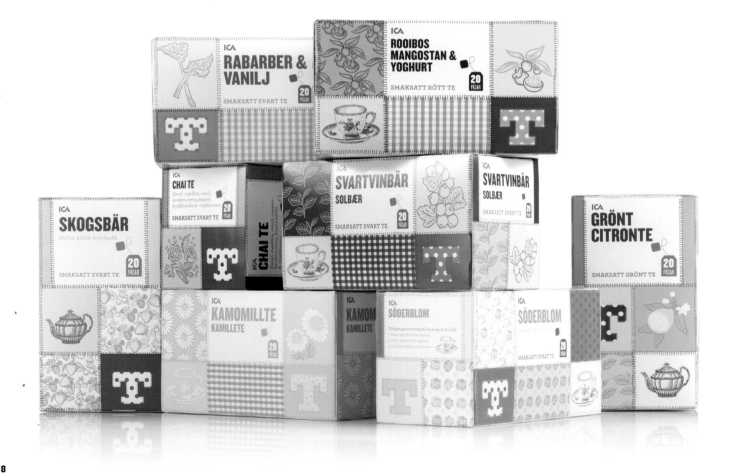

MORRISONS
LOVE IN A CUP

Design Direction: Martyn Hayes
Senior Design: Simon Thorpe
Account Handler: Rebecca Hanson
Company: Elmwood
Country: UK
Category: Distributors'/Retailers' own brands

BRONZE PENTAWARD 2013

CONSUM
JUICES

Design: Albert Puigdemont, Marta Montagut
Company: Puigdemont Roca
Country: Spain
Category: Distributors'/Retailers' own brands

BRONZE PENTAWARD 2014

FROM REAL FRUIT PIECES

TESCO *finest*

Forest fruits
Tea

Blended by experts for a tea
that's deliciously sweet
and tangy.

15

100% SRI LANKAN GREEN TEA LEAVES

TESCO *finest*

Green Tea
with
Mint

A delicate green tea expertly blended
with Oregon peppermint for a
crisp, clean flavour.

15

SPECIALLY SELECTED BY OUR TEA TASTING EXPERT

TESCO *finest*

Earl Grey
Tea

Infused with tangy bergamot
flavour for its famously
refreshing citrus notes.

15

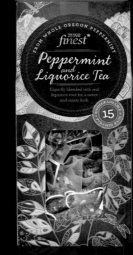

FROM WHOLE OREGON PEPPERMINT

TESCO *finest*

Peppermint
and
Liquorice Tea

Expertly blended with real
liquorice root for a sweet
and minty kick.

15

FROM WHOLE GREEN ROOIBOS

TESCO *finest*

Green Rooibos
with
Pear & Vanilla

For natural sweetness, softened by
our expert blenders with a hint
of vanilla and pear.

15

100% SRI LANKAN GREEN TEA LEAVES

TESCO *finest*

Green
Tea

Specially selected by our expert
taster for a lighter, more
delicate flavour.

15

INFUSED WITH REAL JASMINE PETALS

TESCO *finest*

Green Tea
with
Jasmine

For green tea full of delicate
floral flavour, selected by
our expert taster.

15

WITH WHOLE CAMOMILE FLOWERS

TESCO *finest*

Chamomile
and
Honey Tea

For a pure, delicate flavour, expertly
selected and sweetened with
a touch of honey.

15

FROM WHOLE LEMONGRASS

TESCO *finest*

Lemongrass
and
Ginger Tea

Expertly blended with real root ginger
for really zingy flavour and a
hint of spicy warmth.

15

FROM WHOLE OREGON PEPPERMINT

TESCO *finest*

Peppermint
Leaves

Carefully selected by our expert tea
taster for a fantastically bright,
refreshing flavour.

15

SPECIALLY SELECTED BY OUR TEA TASTING EXPERT

TESCO *finest*

English
Breakfast Tea

A careful blend of Assam, Kenyan and
Ceylon tea for a traditional, strong
and refreshing flavour.

15

TESCO JUICE BAR

Design: Jo Saker, Cathy Ogilvie,
Ellen Munro
Company: Parker Williams
Country: UK
Category: Distributors'/Retailers' own brands

SILVER PENTAWARD 2013

ARDBEG
ESCAPE PACK

Design: Pocket Rocket
Creative Direction/Production: DAPY
Company: DAPY – DO International
Country: France
Category: Casks, cases, gift boxes, ice buckets

SILVER PENTAWARD 2014

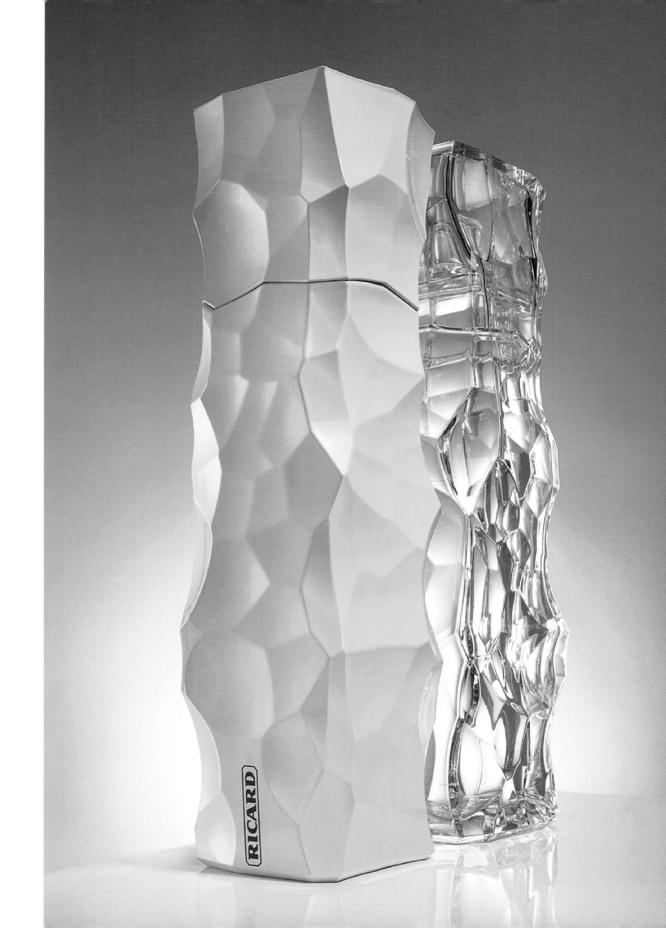

RICARD DUO
BY JAKOB+MACFARLANE

Design: Dominique Jakob,
Brendan MacFarlane
Company: Ricard
Country: France
Category: Casks, cases, gift boxes,
ice buckets

GOLD PENTAWARD 2014

THE HOUSE OF METAXA
5 STARS ON-METAL

Design: The House of Metaxa,
The Brand Union Paris
Company: The House of Metaxa
Country: Belgium
Category: Casks, cases, gift boxes,
ice buckets

BRONZE PENTAWARD 2014

BELVEDERE VODKA
ICE CRUSH

Creative Direction: Jean-Sébastien Blanc,
Vincent Baranger
Design: Martin Lefèvre
Company: 5.5 designstudio
Country: France
Category: Casks, cases, gift boxes, ice buckets

SILVER PENTAWARD 2014

Packaging for beer has become more and more involved in recent years, so this design aimed for a simpler approach, based on two trends on the Romanian market: a general increase in the consumption of beer, and the use of PET bottles or aluminum cans. As beer has now become more popular than wine in Romania, especially beers of German origin, **Volksbier** was chosen as a distinctive new brand name while the eye-catching container is based on a pint glass. Transparent cans are already used for soft drinks and the same PET material here gets very close to glass in its appearance.

Die Verpackung von Bieren wurde in den letzten Jahren immer aufwendiger. Darum verfährt dieses Design nach einem ganz einfachen Ansatz, der zwei Trends auf dem rumänischen Markt aufgreift: den steigenden Bierkonsum und die Verwendung von PET-Flaschen oder Aludosen. Da Bier in Rumänien mittlerweile beliebter ist als Wein, vor allem jenes aus deutscher Herstellung, nannte man die neue Marke **Volksbier** und wählte als Blickfang für das Behältnis einen Bierhumpen. Für Softdrinks werden bereits transparente Dosen eingesetzt, und das PET-Material hier wirkt schon sehr wie Glas.

À l'heure où l'emballage de bières est chaque fois plus élaboré, ce design vise une approche simple fondée sur deux tendances actuelles en Roumanie : la consommation croissante de bières et l'emploi répandu de bouteilles PET ou de canettes d'aluminium. La bière (notamment d'origine allemande) s'étant imposée au vin sur le marché roumain, **Volksbier** a été adopté pour rebaptiser le produit, et l'original emballage rappelle une pinte en verre. Les canettes transparentes sont déjà utilisées pour les boissons rafraîchissantes et le PET simule ici parfaitement le verre.

VOLKSBIER

Design: Cristian Stancu, Viorel Rusu
Company: Remark Studio
Country: Romania
Category: Packaging concept (beverages)
GOLD PENTAWARD 2014

TWICKENHAM FINE ALES

Design: Kevin Daly
Creative Direction: Moyra Casey
Company: Springetts Brand Design Consultants
Country: UK
Category: Packaging concept (beverages)

SILVER PENTAWARD 2014

TROPHY BEER

Design: Galima Akhmetzyanova,
Pavla Chuykina (students)
3D Visualization: Pavel Gubin
School: Auckland University of Technology
Country: Russia
Category: Packaging concept (beverages)

SILVER PENTAWARD 2013

STAR TRADE COFFEE

Design: José Luis García Eguiguren
Company: Gworkshop Design
Country: Ecuador
Category: Packaging concept (beverages)

BRONZE PENTAWARD 2013

REAL DRINKS
GENUINE DRINKS

Design: Kyungmin Park
Company: imkm design
Country: South Korea
Category: Packaging concept (beverages)

SILVER PENTAWARD 2014

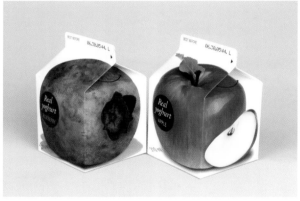

KISS
PURÉE OF VEGETABLES AND FRUITS

Design: Alexandra Istratova
Company: Alexandra Istratova
Country: Russia
Category: Packaging concept (beverages)

GOLD PENTAWARD 2013

HD SCULPT

Design: Greg Hurley, Rick Rangler
Company: Amcor Rigid Plastics
Country: USA
Category: Packaging concept (beverages)

BRONZE PENTAWARD 2014

MOOD OF RED CHINESE LANTERN

Creative Direction: Andrey Kugaevskikh
Art Direction: Roman Dukhovskoy
Design: Natalia Popova
Company: Svoe Mnenie
Country: Russia
Category: Packaging concept (beverages)

SILVER PENTAWARD 2013

GHOST SHIP RUM

Design: Galima Akhmetzyanova,
Pavla Chuykina (students)
School: Auckland University of Technology
Country: Russia
Category: Packaging concept (beverages)

BRONZE PENTAWARD 2014

RISE & SHINE

Design: Cristian Stancu, Viorel Rusu
Company: Remark Studio
Country: Romania
Category: Packaging concept (beverages)

BRONZE PENTAWARD 2013

food

In the jungle that is the world of crisps, crackers and nuts sold in bags, it is imperative to stand out. Amidst fierce competition from national brands on one side and private labels on the other, the Walkers brand (Lay's in many countries) is the market leader in crisps but sought a similar position in the nuts market. To this end, the packs were given a general design representing the face of a tiger in which can be read, as a subliminal image, the name **Tiger Nuts**, cleverly and creatively formed in the distinctive black stripes of a tiger's fur.

Im Dschungel der in Tüten angebotenen Kartoffel-chips, Kräckern und Nüssen muss man sich von der Konkurrenz abheben. Mitten im Wettstreit nationaler Marken auf der einen und Eigenmarken auf der anderen Seite ist Walkers (in vielen Ländern bekannt als Lay's) Marktführer beim Knabbergebäck, strebt aber im Segment der Nusssnacks eine ähnliche Position an. Zu diesem Zweck verlieh man den Verpackungen ein Gestaltungskonzept in Form eines Tigerkopfes, in dem man als subliminales Bild die Worte **Tiger Nuts** lesen kann, sehr geschickt und kreativ eingebettet als Streifen des Tigerfells.

Dans la jungle des chips, biscottes et fruits secs vendus en sachets, il est crucial de se démarquer. Au milieu de cette féroce concurrence des marques nationales d'une part et des labels privés d'autre part, la marque Walkers (Lay's dans de nombreux pays) domine le marché des chips. En quête d'une présence similaire pour les fruits secs, les emballages ont été entièrement repensés, avec une tête de tigre faite, tel un message subliminal, des lettres de **Tiger Nuts** pour représenter les bandes noires de la fourrure de l'animal.

WALKERS
TIGER NUTS

Design: David Annetts, Hayley Barrett, Felicity Walker, Alice Douglas Deane, Jim Burton, Lisa Mathews, Debbie Barber, Michelle Connolly, David Clabon, Rosie Marlow, Chris Mitchell, Chris Weir
Company: Design Bridge
Country: UK
Category: Best of the category food

PLATINUM PENTAWARD 2013

QIAN'S GIFT

Company: Pesign Design
Country: China
Category: Best of the category food
PLATINUM PENTAWARD 2014

In southeast Guizhou, people still follow the age-old ways of growing rice, rejecting chemical products in favor of letting nature look after things and so ensuring the best-quality organic rice is grown. In thus avoiding industrialization the rice packaging too abandons modern manufacturing methods and prefers traditional, high plant-fiber wrappers made by local paper-makers. Indigo is used in the region for dyeing cloth so this was adopted for printing the information on the packaging, all applied by hand without resort to machinery. The distinctive design both respects the environment and goes back to the roots of craft production methods.

In Guizhou im Südwesten Chinas wird der Reis immer noch nach uralter Tradition angebaut. Die Bauern lehnen den Einsatz von Chemikalien ab und lassen der Natur ihren Lauf. Somit produzieren sie einen organischen Reis bester Qualität. Da man Industrialisierung meidet, werden auch bei der Reispackung keine modernen Herstellungsmethoden eingesetzt. Man bevorzugt traditionelle Hüllen aus Pflanzenfasern, von örtlichen Papierherstellern produziert. In dieser Region färbt man Stoffe mit Indigo. Dieser Naturstoff wird auch bei den Produktinfos der Verpackung verwendet – alles per Hand ohne Maschineneinsatz. Das charakteristische Design respektiert die Umwelt und greift auf ursprüngliche Produktionsmethoden zurück.

Dans la province chinoise de Guizhou, les habitants appliquent encore d'anciennes techniques de culture du riz, en bannissant les produits chimiques et en laissant la nature faire son travail pour donner le meilleur des riz organiques. Pas d'industrialisation, donc pas non plus de méthodes de fabrication modernes pour l'emballage : l'enveloppe en fibre végétale est la création de fabricants de papier locaux. L'indigo est employé dans cette région pour teindre les vêtements ; il a aussi été retenu pour imprimer les informations sur le paquet, le tout fait à la main sans la moindre machine. Ce design original est respectueux de l'environnement et renvoie aux origines de production artisanale.

RANA

Client Direction: Carlos Puig Falcó
Creative Management: Nereida de Arcos
Photography/Style: Roig&Portell
Company: Branward
Country: Spain
Category: Cereals

GOLD PENTAWARD 2013

MONSTER HEALTH FOOD

Creative Direction: Peter Asprey
Company: Asprey Creative
Country: Australia
Category: Cereals

SILVER PENTAWARD 2013

WONDER BREAD

Account Direction: Sara Merrifield
Design: Jason Da Silva
Creative Direction: Chris Plewes
Company: Davis
Country: Canada
Category: Cereals

BRONZE PENTAWARD 2014

GUILIN GRUEL
ORGANIC RICE

Company: Lin Shaobin Design
Country: China
Category: Cereals

SILVER PENTAWARD 2014

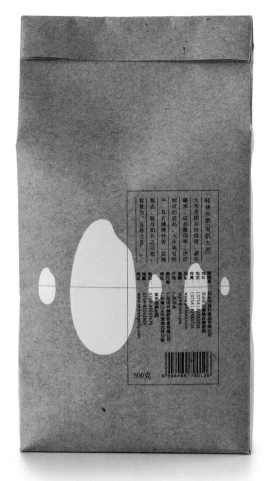
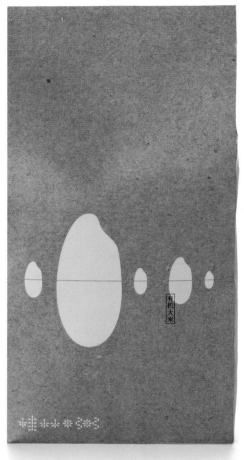

YUCUIFANG

Design: Wu Kuanfu
Company: Shenzhen Excel Package Design
Country: China
Category: Cereals

BRONZE PENTAWARD 2014

BAKEHUSET
NORWEGIAN BREAD

Design: Mathias Disen,
Erling Norderud Hansen
Project Leader: Karianne Stenby
Client Direction:
Caroline Von Hoiningen Huun
Creative Direction: Mathias Disen
Company: Scandinavian Design Group
Country: Norway
Category: Cereals

GOLD PENTAWARD 2014

Norges BRØD

NØKKEN

Grovbrød

Så kom det en gråhest med forgylt sal opp på stranda. Da var nøkken, og ingen annen.

B *Bakehuset*

Norges BRØD

ASKELADDEN

Spelt mellomgrov

«Nei nå orker jeg ikke mer,» sa Trollet. «Du ikke ete,» svarte gutten.

B *Bakehuset*

Norges BRØD

KONGSBRØD

Havrebrød med honning

...og da de kom og fikk es opp ôsa hadde han et opp alt i hop.

B *Bakehuset*

Norges BRØD

VESLEFRIKK

Kornbrød

"Jeg ønsker at ingen kan rikte meg det første jeg ber om" sa Veslefrikk.

B *Bakehuset*

Norges BRØD

HULDRA

Speltloff

Brun stakk hadde a, og lur gikk midt i myra. Kjær og myrynytter vorte hu alder det grøns.

B *Bakehuset*

KOIKE RICE-CLEANING STORE

Executive Creative Direction/Copywriting:
Kenichi Yasuda (sakura.inc)
Creative Direction/Art Direction:
Toshiki Osada (Kreo)
Art Direction/Design: Shogo Seki
Photography: Norio Kitagawa (Tokyo AD Design)
Production: Satoshi Hirai
Company: Shogo Seki
Country: Japan
Category: Cereals
BRONZE PENTAWARD 2013

MYLLYN PARAS 1928

Creative Direction: Alexey Fadeev
Art Direction: Maria Ponomareva
Management: Asya Drozdova
Pre-press: Kurban Garanov
Creative Assistant: Alexey Mikhailov
Company: Depot WPF
Country: Russia
Category: Cereals
SILVER PENTAWARD 2014

ALLINSON
BAKING AND BREAD FLOUR

Creative Direction: Alex Durbridge
Design Strategy: Derek Johnston
Design: Lori Townsend
Photography: Howard Shooter
Company: Family (and friends)
Country: UK
Category: Cereals

SILVER PENTAWARD 2013

In Russia today almost every variety of milk available to buy in stores has a period for extended consumption. As a result the taste is not natural, owing to the large number of preservatives that have been added. Thus, in the consumer's opinion there is no "true" milk. In order to counter this impression a new brand of milk was created, one that was bright and emotionally associated with childhood. The design depicts a world as seen by children, playful, energetic and uncomplicated, and in this way conveys the message that here is a true product with nothing to hide.

In Russland ist heutzutage praktisch jede im Laden erhältliche Sorte Milch verlängert haltbar. Als Folge davon schmeckt sie wegen der großen Zahl zugesetzter Konservierungsstoffe nicht mehr natürlich. Somit gibt es in der Wahrnehmung der Verbraucher keine „echte" Milch mehr. Um diesem Eindruck zu begegnen, wurde eine neue Milchmarke geschaffen, die fröhlich wirkt und emotional mit Kindheit verknüpft ist. Das Design zeigt die Welt, wie sie von Kindern gesehen wird: spielerisch, voller Energie und unkompliziert. So vermittelt es die Botschaft, hier handle es sich um ein Produkt, das nichts zu verbergen hat.

Dans la Russie actuelle, presque tous les types de lait disponibles en magasins ont une date limite de consommation éloignée, et le goût n'est pas naturel en raison des nombreux conservateurs qui ont été ajoutés. Dans l'esprit du consommateur, il n'existe donc pas de « véritable » lait. Pour combattre cette impression, une nouvelle marque de lait a été lancée avec une évocation de l'enfance. Le design illustre le monde tel que vu par les petits : ludique, dynamique et sans complications. Le message transmis est celui d'un produit authentique, sans rien à cacher.

SKY-HIGH

Creative Direction: Alexey Fadeev
Design: Vera Zvereva
Copywriting: Anastasia Tretyakova
Account Management: Ksenia Parkhomenko
Company: Depot WPF
Country: Russia
Category: Dairy products

GOLD PENTAWARD 2013

A-MOLOKO

Design: Vlad Ermolaev
Company: Ermolaev Bureau
Country: Russia
Category: Dairy products

BRONZE PENTAWARD 2013

NATURAL PLAN

Design: Park Sang-Hyun, Kwon Min-Jung,
Park Moon-Soon, Jeon Sun-Young,
Lee Moon-Yong, Jung Ju-Hee, Jeon Hye-Lim
Company: Korea Yakult
Country: South Korea
Category: Dairy products

SILVER PENTAWARD 2013

LURPAK SLOW CHURNED

Chief Creative Officer: Jonathan Ford
Creative Direction: Natalie Chung
Design: Vicki Willatts
Realization: Shaun Jones
Strategy: Rory Fegan
Account Direction: Nicci Cooper
Company: Pearlfisher
Country: UK
Category: Dairy products

SILVER PENTAWARD 2014

DANONE B2B
POP ART IN THE DAIRY WORLD

Creative Direction: Sylvia Vitale Rotta, Camille Riboud
Senior Design: Fanny Bouffier
Company: Team Créatif
Country: France
Category: Dairy products

SILVER PENTAWARD 2013

MALÝ GAZDA

Graphic Design: Juraj Vontorcik,
Juraj Demovic, Livia Lorinczova
Company: Pergamen Trnava
Country: Slovakia
Category: Dairy products

GOLD PENTAWARD 2014

KRAFT SINGLES

Account Direction: Sara Merrifield
Design: Jason Da Silva
Creative Direction: Chris Plewes
Company: Davis
Country: Canada
Category: Dairy products

BRONZE PENTAWARD 2014

ARLA FOODS
ANCHOR CHEDDAR

Design Direction: Steven Shaw
Creative Direction: Andrew Lawrence
Head of Verbal Identity: Simon Griffin
Account Management Direction: Jan Hirst
Account Direction: Deborah Stafford-Watson
Company: Elmwood
Country: UK
Category: Dairy products

SILVER PENTAWARD 2014

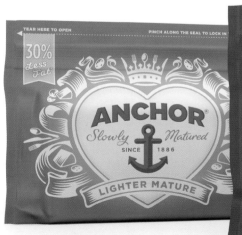
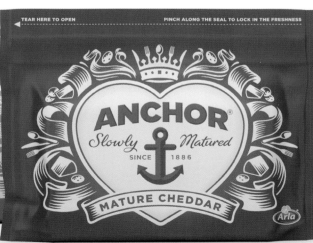
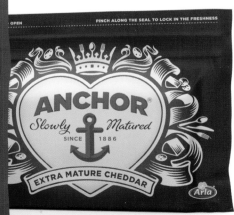

WING-CO

Design: Ben Lambert, Pete Hayes,
Sophie Escribano
Company: PB Creative
Country: UK
Category: Dairy products
BRONZE PENTAWARD 2013

TEMP TEE

Account Direction: Sara Merrifield
Design: Marianne Mastrofini
Creative Direction: Mark Roberts
Company: Davis
Country: Canada
Category: Dairy products
BRONZE PENTAWARD 2014

VERSTEGEN SPICES & SAUCES 'TABLE' SAUCES

Design: Erik de Graaf
Company: Millford
Country: Netherlands
Category: Spices, oils & sauces

GOLD PENTAWARD 2013

BIG KITCHEN

Brand Consultation: Ilya Lazuchenkov,
Tatiana Kharitonova
Brand Analysis: Katerina Palshina
Art Direction: Egor Myznik
Copywriting: Roman Urban
Project Management: Alice Askerova
Company: Plenum Brand Consultancy
Country: Russia
Category: Spices, oils & sauces

SILVER PENTAWARD 2013

JANG

Creative Direction: Jin Eun-son
Art Direction: Kim Nuly
Design: Kim Bo-hyun,
An Ji-Yeon, Oh Areum
Company: Sempio Foods
Country: South Korea
Category: Spices, oils & sauces
SILVER PENTAWARD 2013

TOKYO SA SHI SU SE SO

Art Direction / Graphic Design: Yukihiko Aizawa
Company: Aizawa Office
Country: Japan
Category: Spices, oils & sauces
GOLD PENTAWARD 2014

FORCES SAUCES

Creative Direction: Simon Pendry
Structure Direction: Guy Williams
Design: Bluemarlin team
Company: Bluemarlin
Country: UK
Category: Spices, oils & sauces

SILVER PENTAWARD 2014

NESTLÉ THOMY

Design: Rodrigo Costabeber,
Luis Bartolomei, Leticia Takiyama
Company: B+G
Country: Brazil
Category: Spices, oils & sauces
BRONZE PENTAWARD 2013

KYUSHU KITCHEN
KYUSHU YASAI DRESSING

Art Direction: Akihiro Nishizawa
Design: Izumi Kiyotaki
Company: Eight Branding Design
Country: Japan
Category: Spices, oils & sauces
SILVER PENTAWARD 2014

TRIKALINOS

Creative Direction: Minos Zarifopoulos
Illustration: Ilias Giannopoulos
Company: Office Communication Consultants
Country: Greece
Category: Spices, oils & sauces

BRONZE PENTAWARD 2014

DIABLO

Art Direction: Natalya Basova
Design: Natalya Popova
Company: Viewpoint
Country: Russia
Category: Spices, oils & sauces

BRONZE PENTAWARD 2014

As a new player in the category, **Blue Goose** had to stand out from other organic meat products, and set about this by making its quality plain to see. To promote its health benefits a simple template was created to equate humane preparation with a product that was good for consumers. The stylized design, with hand-drawn cows, chickens and fish, emphasizes a premium, artisanal product, rather than showing the usual farm imagery, while the details inside the animal outlines refer to the natural environment and conditions in which each was raised. The overall visual focus succeeded in significantly increasing distribution in the Canadian market.

Als neuer Player seiner Kategorie wollte sich **Blue Goose** neben anderen Anbietern organischer Fleisch-produkte sichtbar positionieren, am besten und ein-fachsten durch sichtbare Qualität. Zur Hervorhebung der gesundheitlichen Vorteile schuf man ein einfaches Grundmuster, das humane Tierhaltung und Konsumen-tennutzen gleichsetzt. Das stilisierte Design zeigt keine üblichen Bauernhofbilder, sondern betont dieses hand-werkliche Premiumprodukt mit von Hand gezeichneten Kühen, Hühnern und Fischen. Die Details in den Zeich-nungen beziehen sich auf die natürliche Umgebung und die Bedingungen, unter denen die Tiere aufwachsen. Dieser visuelle Fokus sorgte erfolgreich für eine wesent-liche Verbreitung auf dem kanadischen Markt.

Nouveau venu dans la catégorie, **Blue Goose** devait s'imposer sur le marché et faire passer clairement un message de qualité. Pour vanter ses effets salutaires, cette création simple cherche à transmettre l'idée d'une préparation respectueuse et d'un produit sain. Le design stylisé, avec des vaches, des poules et des poissons dessinés à la main, souligne l'aspect artisanal et de qualité, alors que les détails dans le corps des animaux renvoient à l'environnement naturel et aux conditions dans lesquelles ils ont été élevés. L'approche visuelle a réussi à augmenter de façon notable sa distribution sur le marché canadien.

BLUE GOOSE

Executive Creative Direction: Dave Roberts
Creative Direction: Tom Koukodimos
Design: Flavio Carvalho (senior), Anna Sera Garcia (senior), Oleg Portnoy
Copywriting: Pip Scowcroft, Laurent Abesdris
Illustration: Ben Kwok
Typography: Ian Brignell
Production: Karla Ramirez
Graphic Artist: Johnlee Raine
Company: Sid Lee
Country: Canada
Category: Fish, meat, poultry

GOLD PENTAWARD 2014

THALASSIOS KOSMOS

Creative Direction/Design: Gregory Tsaknakis
Company: Mousegraphics
Country: Greece
Category: Fish, meat, poultry

SILVER PENTAWARD 2014

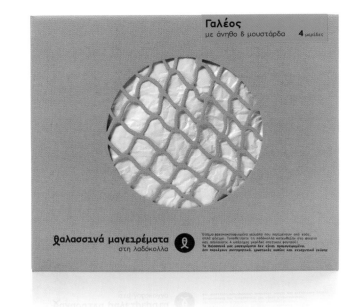

MINDFUL MEATS

Creative Direction: Hamish Campbell
Chief Creative Officer: Jonathan Ford
Strategy Direction: Tess Wicksteed
Senior Design: Kate Caravaty
Company: Pearlfisher
Country: USA
Category: Fish, meat, poultry
BRONZE PENTAWARD 2013

CALLIPO

Creative Direction: Gianfranco Siano
Design Direction: Giacomo Cesana
Design: Massimiliano Frangi
Company: CBA
Country: Italy
Category: Fish, meat, poultry
SILVER PENTAWARD 2013

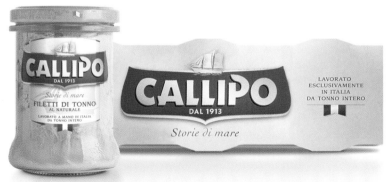

JUSTIN BRIDOU
POPS

Creative Direction: Rob Evers
Design: Aurélie Lacues
Executive Direction/Client Services: Oriane Tristani
Associate Client Direction: Anita Lim
Senior Consultant: Thomas Sauvage
Prod./Imp./Real. Direction: Maureen Baroni
Production Management: Lorette Lacaze
Production Artists: Didier Hongre, Olivier Thoï
Company: Landor Associates
Country: France
Category: Fish, meat, poultry

GOLD PENTAWARD 2013

OSCAR MAYER
BUTCHER THICK CUT BACON

Executive Creative Direction: Christopher Lehmann
Design: Strom Strandell
Design Direction: Anne Vaschetto
Client Associate: Michael Bowman
Client Management: Virginia Hultman
Technical Design: Ed Sarge
Associate Direction Graphic Technology: Scott Hosa
Company: Landor Associates
Country: USA
Category: Fish, meat, poultry

SILVER PENTAWARD 2014

The hearty, smoky goodness of **Butcher Thick Cut Bacon**'s succulent slices was being missed by consumers who could see only packaging and a higher price. To redress this situation it was noticed that most of the key information in this category wasn't on the front, but the back, so by flipping the pack over this effectively tripled the amount of package surface area available and instantly differentiated the brand from every other bacon on the market. To capitalize on this bold reversal, an authentic, butcher-style paper was employed along with carefully crafted traditional type, making it all feel new again.

Die Kunden vermissten die herzhaft-rauchige Güte der saftigen Scheiben von **Butcher Thick Cut Bacon**, weil sie nur die Verpackung und einen höheren Preis wahrnehmen konnten. Als Lösung dieses Problems erkannte man, dass die wesentlichen Infos dieser Kategorie meist nicht vorne, sondern auf der Rückseite zu finden sind. Also drehte man die Schinkenpackung einfach um und verdreifachte so die effektive Packungs-oberfläche. Damit hob sich die Marke sofort von allen Konkurrenzprodukten ab. Zusätzlich wurde authen-tisches Papier im Fleischereistil mit sorgfältig gestalteter traditioneller Schrift eingesetzt. So wirkte das Produkt insgesamt wieder völlig neu.

Le bon goût fumé des délicieuses tranches de **Butcher Thick Cut Bacon** passait inaperçu auprès des consommateurs, qui ne voyaient qu'un emballage et un prix élevé. En fait, il s'est avéré que la plupart des informations clés se trouvaient au dos du paquet. La solution : inverser l'emballage a suffi à tripler l'espace disponible et à immédiatement distinguer la marque de ses concurrents. Pour tirer le plus de profit de ce changement radical, un véritable papier de boucher a été utilisé et une typographie soignée a été choisie afin de donner un air de renouveau à l'ensemble.

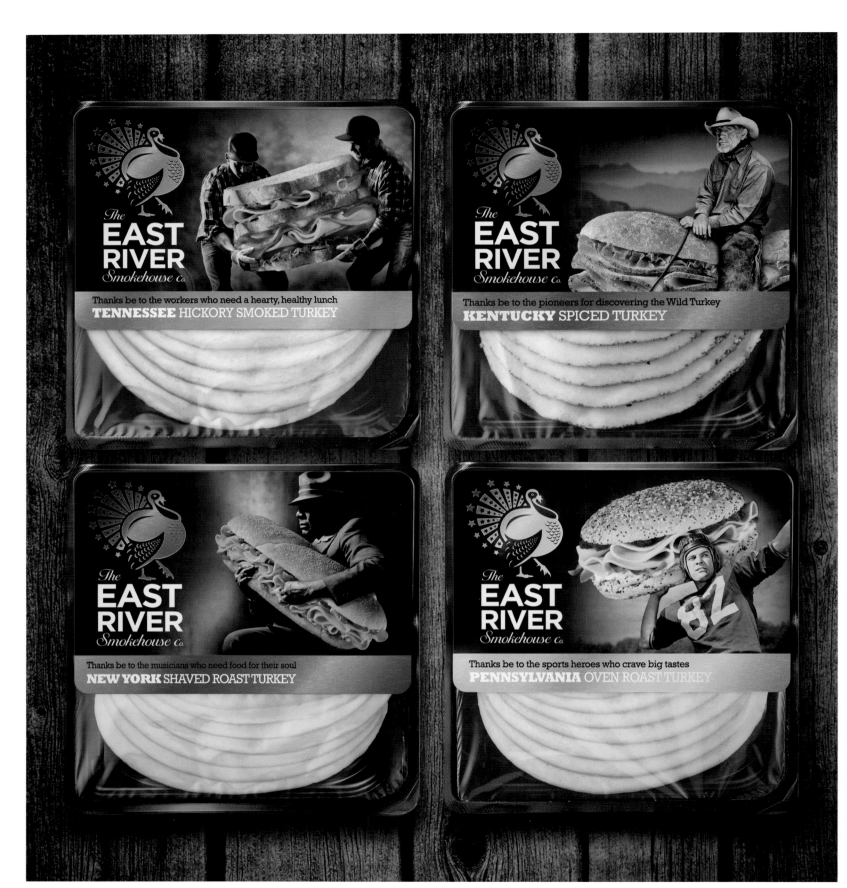

THE EAST RIVER SMOKEHOUSE CO.

Creative Direction: Moyra Casey
Design: James Roast, John Sherwood
Company: Springetts Brand Design Consultants
Country: UK
Category: Fish, meat, poultry

SILVER PENTAWARD 2013

KOKORIKO
BIG POLLO SNACK

Structural Design: María del Sol Poveda Castillo
Art Direction/Graphic Design: Nicolás Rosso Londoño
Concept: María del Sol Poveda Castillo, Juan Sebastián Muñoz Mejía, Nicolás Rosso Londoño
Project Management: Juan Sebastián Muñoz Mejía
Strategic Direction: Mauricio Salazar Vélez
Company: Young Marketing
Country: Colombia
Category: Fish, meat, poultry

BRONZE PENTAWARD 2013

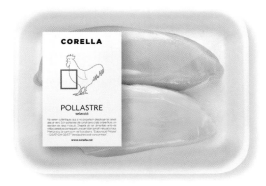

CORELLA

Design: Albert Martinez, Marc Navarro
Company: Fauna
Country: Spain
Category: Fish, meat, poultry
BRONZE PENTAWARD 2014

LOFOTLAM

Creative Direction: Morten Throndsen
Design: Eia Grødal
Company: Strømme Throndsen Design
Country: Norway
Category: Fish, meat, poultry

BRONZE PENTAWARD 2014

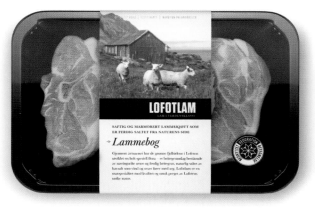

ANTO

Creative Direction: Gustavo Piqueira
Design: Gustavo Piqueira, Samia Jacintho, Ingrid Lafalce
Assistant Design: Ana Lobo, Lilian Meireles
Company: Casa Rex
Country: Brazil
Category: Fruit & vegetables

GOLD PENTAWARD 2013

FELDTHUSEN

Creative Direction: Gregory Tsaknakis
Design: Joshua Olsthoorn
Company: Mousegraphics
Country: Greece
Category: Fruit & vegetables

GOLD PENTAWARD 2014

MIKANZ

Art Direction/Design: Koichi Sugiyama
Copywriting: Yuta Naruse
Illustration: Minako Endo
Photography: Yoshihiro Toyota
Production: Taku Kitano, Junya Narita
Company: Koichi Sugiyama
Country: Japan
Category: Fruit & vegetables

SILVER PENTAWARD 2013

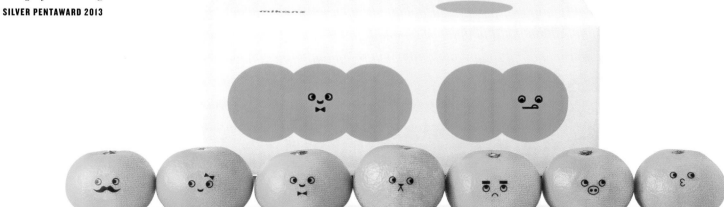

PLUK KRUIDJE
HERBAL HEALTH FOODS

Design: Jon Sonneveld
Company: Mountain Design
Country: Netherlands
Category: Fruit & vegetables

SILVER PENTAWARD 2013

JA NAMEGATA SWEET POTATOES

Design: Katanori Hori
Company: Rengo
Country: Japan
Category: Fruit & vegetables

BRONZE PENTAWARD 2013

food **173**

BEECH-NUT BABY FOOD

Creative Strategy: Eric Staples
Creative Direction: Brody Boyer
Design: Nancy Hourihan, Emily Berry,
Kelly Frazier, Mark Schepker
Production Design: John Steiger
Company: Bluedog Design
Country: USA
Category: Fruit & vegetables

SILVER PENTAWARD 2014

KADOYA
UMEBOSHI 8

Art Direction: Koichi Sugiyama
Design: Minako Endo
Copywriting: Yuta Naruse
Production: Taku Kitano
Company: Maru
Country: Japan
Category: Fruit & vegetables

BRONZE PENTAWARD 2014

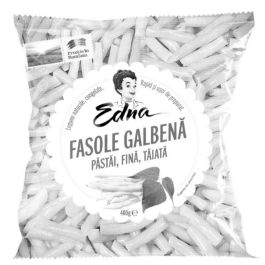
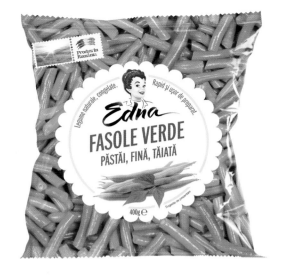

EDNA

Creative Direction / Design: Irinel Ionescu
Design: Raluca Popan
Photography: Paula Feodor
Pre-press: Danubiu Birzu
Project Management: Ana Poiana
Company: Ampro Design Consultants,
Country: Romania
Category: Fruit & vegetables

BRONZE PENTAWARD 2014

BEST CHOICE

Creative Direction: Jürgen Hûughe
Design: Katrien Starckx
Company: Quatre Mains
Country: Belgium
Category: Fruit & vegetables

SILVER PENTAWARD 2014

To create a name and identity for London's first premium burger delivery service, inspiration came from the obsessiveness of the two founders with their search for the perfect ingredients. The basic design was stripped back to black and white, with a blue accent for the key element in the name. On the packaging itself, bright red ketchup lines across a series of images strike out things that simply aren't good enough to be 'chosen' here. The target audience is young professionals in SW London with a healthy disposable income, who eat out and don't mind paying a premium for quality.

Auf der Suche nach Namen und Identität des ersten Londoner Lieferservices für Premium-Burger ließ man sich davon inspirieren, wie obsessiv die beiden Gründer nach perfekten Zutaten suchen. Das Basisdesign baut auf Schwarz und Weiß auf und enthält im Namen einen Blauton als zentrales Element. Auf der Packung selbst streicht ein leuchtender Ketchupstreifen Dinge durch, die nicht gut genug sind, um für dieses Produkt „erwählt" zu werden. Die Marke richtet sich als Zielgruppe an junge Berufstätige im Südwesten Londons mit einem gesunden verfügbaren Einkommen, die gerne auswärts essen und sich die Premiumqualität auch etwas kosten lassen.

Pour créer un nom et l'identité du premier service de livraison de burgers de qualité à Londres, l'inspiration est venue de la quête obsessive des ingrédients parfaits par les deux fondateurs. Le design de base a été dépouillé pour s'en tenir au noir et blanc, avec une touche de bleu pour l'élément clé dans le nom. Sur l'emballage, des lignes rouge ketchup en travers d'une série d'images barrent ce qui n'est pas assez bon pour être dans le produit. Le public cible : de jeunes professionnels du sud-ouest londonien, au pouvoir d'achat élevé, mangeant souvent au restaurant et n'hésitant pas à payer le prix pour avoir de la qualité.

CHOSEN BUN

Creative Direction: Garick Hamm
Design: Craig Kirk
Company: Williams Murray Hamm
Country: UK
Category: Soups, ready-to-eat dishes

GOLD PENTAWARD 2014

RIKEN

Design: Soichi Yamaguchi
Company: Anthem Worldwide
Country: Singapore
Category: Soups, ready-to-eat dishes

BRONZE PENTAWARD 2014

HEINZ
SOUP OF THE DAY

Creative Strategy: Sonya Mandeno
Creative Direction: Tim Wilson
Design: Sara Hayat, Debbie Bognar
Artwork: Paul Copeland
Company: Point 3 Design
Country: Australia
Category: Soups, ready-to-eat dishes

SILVER PENTAWARD 2014

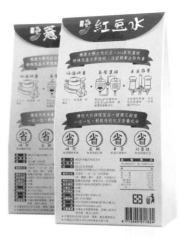

GOOD EATS

Design: Wei Chun-Huan
Company: E-JOY Biotechnology
Country: Taiwan
Category: Soups, ready-to-eat dishes

BRONZE PENTAWARD 2014

KENTUCKY FRIED CHICKEN

Creative Direction: Harri Lemke, Tim Schultheis
Art Direction: Lena Konopka
Design: Ariane Wollny, Carmen Schmitz
Company: LSD Lemkeschultheis Design
Country: Germany
Category: Soups, ready-to-eat dishes

SILVER PENTAWARD 2014

As a 100 % natural and guilt-free snack, and a playful alternative to eating actual fruit, this juice range in squeezable pouches took advantage of new fruit-processing technology to revamp its packaging. The "fruit+process" moves from picking to blending in just 24 hours, with no cooking; the package design follows this sense of directness and, based on the idea that a picture says more than 1,000 words, expresses immediately what the product is: pure blended fruit. It does this by making the packaging into the form of the fruit itself, exactly as it would be found at the greengrocer's.

Als 100 % natürlicher Snack ohne schlechtes Gewissen und als unbeschwerte Alternative zum Genuss echter Früchte nutzt dieses Saftsortiment im Druckbeutel aktuelle Fortschritte der Fruchtverarbeitung. Der Prozess der Weiterverarbeitung zwischen Pflücken und Verschneiden benötigt weniger als 24 Stunden – ohne Kochen. Das Verpackungsdesign greift diese Direktheit auf: Ein Bild sagt mehr als 1000 Worte, und so drückt die Packung sofort aus, um was es hier geht: um reinsten Fruchtsaft! Dafür wird die Verpackung zur Frucht selbst, als hätte man sie gerade beim Obsthändler gefunden.

Cet en-cas sain et 100 % naturel est une nouvelle façon amusante de consommer des fruits frais. La gamme de jus se présente dans des gourdes souples et l'emballage relooké s'inspire du nouveau procédé de traitement des fruits. Le cycle allant de la cueillette au mélange ne dure que 24 heures et n'implique aucune cuisson. Le design obéit à l'esprit de transparence et partant du principe qu'une image vaut plus que mille mots, il montre sans détour ce qu'il renferme: un mélange de fruits pur. L'emballage a la forme du propre fruit, comme sorti de l'étal du maraîcher.

NA! NATURE ADDICTS

Creative Direction: Cécile Lacoste, Jérôme Lanoy
Art Direction: Lise Fenouil
Company: Logic Design
Country: France
Category: Confectionery & sweet snacks

GOLD PENTAWARD 2014

CADBURY DAIRY MILK

Creative Direction: Natalie Chung
Chief Creative Officer: Jonathan Ford
Design Direction: Dan Gladden
Design: Roland Hobbs
Senior Strategist: Rory Fegan
Account Direction: Margit Wettler, Andrew Slade
Account Management: Laura Strusiewicz
Company: Pearlfisher
Country: UK
Category: Confectionery & sweet snacks

GOLD PENTAWARD 2013

**TRIDENT
TWIST**

Creative Direction: David Stroud
Design Direction: Stephen McDavid
Brand Direction: Caroline Wright
Project Lead: Véronique Le Fort
Company: LPK International
Country: Switzerland
Category: Confectionery & sweet snacks

BRONZE PENTAWARD 2013

SMOOCH

Design: Alastair Duckworth
Creative Direction: Anthony Biles
Company: Biles
Country: UK
Category: Confectionery & sweet snacks

SILVER PENTAWARD 2013

STRIDE
FEARLESS FRUIT

Account Direction: Ben Blaber
Design: Kai Muller, Jason Da Silva
Company: Davis
Country: Canada
Category: Confectionery & sweet snacks

SILVER PENTAWARD 2013

IMURAYA GROUP
GOOD LUCK YOKAN

Design: Kaori Takimoto, Miki Imai,
Kanako Matsuyama, Eri Inamura,
Shihomi Ikeda
Company: Rengo
Country: Japan
Category: Confectionery & sweet snacks

BRONZE PENTAWARD 2014

HANDS OFF MY CHOCOLATE

Design: Kim Kamperman
Company: Yellow Dress Retail
Country: Netherlands
Category: Confectionery & sweet snacks

SILVER PENTAWARD 2014

NIBMOR

Creative Direction: Hamish Campbell
Creative Partner/CCO: Jonathan Ford
Executive Vice President: Tess Wicksteed
Company: Pearlfisher
Country: USA
Category: Confectionery & sweet snacks

SILVER PENTAWARD 2014

DENT BY BRYNILD

Managing Direction: Line Støtvig
Creative Direction: Bjørn Rybakken
Project Management: May Britt Lunde Baumann
Design: Alexandra Kloster
Production: Klaus Dalseth
Company: Tangram Design
Country: Norway
Category: Confectionery & sweet snacks

BRONZE PENTAWARD 2013

MATBAM

Design: Ji Sun Kim, Soo Kyung Lee,
Maeng Kwang Seob, Hayeon Park
Company: CJ CheilJedang
Country: South Korea
Category: Confectionery & sweet snacks

BRONZE PENTAWARD 2014

The design for **Kettle Foods'** new range of baked chips centers around their appeal to people's appetite, but in a way that makes sure to communicate the improved health benefits of baked over other forms of chip. Because of this, the packs had to stand out clearly on the shelf, to be distinct from other brands and to announce to consumers the great taste of these chips that are more healthy to eat. The illustration of the baking dish and main flavor ingredients thus communicates the way these chips are made, and works as a subliminal message which suggests that fewer calories can have a taste benefit, rather than be a compromise.

Das Design für das neue Sortiment gebackener Chips von **Kettle Foods** rückt den Appetit auf Knabberzeug in den Blick und vermittelt zugleich, welche gesundheitlichen Vorteile gebackene Chips im Vergleich zu anderen bringen. Deswegen müssen die Packungen im Regal besonders ins Auge fallen und sich von anderen Marken abheben. Kunden sollen erfahren, dass die gesünderen Chips auch noch gut schmecken. Die Backform und die wesentlichen Geschmackszutaten vermitteln plastisch, wie die Chips hergestellt werden. Gleichzeitig fungiert dies als unterschwellige Botschaft, dass weniger Kalorien geschmacklich auch vorteilhaft sind, anstatt nur ein Kompromiss zu sein.

Le design pour la nouvelle gamme de chips de **Kettle Foods** cherche principalement à montrer en quoi elles sont appétissantes, mais avec l'intention d'expliquer les effets salutaires des chips au four comparées aux autres types. Les paquets devaient pour cette raison se démarquer dans les rayons et montrer que ces chips savoureuses étaient aussi plus saines. L'image du plat de cuisson et des principaux ingrédients illustrent comment ces chips sont préparées. Le message subliminal suggère que le fait de réduire les calories n'implique pas forcément un sacrifice, et peut au contraire supposer une amélioration du goût.

KETTLE BAKED CHIPS

Creative Direction: David Turner, Bruce Duckworth
Design Direction: Clem Halpin
Design: Matt Lurcock, Phil Skinner
Photography: Gareth Sambidge
Artwork: James Norris
Retouch: George Marshall
Account Management: Amanda Bothwell,
Monica Annesanti
Company: Turner Duckworth: London & San Francisco
Country: UK, USA
Category: Savory snacks

GOLD PENTAWARD 2014

ICORN

Creative Direction: Alexey Fadeev
Art Direction: Alexandr Zagorskiy
Design: Maria Ponomareva, Lyudmila Galchenko
Account Management: Anastasia Tretyakova
Company: Depot WPF
Country: Russia
Category: Savory snacks

SILVER PENTAWARD 2013

WALKERS DEEP RIDGED

Design: Simon Thorneycroft
Company: Perspective Branding
Country: USA
Category: Savory snacks

BRONZE PENTAWARD 2013

THOMAS J. FUDGE'S

Creative Direction: Perry Haydn Taylor
Company: Big Fish
Country: UK
Category: Savory snacks

SILVER PENTAWARD 2014

TYRRELLS
ARISTO-CRACKLING

Creative Direction: Perry Haydn Taylor
Company: Big Fish
Country: UK
Category: Savory snacks

BRONZE PENTAWARD 2014

ROOTS TO GO

Design Direction: Gaby Tischer
Design: Joel Bento
Company: Spice Design
Country: Brazil
Category: Savory snacks

BRONZE PENTAWARD 2014

BUTTERKIST

Executive Creative Direction: Paul Taylor
Design Direction: Rachel Bright
Design: Daniel Wilson
Account Management: Abigail Scott
Company: BrandOpus
Country: UK
Category: Savory snacks

SILVER PENTAWARD 2013

ÜBERNUTS

Design: Cristian 'Kit' Paul,
Cristian Petre, Adrian Stanculet
Company: Brandient
Country: Romania
Category: Savory snacks
SILVER PENTAWARD 2014

MR. FRANK / MR. CORN / MR. KOGI

Creative Direction: Ji Seon Kim
Art Direction: Kang Gook Lee
Design: You Jung Jang, Min Jung Kim
Company: CJ CheilJedang
Country: South Korea
Category: Savory snacks
BRONZE PENTAWARD 2013

This super-premium, all-wood packaging was developed not so much as a pack for the honey jar, but as an object that may become a permanent piece of a household's kitchenware. In so doing it completely re-invents the idea of the domestic honey-pot. The packaging comprises a cap, a base and four smoothly sanded rings in the middle, all threaded together with a rope handle to create the charming appearance of a beehive, with the jar of honey inside. The region of Armenia it comes from is known for its high-quality honey, produced from meadows no fertilizer has ever touched, thus making this new brand the perfect gift.

Diese Superpremium-Verpackung aus Vollholz wurde weniger als Hülle für ein Honigglas konzipiert, sondern eher als Objekt, das auch dauerhaft in der eigenen Küche nutzbar ist. Dazu erfand man die Idee des häuslichen Honigtopfs komplett neu. Die Verpackung besteht aus Deckel, Basis und vier glattgeschmirgelten, über ein Band miteinander verbundenen Ringen. Zusammen erscheinen sie als bezaubernder Bienenkorb mit Honigglas darin. Die armenische Region, aus der das Lebensmittel stammt, ist für ihren qualitativ hochwertigen Honig bekannt, der auf Wiesen produziert wird, die keinen Kunstdünger kennen. Das macht diese neue Marke zum perfekten Geschenk.

Cet emballage en bois d'extrême qualité a été conçu non pas tant comme une protection pour le pot de miel, mais comme un objet pouvant trouver sa place dans une cuisine ; l'idée du pot de miel familial est ainsi complètement revisitée. L'emballage en bois poncé compte un couvercle, une base et un corps fait de quatre anneaux. Une corde passe par tous ces éléments et finit en poignée, rappel évident d'une ruche, avec le pot de miel à l'intérieur. La région d'Arménie dont il provient est réputée pour son miel d'excellente qualité, produit dans des prairies qui n'ont jamais reçu d'engrais. Le produit forme un cadeau idéal en soi.

BZZZ

Design: Stepan Azaryan, Matt Bartelsian
Company: Backbone Studio
Country: Armenia
Category: Pastry, biscuits, ice-cream, desserts, sugar

GOLD PENTAWARD 2013

When young egg-farmers who'd grown up on a farm east of Oslo wanted to start a family-run ice-cream venture, using eggs from their own hens, milk from a neighbor's farm and local ingredients, just the right packaging was needed for their homemade product. The logo comes from the farm's bell-tower, used during festivities and celebrations, and reflects a food for special occasions and sharing. The packaging uses color coding for the different flavors and can easily be expanded as the range develops, with add-on labels used because of the relatively small-scale production, matched with a hand-applied paper seal that recalls traditional muslin.

Als junge Eierbauern, die auf einer Farm östlich von Oslo aufgewachsen sind, ein familieneigenes Eisgeschäft mit Eiern von eigenen Hennen, Milch von der Nachbarsfarm und Zutaten aus der Gegend gründen wollten, fehlte ihnen für das hausgemachte Produkt nur noch die richtige Verpackung. Das Logo zeigt den für Feiern und Festlichkeiten genutzten Glockenturm der Farm und spielt somit auf ein Lebensmittel an, das für besondere Gelegenheiten und den gemeinsamen Genuss gedacht ist. Die Farbcodes der Packung verweisen auf die verschiedenen Geschmacksrichtungen, einfach erweiterbar, wenn das Sortiment ausgebaut wird. Aufgrund der kleinen Produktionszahlen arbeitet man mit Aufklebeetiketten, zu denen das mit Hand aufgebrachte Siegelpapier passt, das an traditionellen Musselin erinnert.

De jeunes producteurs d'œufs ayant grandi dans une ferme à l'est d'Oslo ont un jour eu l'idée de lancer une entreprise familiale de glaces faites à base d'œufs de leurs propres poules, de lait de la ferme voisine et d'ingrédients locaux. L'emballage se devait d'être à la hauteur de ce produit frais, avec un logo inspiré du clocher de la ferme utilisé pour les fêtes et les célébrations : il traduit un met à partager pour les grandes occasions. L'emballage utilise un code de couleur pour les différents parfums et est facilement déclinable si la gamme doit s'étendre. Les étiquettes, apposées à la main étant donné les petites quantités produites, sont assorties au sceau de papier rappelant la traditionnelle mousseline.

BAMSRUDLAVEN GÅRDSIS

Design: Henrik Olssøn, Erika Barbieri
Company: Olssøn Barbieri
Country: Norway
Category: Pastry, biscuits, ice-cream, desserts, sugar

GOLD PENTAWARD 2014

PAZZO GELATO PREMIUM

Chief Creative Officer: Claude De Peña
Creative Direction: Joamar Meira
Design: Pedro Rocha
Illustration: Julia Zapata, Felipe Rodrigues,
Rafael de Lima (monstro)
Company: Team Créatif
Country: Brazil
Category: Pastry, biscuits, ice-cream,
desserts, sugar

SILVER PENTAWARD 2014

Pazzo (Italian for "crazy") is a brand created 'by crazy people for people crazy about ice-cream' determined to bring their good-quality products to the Brazilian market. After the name, the irreverent approach to the brand's identity is also designed to attract people to try an authentic ice-cream made in the best Sicilian tradition. Classic typography is thus combined with an Italian jester from an old Tarot card, for an eye-catching logo, along with illustrations from the Commedia dell'Arte in a playful or nonsensical style.

Pazzo heißt auf Italienisch „verrückt". Diese Marke wurde geschaffen von „Verrückten und ist für alle, die verrückt nach Eiscreme sind". Man ist fest entschlossen, die qualitativ hochwertigen Produkte auf den brasilianischen Markt zu bringen. Neben dem Namen soll auch der respektlose Umgang mit der Markenidentität Menschen locken, ein authentisches, in bester sizilianischer Tradition hergestelltes Eis zu probieren. Die klassische Typografie, kombiniert mit einem italienischen Hofnarren von einer alten Tarotkarte, ergibt zusammen mit verspielten oder sinnfreien Illustrationen im Stil der Commedia dell'Arte ein auffälliges Logo.

Pazzo (fou, en italien) est une marque créée par de « folles personnes pour les personnes folles de glaces » et qui a décidé de se lancer sur le marché brésilien. Outre le nom, l'approche non conventionnelle de l'identité vise à inciter les consommateurs à goûter une glace authentique faite selon la meilleure tradition sicilienne. La typographie classique a été assortie d'une image de bouffon issue d'un ancien jeu de Tarot pour que le logo soit accrocheur, ainsi que d'illustrations de la Commedia dell'Arte pour un visuel décalé.

LICK

Design: Hayley Bishop
Creative Direction: David Pearman
Company: This Way Up
Country: UK
Category: Pastry, biscuits, ice-cream, desserts, sugar

SILVER PENTAWARD 2014

BRIGADERIA ICE-CREAM

Creative Direction: Gustavo Piqueira
Design: Gustavo Piqueira, Samia Jacintho
Company: Casa Rex
Country: Brazil
Category: Pastry, biscuits, ice-cream, desserts, sugar

BRONZE PENTAWARD 2014

DIVINO

Design Direction: Mary Lewis
Company: Lewis Moberly
Country: UK
Category: Pastry, biscuits,
ice-cream, desserts, sugar

BRONZE PENTAWARD 2013

B&G FOODFACTORY

Design: Joeri Florin, Stéphane Kimpe
Company: Florin Kimpe
Country: Belgium
Category: Pastry, biscuits, ice-cream,
desserts, sugar

SILVER PENTAWARD 2013

PETITZEL SWEET PUDDING

Design: Ji Sun Kim, Hyuk Lyul Kwon,
Hayeon Park, Ah Ryeon Jung
Company: CJ CheilJedang
Country: South Korea
Category: Pastry, biscuits, ice-cream, desserts, sugar
BRONZE PENTAWARD 2014

JUST ENOUGH OF A (VERY) GOOD THING

Creative Direction: Hamish Campbell
Strategy Direction: Tess Wicksteed
Design Direction: Simone Fabricius
Company: Pearlfisher
Country: USA
Category: Pastry, biscuits, ice-cream, desserts, sugar

BRONZE PENTAWARD 2013

BISSON

Design: Christophe Mainguy, Bruno Joly, Hervé Guitaut
Company: Caracas
Country: France
Category: Pastry, biscuits, ice-cream, desserts, sugar

SILVER PENTAWARD 2013

kàllø

LIGHTLY SALTED
WHOLEGRAIN LOW FAT RICE CAKES

kàllø

ORGANIC LIGHTLY SALTED
WHOLEGRAIN LOW FAT RICE CAKES

kàllø

FAIRTRADE ORGANIC UNSALTED
WHOLEGRAIN LOW FAT RICE CAKES

kàllø
ROASTED CHILLI
WHOLEGRAIN LOW FAT RICE CAKES

kàllø
ORGANIC SESAME SEED
WHOLEGRAIN LOW FAT RICE CAKES

kàllø
CARAMEL
WHOLEGRAIN LOW FAT RICE & CORN CAKES

kàllø
SPELT, OATS & OAT BRAN
MULTIGRAIN RICE CAKES

kàllø
CORN CAKES

kàllø
SEA SALT & BALSAMIC
WHOLEGRAIN LOW FAT RICE CAKES

kàllø
BLUEBERRY & VANILLA
WHOLEGRAIN LOW FAT RICE & CORN CAKES

KALLØ

Creative Direction: Perry Haydn Taylor
Company: Big Fish
Country: UK
Category: Food trends

GOLD PENTAWARD 2014

Kallø makes natural, healthy alternatives to things like cakes, biscuits, bread and stock-cubes, but their packaging has in the past been typically rather anonymous. With customers who are intelligent and like to be in control of what they eat it was also important to move on from the old packaging which made them feel like they had 'special needs' rather than being foodies free to enjoy natural nibbles. The revamped design was thus intended to liberate Kallø consumers from any negative feelings and instead give them something to love and be proud of, with these cheerful packs decorated with poems and illustrations.

Kallø bietet eine natürliche, gesunde Alternative für Kekse, Biskuits, Brot oder auch Brühwürfel, doch deren Verpackung war früher oft recht anonym. Für intelligente Kunden, die unbedingt wissen wollen, was sie essen, war es aber auch wichtig, sich von der alten Verpackung zu lösen. Die alte Packung hatte das Gefühl vermittelt, irgendwie bedürftig zu sein, anstatt den Feinschmecker in den Vordergrund zu rücken, der gerne natürlichen Knabberspaß genießt. Das umgestaltete Design sollte somit die Kallø-Kunden von negativen Gefühlen befreien und ihnen mit den fröhlichen Verpackungen, geschmückt mit Gedichten und Illustrationen, etwas an die Hand geben, das sie lieben und worauf sie stolz sein können.

Kallø fabrique des gâteaux, des biscuits, du pain et, des cubes de bouillon à la fois sains et naturels ; ses emballages étaient toutefois sans personnalité. Les consommateurs étant de plus en plus attentifs et soucieux de ce qu'ils mangent, il était important pour la marque d'évoluer vers un design en accord avec les besoins des clients qui préfèrent être considérés des gourmets appréciant les en-cas naturels plutôt qu'ayant des besoins spéciaux. La refonte du design a donc cherché à libérer les consommateurs de Kallø de sentiments négatifs en leur offrant des produits agréables aux emballages colorés et décorés de poèmes et d'illustrations.

THE PRIMAL KITCHEN

Design: Claudio Vecchio, Will Gladden
Company: Midday
Country: UK
Category: Food trends

BRONZE PENTAWARD 2014

HEINZ ORGANIC

Creative Strategy: Sonya Mandeno
Creative Direction: Tim Wilson
Design: Debbie Bognar, Sarah Hendy
Illustration: Georgina Luck
Artwork: Heath McGregor
Company: Point 3 Design
Country: Australia
Category: Food trends

SILVER PENTAWARD 2014

TRUEVIBE ORGANICS

Creative Direction: Alex Durbridge
Strategy Direction: Derek Johnston
Design: Lori Townsend, Trang Lee, Dina Hassan, Harriet Stansall
Company: Family (and friends)
Country: UK
Category: Food trends

BRONZE PENTAWARD 2014

HARMONIAN

Creative Direction: Gregory Tsaknakis
Design: Joshua Olsthoorn
Company: Mousegraphics
Country: Greece
Category: Food trends

SILVER PENTAWARD 2014

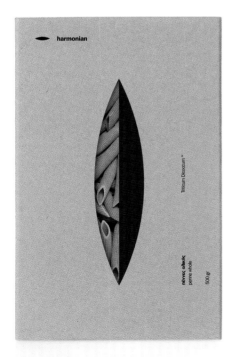

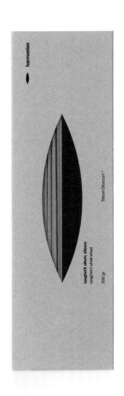
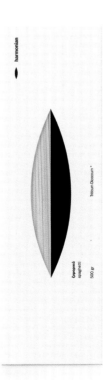

**CRISTAL UNION
DADDY SUCRE**

Design: CB design team
Company: Sleever
Country: France
Category: Limited editions,
limited series, event creations

SILVER PENTAWARD 2014

CRISTAL UNION
DADDY SUCRE "PRISONNIERS"

Design: CB'a design team
Company: Sleever
Country: France
Category: Limited editions, limited series,
event creations
GOLD PENTAWARD 2013

MOSCOW FARMER

Executive Creative Direction: Andrew Ushakov
Art Direction: Alexandra Istratova
Illustration: Alexandra Istratova, Alexander Koshkin
Copywriting: Darya Ushakova
Company: Geometry Global
Country: Russia
Category: Limited editions, limited series,
event creations

SILVER PENTAWARD 2014

MAROU FAISEURS DE CHOCOLAT AIR FRANCE

Design: Chi-An De Leo, Joshua Breidenbach,
Klara Pettersson, Jennifer Chan
Company: Rice Creative
Country: Vietnam
Category: Limited editions, limited series,
event creations

BRONZE PENTAWARD 2014

HEINZ
GROWN, NOT MADE

Creative Direction: Alexey Fadeev
Art Direction: Maria Ponomareva
Pre-press: Kurban Garanov
Management: Anastasia Tretyakova
Company: Depot WPF
Country: Russia
Category: Limited editions, limited series, event creations

GOLD PENTAWARD 2014

LYLE'S BLACK TREACLE

Design: Asa Cook, Dan Norris, Gavin Daniels, Rory Harker, Becca Probert, Becca Yorke, Julia Howard
Company: Design Bridge
Country: UK
Category: Limited editions, limited series, event creations

SILVER PENTAWARD 2013

CALVÉ UNILEVER NEDERLAND BARBEQUE SAUCES

Design: Peter Guldemond
Company: Mountain Design
Country: Netherlands
Category: Limited editions, limited series, event creations

BRONZE PENTAWARD 2013

LIMA
SOY SAUCE "MAIKO"

Creative Direction: Jürgen Hûughe
Design: Kobe De Keyzer, Vicky Acke
Technical Artwork: Thomas Minnaert
Company: Quatre Mains
Country: Belgium
Category: Limited editions, limited series, event creations

SILVER PENTAWARD 2013

This redesign for a range of flours for **Pams** needed a fresh idea but also something that stayed true to the company spirit of simple, everyday pleasures. With products in various categories yet no one particular 'look', identity is maintained through a consistent style which is clean, modern and down to earth. Flour packaging tends to be very formulaic, with uninspiring designs dominated by big close-up photography. These new packs capture a sense of kitchen nostalgia with their familiar baking items, handmade type, sober colors and a good spoonful of utilitarian chic. The result is a refreshing and delightful take on a basic everyday item.

Für die Neugestaltung eines Mehlsortiments war eine unverbrauchte, frische Idee nötig, die aber gleichzeitig die Philosophie des Unternehmens **Pams** gut vermitteln konnte: den Geist den kleinen Vergnügens im Alltag. Stammen Produkte aus verschiedenen Kategorien, teilen aber keinen speziellen „Look", hält man ihre Identität durch einen aufgeräumt-klaren, modernen und bodenständigen Stil konsistent. Mehlpackungen neigen meist dazu, sehr formelhaft zu sein mit oft uninspirierten Designs, geprägt von großen Nahaufnahmen. Bei diesen neuen Packungen hingegen klingt mit den vertrauten Backutensilien, der Handschrift, den dezenten Farben und einer kräftigen Prise zweckmäßigem Chic eine gute Küchennostalgie an. So wird ein profanes Grundnahrungsmittel wieder frisch und besonders.

Le redesign d'une gamme de farines pour **Pams** demandait une idée nouvelle, tout en restant fidèle à l'esprit de plaisirs quotidiens simples. La compagnie avait des produits dans diverses catégories mais aucun look particulier. L'identité a donc été conservée avec un style épuré, moderne et simple à la fois. En général, les paquets de farine sont assez conventionnels et le design reste banal, souvent avec des gros plans. Ces nouveaux paquets évoquent une certaine nostalgie culinaire grâce aux accessoires familiers, la police faite à la main, les couleurs sobres et une bonne dose de chic pratique. Le résultat est un regard frais et agréable sur un ingrédient quotidien.

PAMS FLOUR

Creative Direction/Design: Paula Bunny
Illustration: Angela Keoghan
Company: Brother Design
Country: New Zealand
Category: Distributors'/Retailers' own brands

GOLD PENTAWARD 2014

DELHAIZE
SOUPS

Art Direction: Nacho Lavernia, Alberto Cienfuegos
Company: Lavernia & Cienfuegos
Country: Spain
Category: Distributors'/Retailers' own brands
GOLD PENTAWARD 2013

Bringing to life the principal ingredient of each variety of this brand of soup, using vivid, photorealistic images, adds a distinctive touch of good humor before eating. The recurring theme of the waiter's hand presenting the bowl sends a positive message of good service and quality. The black and white photography also helps to unify the range, and is complemented by the use of simple bold typography to balance the design. The size of the ingredients, shown in color, has been exaggerated in relation to the plate to emphasize the high proportion of natural content in each and every pot.

Die wesentlichen Zutaten der verschiedenen Sorten dieser Suppenmarke werden anhand fotorealistischer Bilder lebendig. Das sorgt für eine gute Prise Humor, bevor man sich ans Essen macht. Als roter Faden wird die Hand des Kellners gezeigt, die die Suppenschale serviert und so die positive Botschaft von guter Qualität und gutem Service vermittelt. Die Schwarz-Weiß-Fotografie vereinheitlicht das Sortiment und sorgt ergänzt durch kraftvolle Typografie für ein ausgewogenes Design. Die Größe der farbig dargestellten Zutat wurde im Verhältnis zum Teller übertrieben, was den hohen Anteil an natürlichen Inhalten in jedem Suppentopf betont.

L'ingrédient principal de chaque variété de cette marque de soupes prend vie dans des images photoréalistes aux couleurs vives, ce qui ajoute une agréable touche d'humour avant de les déguster. Le thème récurrent de la main du serveur présentant le bol transmet un message de bon service et de qualité. La photo en noir et blanc offre également une présentation homogène de la marque ; elle est assortie de caractères gras pour équilibrer le design. La taille des ingrédients apparaissant en couleurs a été exagérée par rapport à l'assiette pour souligner la proportion élevée de contenu naturel dans chaque emballage.

CONTINENTE SKETCHED POTATO CHIPS

Design: Sonae design team
Company: Sonae MC
Country: Portugal
Category: Distributors'/Retailers' own brands

BRONZE PENTAWARD 2014

EROSKI CHILDREN'S CEREALS

Design: Paco Adin
Company: Supperstudio
Country: Spain
Category: Distributors'/ Retailers' own brands

SILVER PENTAWARD 2014

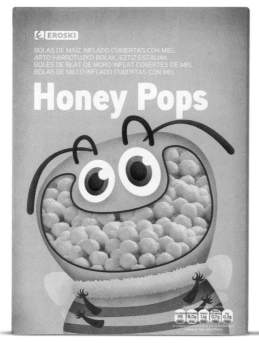

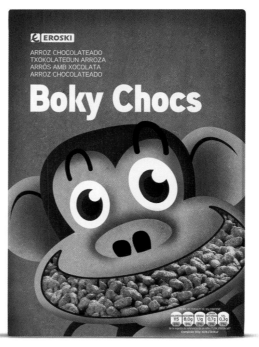

LIANGPINPUZI

Design: Fengliu, Liang Yuan, Shan Cong
Company: KHT Brand Consulting & Management
Country: China
Category: Distributors'/Retailers' own brands

BRONZE PENTAWARD 2014

PEACOCK FRUIT

Design: Jeoung Eun Shin
Company: Emart
Country: South Korea
Category: Distributors'/
Retailers' own brands

SILVER PENTAWARD 2014

EMART
GRAIN PRODUCTS

Creative Direction: Hyunjoo Choi
Design: Seungje Choi, Eunjin Oh
Company: Emart
Country: South Korea
Category: Distributors'/
Retailers' own brands

SILVER PENTAWARD 2013

MARKS & SPENCER
SIMPLY M&S

Design: Peter Knapp, Ryan Shaw
Company: Landor Associates
Country: UK
Category: Distributors'/
Retailers' own brands

BRONZE PENTAWARD 2013

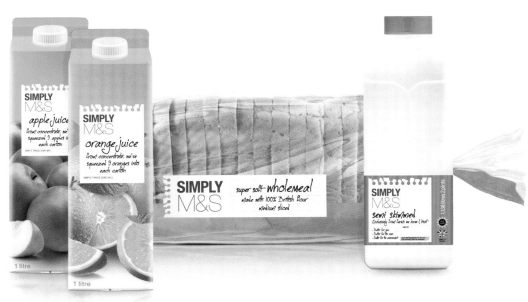

HUSETS

Design: Are Kleivan, Christian Schnitler
Company: The Metric System Design Studio
Country: Norway
Category: Cross-category ranges

BRONZE PENTAWARD 2013

GARANT BY AXFOOD
ECOLOGICAL PRODUCTS

Art Direction/Design: Stefan Sundstrom
Original Artwork/Design: Malin Ringsby, Linn Svensson,
Mathias Jonsson, Karl Mattisson, Johan Haag
Creative Direction: Marie Wollbeck
Account Direction: Susanne Oberg Dimic
Strategic Direction: Torbjorn Nordkvist
Project Management Design: Jenny Wenngren (Axfood)
Photography: Fabian Bjornstjerna
Company: BAS
Country: Sweden
Category: Cross-category ranges

SILVER PENTAWARD 2013

A high-quality, private label owned by Axfood, **Garant** developed the design for its range of ecological products by highlighting each one to attract environmentally conscious and knowledgeable consumers. Shoppers can rate and comment on the products online (tyckomgarant.se) and Axfood can then respond and adapt to what customers want. Today there are about 800 items, with packaging to suit everyday ecological living. The special handmade typeface makes product names and information clearly identifiable, whilst vibrant color combinations make the brand visible and contemporary. As a result Garant Eco has improved sales, increased the brand's popularity and created buzz.

Garant ist eine Eigenmarke hoher Qualität, die zu Axfood gehört. Für dessen Sortiment ökologischer Produkte wurde ein Design entwickelt, das diese jeweils hervorhebt, um gebildete und umweltbewusste Verbraucher anzusprechen. Die Käufer können die Produkte online bewerten und kommentieren (tyckomgarant.se). Darauf kann Axfood reagieren und Kundenwünsche aufgreifen. Heute sind etwa 800 Produkte mit einer dem ökologisch bewussten Alltag angepassten Verpackung erhältlich. Mit dem speziellen, handgezeichneten Schriftbild werden Produktnamen und Informationen klar identifizierbar, und durch die leuchtenden Farbkombinationen ist die Marke gut erkennbar und modern. Als Folge verbesserten sich die Verkäufe von Garant Eco, die Beliebtheit der Marke stieg und sorgte für viel Rummel.

Label privé de grande qualité appartenant à Axfood, **Garant** a conçu le design de sa gamme de produits écologiques en mettant chacun d'eux en avant pour séduire les consommateurs informés et responsables en matière d'environnement. Les clients peuvent évaluer et commenter les produits en ligne (tyckomgarant.se) ; Axfood leur répond et s'adapte aux requêtes reçues. Il existe à l'heure actuelle environ 800 articles dont l'emballage respecte un style de vie écologique. La police de caractères rend clairement identifiables les noms des produits et les informations ; les combinaisons de couleurs vives assurent la visibilité et donnent une touche contemporaine. Garant Eco a su augmenter ses ventes, tout comme la popularité de la marque.

WOOLWORTHS GOLD

Design: Claire Stenvert (senior), Jessica Parisi
Creative Direction: Gavin Greenhalf
Styling: Gemma Lush
Photography: Andrew Dougal Stavert
Account Management: Jane Eaton
Head of Own Brand Packaging Design:
Suzy Lake (Woolworths)
Design Specialist: Sandra Dagher (Woolworths)
Company: Marque Brand Consultants
Country: Australia
Category: Cross-category ranges

BRONZE PENTAWARD 2014

TESCO FINEST
GROCERY

Design: Melanie Kendall, Jesse Moran,
Helena Bland, Jon Sleeman, Paul Watson
Art Direction: Simon Pemberton
Company: Pemberton & Whitefoord
Country: UK
Category: Cross-category ranges

GOLD PENTAWARD 2014

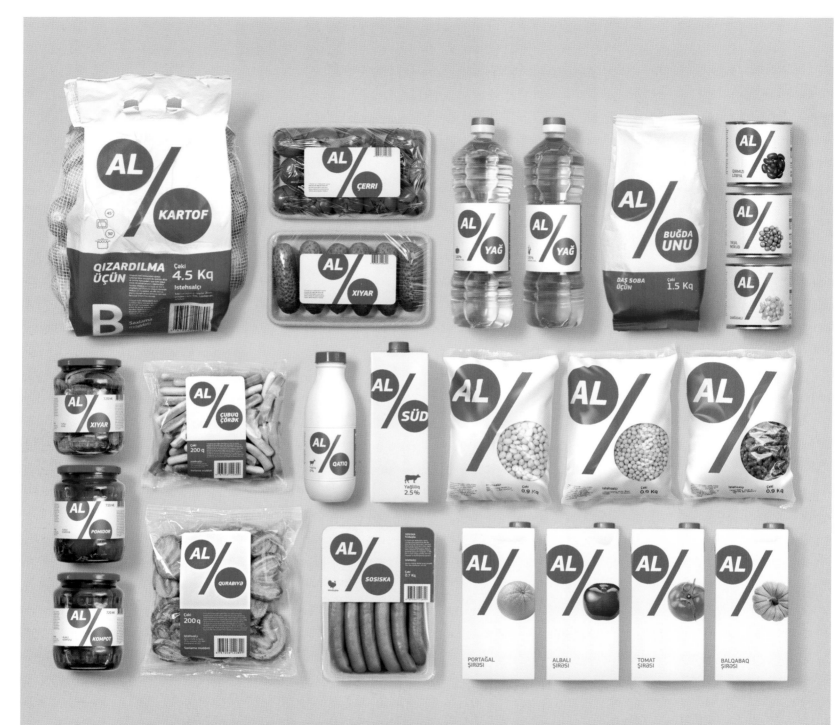

AL MARKET

Design: Andrey Tarakanov, Farhad Kuchkarov
Company: Tomatdesign
Country: Russia
Category: Cross-category ranges

SILVER PENTAWARD 2014

EROSKI PACKAGING RANGE

Design: Paco Adin
Company: Supperstudio
Country: Spain
Category: Cross-category ranges

SILVER PENTAWARD 2014

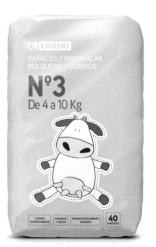

KRAFT
MAC & CHEESE

Account Direction: Sara Merrifield
Creative Direction: Chris Plewes
Design Direction: Jason Da Silva
Company: Davis
Country: Canada
Category: Packaging concept (food)

SILVER PENTAWARD 2014

BLA-BLA COOKIES

Design: Oksana Paley, Adeliya Koldarova,
Zaira Panaeva, Daria Sapozhnikov (students)
Teacher: Leonid Slavin
School: British Higher School of Art and Design,
Moscow
Country: Russia
Category: Packaging concept (food)

BRONZE PENTAWARD 2013

In order to promote the idea of sustainability for this general foodstuff the emphasis was put squarely on its freshness by means of the design showing an egg being "just laid". The three images of hens a-laying indicate the three different sizes of eggs available. The use of the standard egg-box helps to convey the idea of freshness, with the fastening bump becoming a representation of the egg itself so that consumers can better understand the natural process of egg-laying.

Um für dieses Grundnahrungsmittel das Konzept der Nachhaltigkeit in den Vordergrund zu stellen, bestimmt die Frische des Produkts das Design: Die Verpackung zeigt ein „frisch gelegtes" Ei. Drei Bilder von Hennen im Legeeinsatz kennzeichnen die verschiedenen Eiergrößen. Das Standardformat der Eierkartons hilft die Frische unmittelbar zu vermitteln. Der Kartonverschluss selbst repräsentiert bereits das Produkt. Dem Verbraucher wird so der natürliche Prozess des Eierlegens näher gebracht.

Pour mettre en avant, l'idée de développement durable de cet aliment de base, l'accent est mis sur la fraîcheur par l'image de l'oeuf pondu « en direct ». Les trois images de poules en train de pondre correspondent aux trois tailles d'oeufs disponibles. L'utilisation de la boîte standard véhicule l'idée de fraîcheur ; le système de fermeture est symbolisé par un oeuf afin que les consommateurs perçoivent mieux encore le processus naturel de ponte.

JUST LAID

Design: Kevin Daly
Illustration: Peter O'Connor
Company: Springetts Brand Design Consultants
Country: UK
Category: Packaging concept (food)

GOLD PENTAWARDS 2014
SPECIAL LARS WALLENTIN HAHAHA PRIZE

SPROUT

Creative Direction: Moyra Casey
Design: Kelly Bennett
Visualization: Peter O'Connor
Company: Springetts Brand Design Consultants
Country: UK
Category: Packaging concept (food)

GOLD PENTAWARD 2013

Sprout set out to break new ground in the baby food category with the introduction of a fresh, chilled range of part-prepared baby food, similar to formats available for adult consumption. This would allow parents to make up the meals quickly and easily at home. The name is intended to convey the integrity of the ingredients and how the right food is key to healthy development. Building on this idea, the creative execution is a playful, literal expression of "you are what you eat". The baby is shown as happy, healthy and flourishing with the help of nature's best ingredients, an image designed to be both reassuring and emotionally engaging, as well as making people smile.

Sprout macht sich daran, in der Kategorie Babynahrung Neuland zu betreten, und führte ein frisches, gekühltes Sortiment mit teilweise vorgekochter Babynahrung ein. Solche Formate gibt es bereits als Produkte für Erwachsene. So können Eltern die Mahlzeiten schnell und einfach zu Hause zubereiten. Der Name soll die Integrität der Zutaten vermitteln und richtige Nahrung als Schlüssel zu einer gesunden Entwicklung. Die kreative Ausführung greift dieses Konzept auf und setzt den Spruch „Du bist, was du isst" spielerisch und buchstäblich um. Man sieht das gesunde und glückliche Baby, das mithilfe bester natürlicher Zutaten wächst und gedeiht. Dieses Bild verleiht Bestätigung, schafft emotionale Bindung und entlockt ein Lächeln.

Sprout cherchait à innover dans le domaine des aliments pour bébés en lançant une gamme de préparations au design frais et dans des formats semblables à ceux pour les adultes. L'idée était de permettre aux parents de préparer rapidement les repas. Le nom vise à évoquer l'intégrité des ingrédients et à faire savoir qu'une alimentation saine est la clé d'une bonne croissance. Le résultat est l'expression littérale de « vous êtes ce que vous mangez » : les bébés apparaissent contents, en bonne santé et épanouis grâce aux meilleurs ingrédients qu'offre la nature. L'image est conçue pour être rassurante et stimulante, mais aussi pour faire sourire.

EAT&GO

Design: Olga Gambaryan, Diana Gibadulina,
Alexander Kischenko, Andronik Poloz (students)
School: British Higher School of Art and Design,
Moscow
Country: Russia
Category: Packaging concept (food)

SILVER PENTAWARD 2013

SHMAT
MEAT SNACKS

Design: Ruslan Simashev (student)
School: British Higher School of Art and Design, Moscow
Country: Russia
Category: Packaging concept (food)

BRONZE PENTAWARD 2014

HANS & HOLLY

Design: Series Nemo team
Company: Series Nemo
Country: Spain
Category: Packaging concept (food)

SILVER PENTAWARD 2013

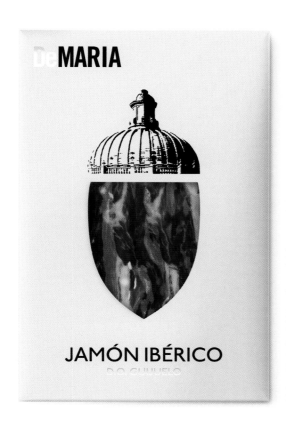
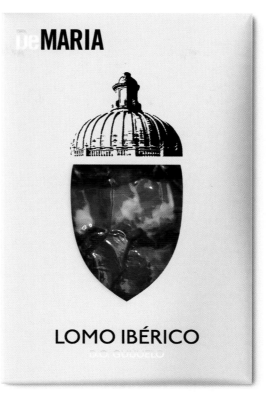

JAMÓN IBÉRICO

LOMO IBÉRICO

DEMARIA

Design: Gaizka Ruiz
Creative Direction: Enric Aguilera
Company: Enric Aguilera Asociados
Country: Spain
Category: Packaging concept (food)
BRONZE PENTAWARD 2013

OPPO

Design: Gary Martin, Peter Knapp,
Mark Wood, Benjamin Marshall
Company: Landor Associates
Country: UK
Category: Packaging concept (food)
SILVER PENTAWARD 2014

YOUR WAY JERKY

Design: Oleg Safronov (student)
School: British Higher School of Art and Design, Moscow
Country: Russia
Category: Packaging concept (food)

SILVER PENTAWARD 2014

BAXTERS FAVOURITES

Design: Kelly Bennett
Creative Direction: Moyra Casey
Company: Springetts Brand Design Consultants
Country: UK
Category: Packaging concept (food)

BRONZE PENTAWARD 2014

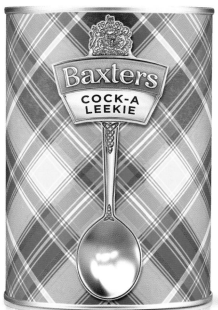

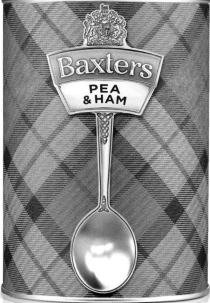
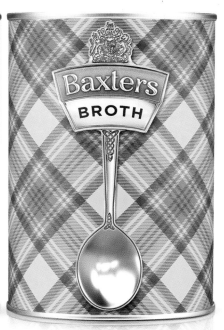

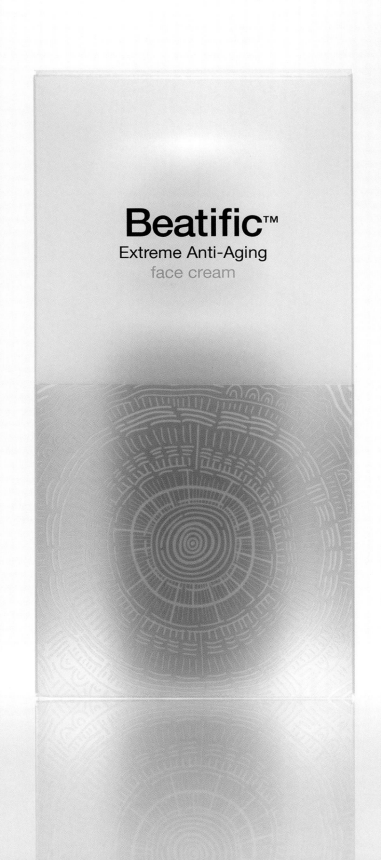

Best of the category

Garments

Health care

body

Body care

Beauty

Distributors'/Retailers' own brands

Packaging concept

STRONG NUTRIENTS

Design: Karen Welman
Illustration: Andy Lyons, Handsome Frank
Company: Pearlfisher
Country: UK
Category: Best of the category body

PLATINUM PENTAWARD 2013

Strong is a brand of high-quality food supplements developed to promote health and beauty at the cellular level for a younger, stronger and more dynamic body. The design's objective was to stand out from functional brands and create the concept of "beauty from within" by evoking the ultimate benefits of choosing Strong over other products. The labeling showcases a range of beautiful and elegant birds (as well as Pegasus) which are known for their hidden strength, with the illustrations rendered in a stylized and timeless manner. The resulting designs are visually striking, creating high visibility for both retail and e-commerce.

Strong ist eine Marke qualitativ hochwertiger Nahrungsergänzungsmittel. Für einen jüngeren, stärkeren und dynamischeren Körper stärken sie Gesundheit und Aussehen auf zellulärer Ebene. Die Designvorgabe war, sich von funktionalen Marken abzuheben und das Konzept einer „Schönheit von innen" zu schaffen. Dazu betonte man die ultimativen Vorteile von Strong gegenüber anderen Produkten. Die Etiketten zeigen verschiedene schöne und elegante Vögel (zudem einen Pegasus), die für ihre verborgene Kraft bekannt sind. Die Illustrationen sind in stilisierter und zeitloser Art ausgeführt. Im Ergebnis sind die Designs visuell überzeugend und sorgen sowohl im Einzel- als auch im Onlinehandel für einen hohen Wahrnehmungsgrad.

Strong est une marque de compléments alimentaires de grande qualité élaborés comme source de santé et de beauté au niveau cellulaire, avec la promesse d'un corps plus jeune, plus fort et plus dynamique. L'objectif du design était de se distinguer des marques fonctionnelles et de créer un concept de « beauté de l'intérieur » en expliquant tous les bienfaits de Strong comparé à la concurrence. L'étiquetage présente une série d'oiseaux élégants (ainsi que Pégase), connus pour leur force cachée. Les illustrations sont reproduites de façon stylisée et intemporelle, avec un fort impact visuel et une grande visibilité, en magasin comme en ligne.

In developing this new skincare line for middle-to upper-class consumers, a name was sought that would express its equal blend of the aesthetic and the scientific. Inspired by art history, the word 'beatific' was chosen, meaning blessed and indicating a communion with the divine, so as to be able to share its spiritual light and glory. With this name then signposting the meeting-point of Beauty and Science, the rest of the design followed accordingly: the abstract and ethereal light patterns on the packaging; the use of semi-transparent, translucent material; the 4-color iridescent palette; and the elegant and sober typography.

In der Entwicklung dieser neuen Hautpflegelinie für Kunden aus der Mittel- und Oberklasse suchte man einen Namen, der Ästhetik und Wissenschaft in ausgewogener Mischung verdeutlicht. Inspiriert durch die Kunstgeschichte entschied man sich für „beatific", das auf Seligkeit anspielt und auf die Verbindung mit dem Göttlichen verweist, als könne man dessen spirituelles Licht und Herrlichkeit teilen. Im Namen schon verschmelzen also Schönheit und Wissenschaft, und dem schließt sich das restliche Design an: die abstrakten und ätherischen Lichtmuster der Verpackung, das halbtransparente, durchscheinende Material, die schillernde Vierfarbpalette mit ihrer eleganten und nüchternen Typografie.

Pour cette nouvelle ligne de produits cosmétiques s'adressant à une clientèle de classe moyenne à supérieure, le nom devait transmettre l'équilibre entre esthétique et science. Synonyme de béni, « beatific » s'inspire de l'histoire de l'art et traduit la communion avec le Divin, capable de faire partager sa lumière spirituelle et sa gloire. Ce mariage entre beauté et science a dicté le reste du design : un graphisme abstrait et éthéré, un matériau d'emballage translucide et semi-transparent, une palette de 4 couleurs irisées et une typographie sobre et élégante.

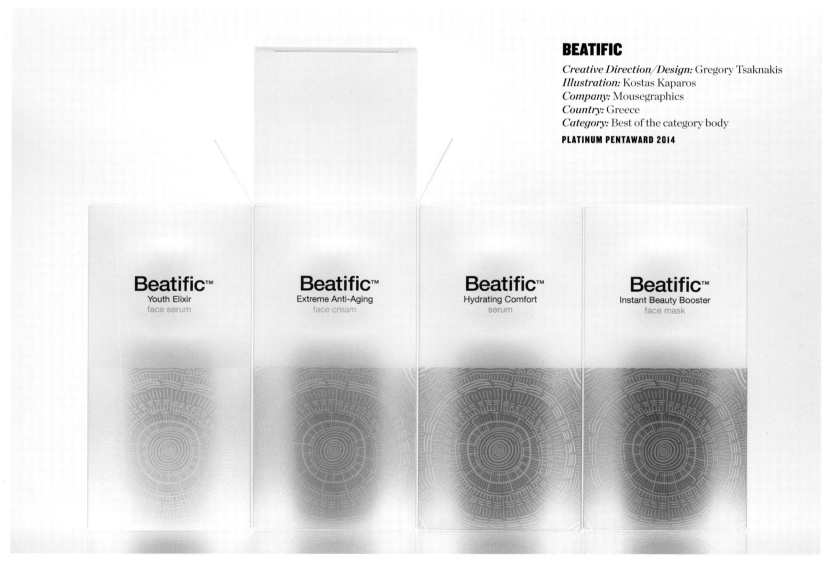

BEATIFIC

Creative Direction/Design: Gregory Tsaknakis
Illustration: Kostas Kaparos
Company: Mousegraphics
Country: Greece
Category: Best of the category body

PLATINUM PENTAWARD 2014

Beatific™
Youth Elixir
face serum

Beatific™
Extreme Anti-Aging
face cream

Beatific™
Hydrating Comfort
serum

Beatific™
Instant Beauty Booster
face mask

SOC is a Japanese brand of socks whose slogan is "An inspiration born from your foot". The package has been designed so that it is able to contain socks of all sizes and display the different styles, and was created according to the art of traditional Japanese folding, so that it may be opened without destroying the packaging. The form is compact and uses a minimum of paper, is reusable after purchase, inexpensive to produce and is still attractive: much like the values of SOC itself.

Die japanische Strumpfmarke SOC wirbt mit dem Slogan „inspiriert von deinen Füßen". Das Design kann Socken in allen Größen aufnehmen und die verschiedenen Styles bleiben sichtbar. Es wurde in der Kunst des japanischen Papierfaltens geschaffen: So kann man die Verpackung öffnen, ohne sie zu beschädigen. In kompakter Form und mit wenig Papierverbrauch kann sie nach dem Kauf anderweitig verwendet werden, ist preisgünstig in der Herstellung und trotzdem attraktiv – genau diese Werte verkörpert auch SOC selbst.

SOC est une marque japonaise de chaussettes dont le slogan est « Une inspiration née de votre pied ». L'emballage a été pensé pour contenir des chaussettes de toutes les tailles et présenter les divers styles disponibles. Il a été créé selon le traditionnel art du pliage japonais pour s'ouvrir sans être abîmé. Sa forme est compacte, demande un minimum de papier, il est réutilisable, sa production est bon marché et le résultat est attrayant : telles sont aussi les valeurs de SOC.

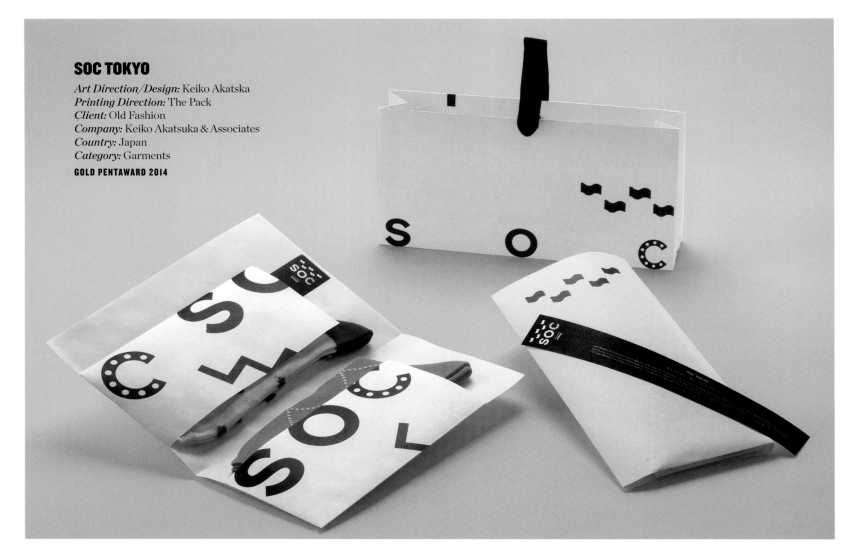

SOC TOKYO

Art Direction/Design: Keiko Akatska
Printing Direction: The Pack
Client: Old Fashion
Company: Keiko Akatsuka & Associates
Country: Japan
Category: Garments

GOLD PENTAWARD 2014

SHISEIDO FUROSHIKI

Creative Direction: Yoji Nobuto
Art Direction/Design: Ippei Murata
Typography: Yutaka Kobayashi
Production: Kumiko Suzuki
Company: Shiseido
Country: Japan
Category: Garments

SILVER PENTAWARD 2014

At **Shiseido**, there is what could be called the 'Shiseido style of letters', a set of letter forms used for products and advertising which have been re-drawn and adapted over the years by new generations of designers. The furoshiki is a traditional way of wrapping and carrying gifts using a single piece of cloth, while the delicate colors and bold lines shown here employ yuzen dyeing techniques from Kyoto. The result is that letters that were originally used in decorative combinations now become beautiful abstract patterns. Furthermore, the paper used to package each furoshiki itself uses just one sheet of paper, hand-folded in the same style.

Bei **Shiseido** lässt sich von einer Art „Buchstaben im Shiseido-Stil" sprechen. Deren Formen hat man für Produkte und Werbung eingesetzt und im Laufe der Jahre von Designer-Generationen immer wieder neu zeichnen und anpassen lassen. Als Furoshiki bezeichnet man die Tradition, Geschenke oder andere Gegenstände in ein tragbares Tuch zu wickeln. Gut zu sehen sind die mit der Yuzen-Färbetechnik aus Kyoto aufgebrachten zarten Farben und kräftigen Linien. So werden ursprünglich in dekorativen Kombinationen verwendete Buchstaben nun zu wunderschönen abstrakten Mustern. Überdies packt man die Furoshiki jeweils in nur ein Blatt Papier, das im gleichen Stil per Hand gefaltet ist.

Chez **Shiseido**, il existe ce que l'on pourrait appeler une « police de caractère maison », une typographie utilisée pour les produits et les campagnes publicitaires, conçues et adaptées depuis des années par des généra-tions de designers. Le furoshiki est une méthode tradi-tionnelle d'emballage de cadeaux à l'aide d'un morceau de tissu. Les couleurs douces et les lignes franches emploient les techniques de teinture yuzen de Kyoto. Résultat : les lettres qui étaient utilisées dans des arrangements décoratifs forment désormais de superbes motifs abstraits. Le papier enveloppant chaque furoshiki n'a qu'une feuille d'épaisseur, pliée à la main dans le même style.

GAUZE MUFFLER

Art Direction/Graphic Design: Koji Matsumoto
Company: Grand Deluxe
Country: Japan
Category: Garments

SILVER PENTAWARD 2014

ARGENTUM

Creative Direction: Andrey Kugaevskikh
Design: Masha Solyankina
Company: Svoe Mnenie
Country: Russia
Category: Garments

BRONZE PENTAWARD 2014

ADIDAS PERFORMANCE

Creative Direction: Maxim Kolyshev
Art Direction: Andrey Zaitsev
Company: TBWA\\Moscow
Country: Russia
Category: Garments

BRONZE PENTAWARD 2014

VIZIT

Creative Direction: Valery Melnik
Design: Roman Luzanov
Account Management: Tatyana Sandler
Company: Vozduh Advertising Agency
Country: Russia
Category: Health care

GOLD PENTAWARD 2014

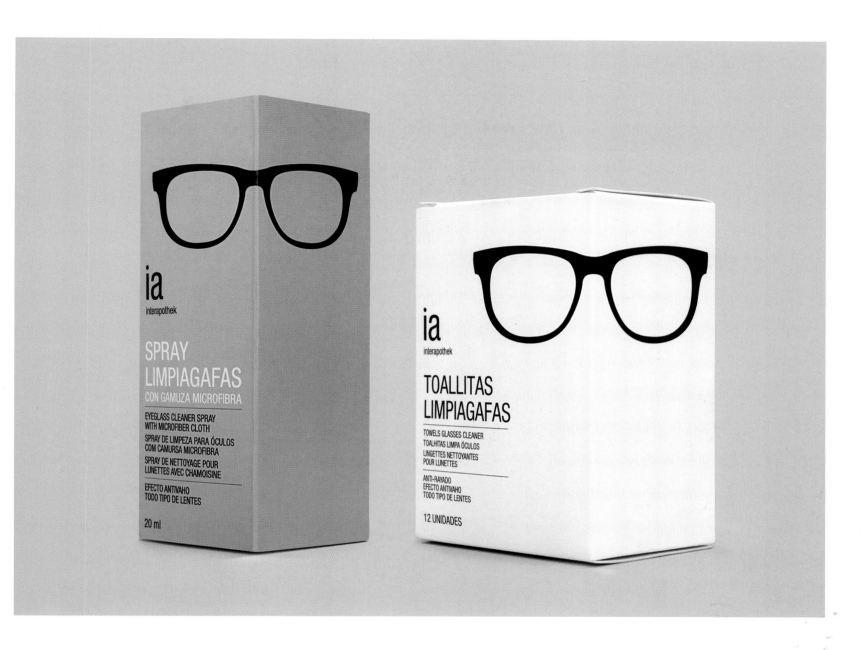

ia
interapothek

SPRAY
LIMPIAGAFAS
CON GAMUZA MICROFIBRA

EYEGLASS CLEANER SPRAY
WITH MICROFIBER CLOTH

SPRAY DE LIMPEZA PARA ÓCULOS
COM CAMURSA MICROFIBRA

SPRAY DE NETTOYAGE POUR
LUNETTES AVEC CHAMOISINE

EFECTO ANTIVAHO
TODO TIPO DE LENTES

20 ml

ia
interapothek

TOALLITAS
LIMPIAGAFAS

TOWELS GLASSES CLEANER
TOALHITAS LIMPA ÓCULOS
LINGETTES NETTOYANTES
POUR LUNETTES

ANTI-RAYADO
EFECTO ANTIVAHO
TODO TIPO DE LENTES

12 UNIDADES

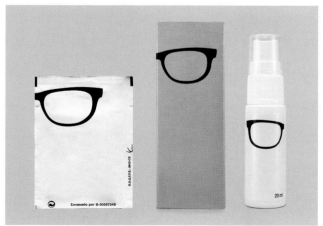

IA
OPTICAL RANGE FOR PHARMACIES

Creative Direction: Eduardo del Fraile
Design: Eduardo del Fraile, Antonio Marquez
Company: Eduardo del Fraile
Country: Spain
Category: Health care

SILVER PENTAWARD 2013

Obesity is the number one enemy in today's western societies and the health of their citizens. Nomobese's mission is to put an end to obesity. An intense personal program guides, coaches and trains the user to attain a better lifestyle and a healthier weight. The **Starters Kit** includes a personal diary, for help and motivation, whilst the general design employs a set of confrontational visuals. At first sight the pack makes this look appetizing and good fun, but a second look reveals the true meaning: an unhealthy lifestyle and bad nutrition can — and will — kill you in the end, a powerful reminder to get rid of old habits and kiss obesity goodbye!

Fettleibigkeit ist in den heutigen westlichen Gesellschaften Feind Nummer eins für die Gesundheit seiner Bürger. Nomobeses Mission ist es dem Übergewicht ein Ende zu bereiten. Ein intensives persönliches Programm leitet und begleitet den Anwender, um durch Training einen besseren Lebensstil und ein gesünderes Gewicht zu bekommen. Das **Starters Kit** enthält als Hilfe und Motivation ein persönliches Tagebuch, während das Design insgesamt auf konfrontative Bildgebung setzt. Auf den ersten Blick wirkt die Verpackung appetitlich und spaßig, aber dann wird die wahre Bedeutung klar: Ein ungesunder Lebensstil und schlechte Ernährung können – und werden – einem schließlich das Leben kosten. Eine äußerst wirksame Erinnerung daran, sich von alten Gewohnheiten zu trennen und dem Übergewicht eine Abfuhr zu erteilen!

L'obésité est l'ennemi juré actuel des sociétés occidentales et de la santé de leurs citoyens, et Nomobese s'est donné pour mission de l'éradiquer. Un programme personnalisé intensif oriente l'utilisateur pour améliorer son mode de vie et atteindre un poids sain. Le **Starters Kit** inclut un carnet personnel d'aide et de motivation, et son design cherche à faire réagir. Au premier abord, les images sont appétissantes et amusantes ; mais en y regardant de plus près, la vérité s'impose : un style de vie malsain et une alimentation déséquilibrée peuvent et finissent par tuer à la longue. Il n'y a pas de meilleur rappel pour combattre les mauvaises habitudes et dire adieu à l'obésité !

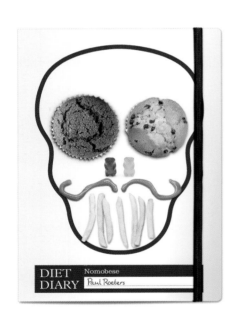

NOMOBESE STARTERS KIT

Creative Direction: Paul Roeters
Design: Roger Huskens
Company: Studio Kluif
Country: Netherlands
Category: Health care

GOLD PENTAWARD 2013

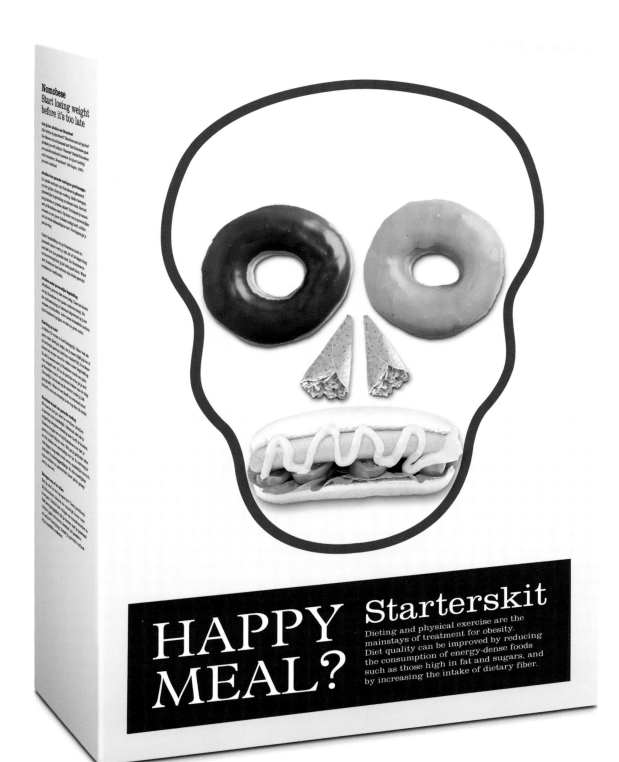

HAPPY MEAL?

Starterskit

Dieting and physical exercise are the mainstays of treatment for obesity. Diet quality can be improved by reducing the consumption of energy-dense foods such as those high in fat and sugars, and by increasing the intake of dietary fiber.

SNOW JUAN

Design: Xiaohui Xi
Company: Xi Xiaohui Design
Country: China
Category: Health care

BRONZE PENTAWARD 2014

BASHFUL CONDOMS

Creative Direction/Design: Tracy Kenworthy
Design: Geoff Bickford
Company: Dessein
Country: Australia
Category: Health care

SILVER PENTAWARD 2014

LOTUS ULTRASONIC SCALPEL

Creative Direction: Bob Mytton
Design: Ed Robin
Company: Mytton Williams
Country: UK
Category: Health care

SILVER PENTAWARD 2013

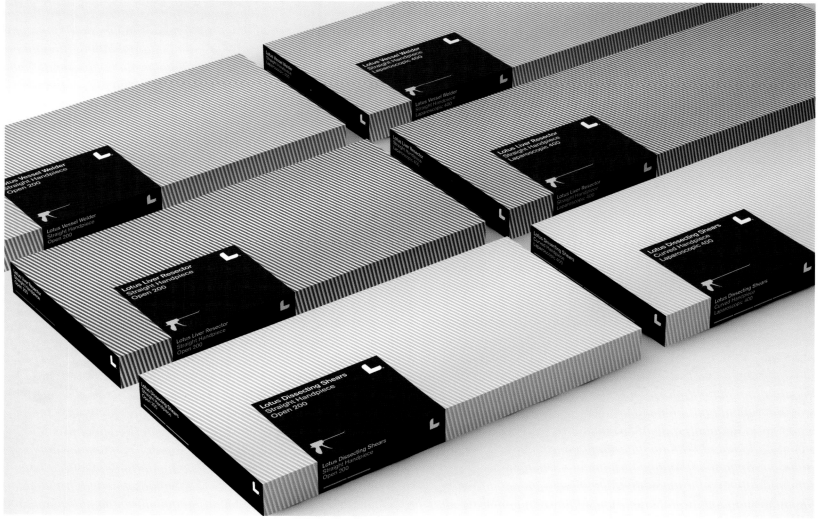

KLEENEX
CHRISTMAS COLLECTION

Design: David Jones
Creative Direction: David Jones, Mark Girvan
Client: Kleenex
Brand Management: Jennifer Beral
Company: Buddy Creative
Country: UK
Category: Health care

SILVER PENTAWARD 2014

KLEENEX
KIDS COLLECTION

Design: Mark Girvan, David Jones, Will Day
Company: Buddy Creative
Country: UK
Category: Health care

BRONZE PENTAWARD 2013

PUFFS WINTER OLYMPIC

Art Direction: Jamey Wagner
Design: Jen Rossignol, Bart Laube,
Jean Campbell, Theresa Seitz, Katie Carter
Company: Interbrand
Country: USA
Category: Health care

BRONZE PENTAWARD 2014

ANSELL
LIFESTYLES, MANIX AND UNIMIL

Creative Direction: Alice Tacconi
Art Direction: Mirco Onesti
Structural Design: Gustavo de Souza Messias
Project Management: Peter Solomon
Illustration: Valerio Tizzi
Graphic Design: Luca Mazzoleni
Company: Reverse Innovation
Country: Italy
Category: Body care

GOLD PENTAWARD 2013

HOYU 3210 OUIOUI

Art Direction: Hanae Yamamuro, Go Nakano
Art Direction/Design: Kumi Imai
(Apis Laboratory)
Copywriting: Ken Matsuda
Illustration: Yuko Kondo
Account Team Lead: Nobuyuki Tanaka
Senior Account Executive: Shigeharu Matsuoka
Account Executive: Junki Arai
Company: Asatsu-DK
Country: Japan
Category: Body care

SILVER PENTAWARD 2013

This styling-product line is aimed at fashion-sensitive youngsters, with each of the six varieties providing a different holding power and finish. Beyond altering a person's external appearance, a change of hairstyle with real styling freedom can awaken deeper, dormant instincts, bringing both the hair and the person to life. The tubes feature whimsical animal-headed characters, created by illustrator Yuko Kondo, each symbolizing a different instinct. In addition, personalities, professions and relationships were assigned to each character and a special world was created on Facebook to reinforce engagement with the target group and multiply the positive effects of word-of-mouth.

Diese Linie an Hairstyling-Produkten in sechs Varianten bezüglich Festigkeit und Finish richtet sich an die modebewussten Youngsters. Neben äußerlicher Veränderung lässt ein anderer Haarstil, der beim Stylen und Frisieren mit echter Freiheit punktet, tief schlummernde Instinkte erwachen und erweckt sowohl das Haar zum Leben als auch die Person, die es trägt. Die Tuben zeigen schrullige Typen des Illustrators Yuko Kondo, dessen Tierköpfe jeweils einen anderen Instinkt symbolisieren. Außerdem bekommt jeder Charakter seine eigene Persönlichkeit, Beruf und Beziehung zugeordnet. Auf Facebook wurde eine spezielle Welt geschaffen, um die Beschäftigung mit der Zielgruppe zu verstärken und die positiven Effekte der Mundpropaganda zu vervielfachen.

Cette ligne de produits coiffants s'adresse aux jeunes soucieux de leur look, chacun des six types offrant une tenue et une finition différentes. Outre le changement d'image, une nouvelle coiffure que l'on peut modeler à son gré peut réveiller des instincts enfouis et faire s'exprimer les cheveux comme la personne en soi. Œuvres de l'illustrateur Yuko Kondo, les personnages fantastiques à tête d'animal symbolisent divers instincts. Chaque personnage a une personnalité, une profession et des amis, et un monde spécial a été créé sur Facebook pour atteindre plus facilement la cible de marché et décupler les avantages du bouche à oreille.

TROJAN

Structural Design: Peter Clarke, Jesse Kruska
Graphic Design: Colangelo, Jim O'Neill
Company: Product Ventures
Country: USA
Category: Body care

SILVER PENTAWARD 2013

SHISEIDO PROFESSIONAL
THE HAIR CARE SALON SOLUTIONS

Creative Direction/Design: Aoshi Kudo
Company: Communication Design Laboratory
Country: Japan
Category: Body care

BRONZE PENTAWARD 2014

KERASYS NATURING

Design: Chang Hee Seo, Youn Jae Oh,
Ae Ra Sin, Tae Hee Le
Company: Aekyung
Country: South Korea
Category: Body care

BRONZE PENTAWARD 2014

KERASYS PERFUME

Design: Taehee Lee, Aera Sin, Hana Lee
Illustration: Yellena James
Company: Aekyung
Country: South Korea
Category: Body care

BRONZE PENTAWARD 2013

GIVING
HERB SERIES

Design: Yun Shi (senior), Jingliang Chen, Donglei Guo, Yunjie Han
Company: Shanghai Jahwa United
Country: China
Category: Body care
SILVER PENTAWARD 2014

LUCIDO-L POWDER IN MILK

Creative/Art Direction: Zenji Hashimoto
Design: Midori Hirai, Chiaki Nomi, Anna Kuramochi
Account Management: Koichi Furusawa
Company: Cloud8
Country: Japan
Category: Body care
SILVER PENTAWARD 2014

**BIC
SOLEIL SHAVE & TRIM**

Design: A Touch of Mojo
Design Development Lead: BIC France
Client: BIC USA Brand Design
Company: BIC USA
Country: USA
Category: Body care

BRONZE PENTAWARD 2013

Mr. Parker is a new range that provides the discerning modern gentleman with everything needed for the best possible shave. It consists of a ready-fitted razor, replacement blade cartridges and a soothing shaving foam. The use of clean typography reflects a clean shave, and is combined with solid colors in bands which correspond to the international code for barbershops. The use of a moustache is a smart signature for the friendly logo and presents the range as a product with a highly personable appearance.

Mr. Parker ist ein neues Sortiment, das dem anspruchsvollen modernen Gentleman alles für die bestmögliche Rasur liefert. Enthalten sind ein einsatzbereiter Rasierer, Ersatzklingen und milder Rasierschaum. Die klare Typografie entspricht einer sauberen Rasur, kombiniert mit kraftvollen, zum internationalen Code der Friseurläden passenden Farbbändern. Der Schnurrbart ist ein smartes Element in dem freundlichen Logo, welches dem gesamten Sortiment ein höchst sympathisches Auftreten ermöglicht.

Mr. Parker est une nouvelle ligne de produits offrant à l'homme moderne exigeant tout ce dont il a besoin pour un rasage parfait. Elle se compose d'un rasoir prêt à l'emploi, de cartouches de lames de rechange et d'une mousse de rasage apaisante. Le recours à une typographie franche annonce un rasage de près, et la combinaison de couleurs vives en bandes rappellent le code international des enseignes de barbiers. La moustache est un logo amusant bien trouvé, symbole d'une gamme de produits intéressante.

MR. PARKER

Creative Direction: Morten Throndsen
Design: Sandro Kvernmo, Bendik Høibraaten
Company: Strømme Throndsen Design
Country: Norway
Category: Body care

GOLD PENTAWARD 2014

DOVE MEN + CARE FACE CARE

Creative Direction: Laurent Hainaut, JB Hartford
Art Direction: Michelle Mak
Design: Kei Hayashi
Production Direction: Linda Tseng
Client/SVP Marketing: Steve Miles
Client Brand Direction: Jennifer Bremner
Client Design Management: Matthew Okin
Company: Raison Pure International
Country: USA
Category: Beauty

GOLD PENTAWARD 2013

WAREW

Creative/Art Direction: Eisuke Tachikawa (Nosigner)
Design: Eisuke Tachikawa, Takeshi Kawano
Photography: Hatta, Takeshi Kawano
Company: Nosigner
Country: Japan
Category: Beauty

GOLD PENTAWARD 2014

Warew, meaning 'authentic Japanese style', is a range of skincare products that seek to bring out the inner beauty, using natural, local ingredients and thus setting new standards in the Japanese market. As beauty exists in simplicity or in the invisible spirit, deep vermilion and white were chosen as the brand colors based on the shiromuku, a kimono worn when a woman is at her most beautiful, a bride. The idea of gesture is present too with the packaging designed to evoke the beautiful shosa movement, like the subtle steps of a tea ceremony. The logo recalls both the national flag and a hand mirror, reflecting the essence of Japanese beauty.

Warew („authentisch japanischer Stil") ist ein Hautpflegesortiment, das innere Schönheit zum Leuchten bringen will. Dafür nutzt es natürliche, lokale Ingredienzen und setzt somit neue Standards auf dem japanischen Markt. Da Schönheit in der Einfachheit oder im unsichtbaren Geist existiert, wählte man als Markenfarben ein dunkles Zinnoberrot und Weiß. Die Farben basieren auf dem Shiromuku-Kimono, den eine Frau dann angelegt, wenn sie am schönsten ist: zur Hochzeit. Auch die Idee der Geste wird aufgegriffen, indem die schönen Shosa-Bewegungen wie bei den subtilen Handlungen der Teezeremonie im Design der Verpackung anklingen. Das Logo spielt sowohl auf die japanische Flagge als auch einen Handspiegel an und reflektiert somit die Essenz japanischer Schönheit.

Warew signifie « style japonais authentique » ; c'est aussi une ligne de produits cosmétiques faits d'ingrédients locaux naturels et cherchant à révéler la beauté intérieure. La marque crée en cela un précédent sur le marché japonais. Il existe une beauté dans la simplicité et dans l'invisible : le blanc et un vermillon intense ont été retenus pour l'identité, tel le shiromuku, ce kimono que portent les femmes le jour de leur mariage. La gestuelle est également présente en évoquant le mouvement shosa, tel le déroulement d'une cérémonie du thé. Le logo rappelle à la fois le drapeau national et un miroir de poche reflétant toute l'essence de la beauté japonaise.

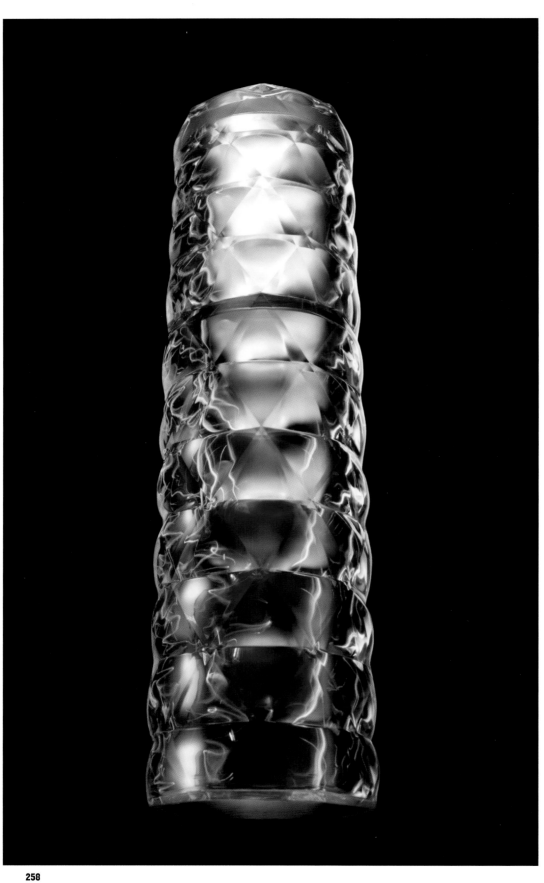

POLA
BA GRANDLUXE 2

Creative Direction: Takashi Matsui,
Chiharu Suzuki
Art Direction: Haruyo Eto
Design: Kentaro Ito, Rumie Ito
Company: Pola
Country: Japan
Category: Beauty

BRONZE PENTAWARD 2014

LIESE

Creative Direction: Masako Hirasawa
Design: Akiko Saito
Product Design: Yohei Shimura
Company: Kao
Country: Japan
Category: Beauty

SILVER PENTAWARD 2013

ETUDE
ETOINETTE LINES

Design: Jung Mi Jung, Mijin Lee,
Sylvie de France
Marketing: Hye Yeon Ji
Company: Etude
Country: South Korea
Category: Beauty

BRONZE PENTAWARD 2013

TOKO-DO
GARLINU.F

Art Direction: Yuji Numazawa
Copywriting: Tomoki Yomogita
Design: Saki Suzuki, Nanami Yamada
Printing Direction: Kumsno Yusuke
Company: Dentsu
Country: Japan
Category: Beauty

BRONZE PENTAWARD 2013

ETUDE
FEDORA HAIR WAX

Design: Jung Mi Jung, Lee Jae Myung,
Sul Semi, Min Anna
Company: Etude
Country: South Korea
Category: Beauty

SILVER PENTAWARD 2013

PRÉDIA
SPA ET MER SKINCARE SERIES

Creative Direction: Kazuhiro Niikura
Art Direction: Rieko Morita
Design: Henri Harada
Company: Kose
Country: Japan
Category: Beauty

BRONZE PENTAWARD 2014

MASH BEAUTY LAB
F ORGANICS

Art Direction/Design:
Hirokazu Kobayashi, Haruna Yamada
Company: Spread
Country: Japan
Category: Beauty

SILVER PENTAWARD 2014

KIA
EAU DE TOILETTE

Design: Aekyung creative design team,
Kum-Suk Jang, Young Soo Jung,
Sung Eun Hong
Company: Aekyung
Country: South Korea
Category: Beauty
SILVER PENTAWARD 2014

The idea of people gathering together around food during holidays was part of the inspiration for the design for this special collection. The resulting gift packaging had a quirky and surprising edge to it that appealed to the Björn Borg target audience of 18-25-year-olds around the world, and communicated the happy, teasing and playful spirit of the brand. The importance of the underwear being visible determined the use of the clear transparent plastic packaging, while the graphic design and word-play was intended to trigger curiosity in the young consumers.

Die Vorstellung von Menschen die sich während der Ferien zum Essen zusammenfinden, inspirierte diese spezielle Kollektion. So entstand diese Geschenkverpackung mit schrulliger und überraschender Note, die das weltweite Zielpublikum der 18–25-Jährigen anspricht und den fröhlichen, scherzhaften und spielerischen Spirit der Marke Björn Borg kommuniziert. Die Unterwäsche sollte unbedingt sichtbar sein, und deswegen wurde eine durchsichtige Plastikverpackung verwendet, Grafikdesign und Wortspiele sollten die Neugier der jüngeren Verbraucher wecken.

Le principe de personnes réunies autour d'une table pour les pour les vacances, a inspiré le design de cette collection spéciale. L'emballage cadeau est original et surprenant, capable de plaire partout dans le monde au public cible de Björn Borg des 18–25 ans. Il vise aussi à transmettre l'esprit joyeux, taquin et ludique de la marque. Les sous-vêtements devaient à tout prix être visibles, d'où le choix du plastique transparent. Le design graphique et le jeu de mots visent à piquer la curiosité des jeunes consommateurs.

A TASTY HOLIDAY

Art Direction/Copywriting: Ida Norrby
Company: Björn Borg
Country: Sweden
Category: Distributors'/Retailers' own brands

GOLD PENTAWARD 2013

ETNIA FRAGRANCES

Creative Direction: Alberto Cienfuegos,
Nacho Lavernia
Design: Raul Edo
Company: Lavernia & Cienfuegos
Country: Spain
Category: Distributors'/Retailers' own brands

SILVER PENTAWARD 2014

The sense of smell has an amazing ability to conjure up memories, whilst few things are nicer than to reminisce about favorite trips abroad. **Etnia**'s fragrance collection was thus inspired by some of the trendiest parts of the world's famous cities, from London's well-known and vibrant Brick Lane to Peking's unexpected and avant-garde 798 Factory. The range consists of a number of these trend-setting localities, with the rounded bottles evoking travel and the global reach of these cities, and at the same time serving as a magnifying-glass to view the map of each neighborhood, as seen from the inside of the bottle and reverse of the label.

Der Geruchssinn hat die erstaunliche Fähigkeit, Erinnerungen wachzurufen. Und an kaum etwas denkt man so gerne zurück wie an besondere Fernreisen. Die **Etnia** Duft Kollektion ließ sich somit von den trendigsten Teilen der berühmtesten Städte der Welt inspirieren: der berühmten Londoner Brick Lane oder ganz unerwartet von der Avantgarde aus dem Pekinger Kunstbezirk Fabrik 798. Zum Sortiment gehören verschiedene dieser Trendsetter-Städte. Die runden Flaschen gemahnen ans Reisen und die globale Wirkung dieser Orte. Sie dienen gleichzeitig als Vergrößerungsglas, durch das man den Stadtplan auf der Rückseite des Etiketts durch die Flasche hindurch betrachten kann.

L'odorat a cette capacité incroyable de rappeler des souvenirs, et il est des plus agréables de revivre en pensées nos meilleurs voyages. La collection de parfums **Etnia** s'est inspirée des lieux les plus en vogue de villes célèbres, comme Brick Lane, quartier londonien réputé et dynamique, ou Espace 798, district original et d'avant-garde à Pékin. La gamme fait référence à plusieurs de ces endroits tendance : le flacon arrondi évoque les voyages et la portée globale de ces villes. Il fait aussi office de loupe pour observer le plan de chaque quartier visible à l'intérieur, au dos de l'étiquette.

EVOKA

Creative Direction: Anthony Biles
Design: Alastair Duckworth
Company: Biles
Country: UK
Category: Distributors'/
Retailers' own brands

BRONZE PENTAWARD 2014

NATURALINE COSMETICS

Creative Direction: Silvana Conzelmann
Company: Schaffner & Conzelmann
Country: Switzerland
Category: Distributors'/Retailers' own brands

BRONZE PENTAWARD 2013

SEPHORA
BATH

Design: Marie-Christine Gendron
Company: Sephora
Country: France
Category: Distributors'/
Retailers' own brands

BRONZE PENTAWARD 2013

SENSITIVE

BE GENTLE
TO YOUR TEETH!

WHITENING

SMILE LIKE
A STAR!

**MULTI
PROTECTION**

YOU DESERVE
COMPLETE CARE!

KIDS 5-12

MAKES YOUR
TEETH STRONG!

FLUOR

EVERY DAY
A CLEAN SMILE!

FRESH

CRAZY COOL
MINT

HEMA TOOTHPASTE

Creative Direction: Paul Roeters
Design: Max Kortsmit
Company: Studio Kluif
Country: Netherlands
Category: Distributors'/Retailers' own brands

SILVER PENTAWARD 2013

COWSHED CHEEKY

Chief Creative Officer: Karen Welman
Creative Direction: Sarah Cattle
Design Direction: Poppy Stedman
Head of Words: Sylvie Saunders
Strategy: Jenny Dean
Company: Pearlfisher
Country: UK
Category: Distributors'/
Retailers' own brands

GOLD PENTAWARD 2014

MADE IN SEPHORA

Design: Solenne Joubert
Product Management: Pauline Prebois
Company: Sephora
Country: France
Category: Distributors'/Retailers'
own brands
SILVER PENTAWARD 2013

CRABTREE & EVELYN
EAU DE PARFUM

Creative Direction: Mary Lewis
Company: Lewis Moberly
Country: UK
Category: Distributors'/
Retailers' own brands
BRONZE PENTAWARD 2014

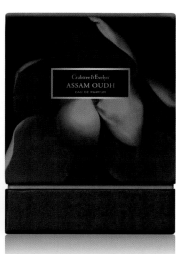

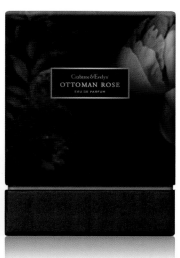

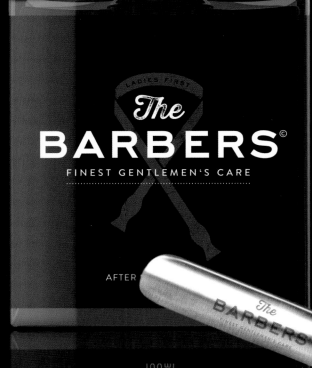

The

BARBERS ©

FINEST GENTLEMEN'S CARE

AFTER

100 ml
AFTER SHAVE LOTION

THE BARBERS GENTLEMEN'S CARE

Design: Soeren Uherek, Tibor Hegedues
Company: Soerentibor
Country: Germany
Category: Packaging concept (body)

GOLD PENTAWARD 2013

BOOK AND PILL

Design: Yunsung Lee (student)
School: Konkuk University
Country: South Korea
Category: Packaging concept (body)

SILVER PENTAWARD 2013

ARBORIS
CONCEPT FOR FRESH COSMETICS

Art Direction: Nadie Parshina
Naming: Svetlana Chugunova
Company: Ohmybrand
Country: Russia
Category: Packaging concept (body)

BRONZE PENTAWARD 2013

VZHIK

Creative Direction: Sergey Redin
Lead Design: Aleksandr Pachkin
Company: Redindesign
Country: Russia
Category: Packaging concept (body)

BRONZE PENTAWARD 2014

TWISTER SISTERS

Design: Olga Voronchikhina (student)
School: British Higher School of Art
and Design, Moscow
Country: Russia
Category: Packaging concept (body)

SILVER PENTAWARD 2014

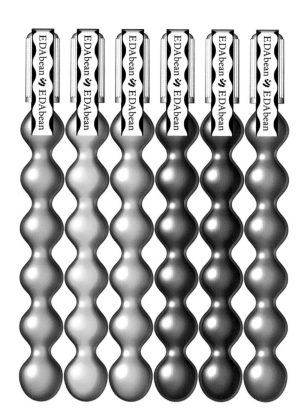

EDA BEANS
EDAMAME CONTAINER

Design: Mutsushi Hirano, Sayaka Shiraishi
Company: Toyo Seikan
Country: Japan
Category: Packaging concept (body)

BRONZE PENTAWARD 2014

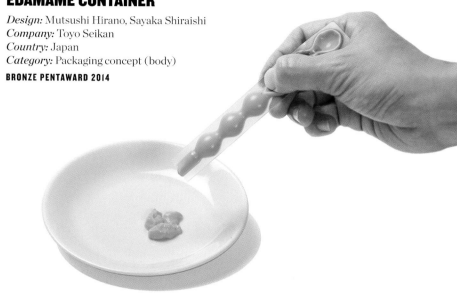

BANDIFUL

Design: Vivi Feng, Yu Ping Chuang (students)
Teacher: Eric O'Toole
School: Pratt Institute
Country: USA
Category: Packaging concept (body)

SILVER PENTAWARD 2013

FOOTSTEPS

Design: Mychko Yuliana (student)
School: British Higher School
of Art and Design, Moscow
Country: Russia
Category: Packaging concept (body)
GOLD PENTAWARD 2014 BIC STUDENT PRIZE

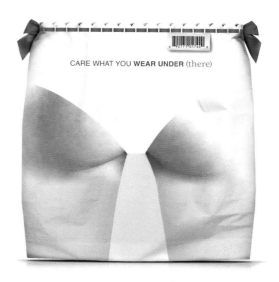

CARE WHAT YOU **WEAR UNDER** (there)

COTTON FEEL PADS WITH TABS
Care what you wear under there.

REGULAR COTTON FEEL PADS
Care what you wear under there.

EVERYDAY COTTON FRESH LINERS
Care what you wear under there.

12 LIGHT TAMPONS WITH APPLICATOR
Care what you wear under there.

12 REGULAR TAMPONS WITH APPLICATOR
Care what you wear under there.

UNDER THERE WEAR

Design: Kelly Bennett,
Chris MacDonald, Moyra Casey
Company: Afterhours
Country: UK
Category: Packaging concept (body)

SILVER PENTAWARD 2014

Best of the category
Perfumes
Make-up, body care, beauty products
Spirits
Fine wines, champagne

luxury

Casks, coffrets, gift boxes
Gourmet food
Limited editions, limited series, collectors' items
Distributors'/Retailers' own brands

THE BALVENIE 50

Creative Partner: Mark Paton
Design: Andy Giddings
Company: Here Design
Country: UK
Category: Best of the category luxury

PLATINUM PENTAWARD 2013
LUXEPACK PRIZE

David Stewart is known around the world by lovers of Scotch whisky and to celebrate the 50th anniversary of his arrival at the Balvenie distillery a limited edition of 88 bottles, with a sale price of £20,000, was produced from a rare cask of **Balvenie** single malt distilled in 1962. Scottish cabinetmaker Sam Chinnery was employed to make a cylinder to hold the bottle composed of 49 layers of wood, from local trees, and one of brass, on which was engraved the history of this exceptional single malt. Inside, a certificate of authenticity was inserted beneath a brass plate. Significant dates in the production of this whisky were mentioned on the label of the bottle, made of blown glass, and the wooden stopper was also handmade by the craftsman.

David Stewart ist bei Liebhabern von Scotch-Whisky weltweit bekannt. Um den 50. Jahrestag seines Eintritts in der Balvenie Distillery zu feiern, wurde eine Sonderauflage von 88 Flaschen mit einem Verkaufspreis von £ 20.000 produziert. Die Abfüllung stammt aus einem seltenen Fass mit einem 1962 gebrannten **Balvenie** Single Malt. Der schottische Kunsttischler Sam Chinnery fertigte für die Flasche einen Zylinder, der aus 49 Holzschichten aus Bäumen der Region besteht sowie einer Messingscheibe, in der die Geschichte dieses außergewöhnlichen Single Malt eingraviert ist. Im Inneren wurde das Echtheitszertifikat unter einer Messingplatte eingefügt. Das Etikett auf der Flasche aus mundgeblasenem Glas erwähnt wesentliche Daten zur Produktion dieses Whiskys, und auch der hölzerne Verschluss stammt von Chinnery.

David Stewart est connu dans le monde entier par les amateurs de Scotch. Pour célébrer le 50e anniversaire de son arrivée à la distillerie Balvenie, une édition limitée de 88 bouteilles (prix de vente : 20 000 £) a été produite à partir d'un fût rare de single malt **Balvenie** distillé en 1962. L'ébéniste écossais Sam Chinnery a été sollicité pour fabriquer un cylindre comptant 49 couches de bois d'arbres locaux et une couche de laiton sur laquelle est gravée l'histoire de cet exceptionnel single malt. À l'intérieur, un certificat d'authenticité a été glissé sous une plaque en laiton. Les principales dates de production de ce whisky sont inscrites sur l'étiquette de la bouteille en verre soufflé ; le couvercle en bois a également été fabriqué à la main par l'artisan.

A prestigious new packaging was required for this premium sliced ham so that **Extrem**'s top product could be bought as a special gift at the same time as the brand was repositioning itself in gourmet stores around the world. The packaging needed to convey the product's extremely high quality in order for it to stand comparison with other high-end delicacies, such as caviar and foie gras. The resulting design, in matt black and with a contrasting golden handle in the form of a pig, doubles as an elegant serving-tray for presenting the finest cuts of Iberian ham in the very smartest style.

Dieser in Scheiben geschnittene Premium-Schinken benötigte eine prestigeträchtige, neue Verpackungsform. Denn dieses Topprodukt von **Extrem** sollte im selben Moment, als sich die Marke in Gourmetgeschäften weltweit gerade neu positionierte, auch als Geschenk gekauft werden können. Die Verpackung musste die besonders hohe Qualität des Produkts vermitteln, damit es verglichen mit anderen Top-Köstlichkeiten wie Kaviar und Foie Gras dem Kunden sofort ins Auge springt. Das resultierende Design in mattem Schwarz mit dem kontrastierenden goldenen Griff in Schweine-Form dient gleichzeitig als elegante Servierschale, um den besten iberischen Schinken außergewöhnlich smart zu präsentieren.

Produit phare d'**Extrem**, ce jambon en tranches de qualité supérieure méritait un nouvel emballage prestigieux digne d'un présent, alors que la marque tentait de se repositionner dans les épiceries fines du monde entier. L'emballage devait être à la hauteur de la qualité exceptionnelle du produit pour le mettre au niveau d'autres aliments raffinés comme le caviar et le foie gras. D'un noir mat sur lequel tranche la poignée dorée en forme de cochon, le design imaginé sert également de plateau de service pour présenter en toute élégance le meilleur du jambon ibérique.

AGRICULTURAS DIVERSAS SLU EXTREM

Creative Direction: Alberto Cienfuegos, Nacho Lavernia
Design: Raul Edo
Company: Lavernia & Cienfuegos
Country: Spain
Category: Best of the category luxury

PLATINUM PENTAWARD 2014
LUXEPACK PRIZE

DIPTYQUE
EAU DE PARFUM

Creative Direction: Sébastien Servaire
Design: Candido De Barros
Graphic Design: Justine Dauchez, Yael Audrain
Company: R'Pure Studio/Servaire
Country: France
Category: Perfumes

SILVER PENTAWARD 2013

The light and airy delicacy of **Daisy Dream** is inspired by the boundless spirit of blue skies and meadow flowers. At the same time, this floral, fruity fragrance reflects an irresistible mixture of intricate details, elegance and femininity which delivers a fresh interpretation of the daisy motif. The glass bottle design is enveloped in a shawl of laced daisies and is topped with a silver cap adorned with further flowers with gold centers.

Daisy Dream mit seiner leichten und luftigen Zartheit lässt sich von der grenzenlosen Weite des blauen Himmels und den Wiesenblumen inspirieren. Gleichzeitig spiegelt der florale und fruchtige Wohlgeruch die unwiderstehliche Mischung diffiziler Details, Eleganz und Weiblichkeit. Die Glasflasche dicht von Gänseblümchen ummantelt, obenauf sitzt einsilbernen Verschluss, verziert mit weiteren Blüten mit goldenem Stempel.

Le design aérien et délicat de **Daisy Dream** s'inspire des étendues de ciel bleu et de prairies en fleurs. Ce parfum à la fois floral et fruité diffuse un mélange irrésistible de détails complexes, d'élégance et de féminité pour une réinterprétation de la marguerite. Le flacon en verre est enveloppé d'un châle de marguerites entrelacées et chapeauté d'un bouchon argenté orné de ces fleurs au cœur d'or.

MARC JACOBS
DAISY DREAM

Creative Direction: Sam O'Donahue
Design: Peter Ash, Felix De Voss
Company: Established
Country: USA
Category: Perfumes

GOLD PENTAWARD 2014

DAISY DREAM
MARC JACOBS

DIPTYQUE
ELECTRIC DIFFUSER

Art Direction: Caroline Colin
Art Direction Animation/Illustration: Juliette Lavat
Marketing Direction: Sébastien Servaire
Product Development Direction: Erwann Pivert
Company: R'Pure Studio/Servaire
Country: France
Category: Perfumes

SILVER PENTAWARD 2014

CLÉ DE PEAU BEAUTÉ
ROSE SYNERGIQUE

Creative Direction: Izumi Matsumoto
Art Direction: Mao Komai
Design: Benoît-Pierre Emery,
Damian O'Sullivan, Mao Komai
Company: Shiseido
Country: Japan
Category: Perfumes

SILVER PENTAWARD 2014

DIPTYQUE
LE SABLIER

Creative Direction: Sébastien Servaire
Design: Candido De Barros
Art Direction: Justine Dauchez
Graphic Design: Wann Pivert
Company: R'Pure Studio/Servaire
Country: France
Category: Perfumes

GOLD PENTAWARD 2013

The prestigious niche brand perfumer **Diptyque** was looking to create a new way of diffusing home scents which would be an alternative to their world-famous candles. The new product would also have to fit in with the subtle narrative universe the brand has shaped for more than 50 years, by developing "curiosities" within the perfume category. The resulting design used gravity and capillarity to spread the perfume through a piece of felt, from where it then evaporates into the room. The timeless design, with a nod to the hourglass, allows an immediate understanding of how it operates as the scent diffuses at the same rate as the perfume can be seen to fall, drop by drop. Made entirely from recycled materials, it also requires no power source.

Der angesehene Parfümhändler für Nischenmarken **Diptyque** wollte als Alternative zu seinen weltberühmten Kerzen auf neue Weise Duftstoffe für Zuhause vertreiben. Das neue Produkt sollte sich ins subtile Erzähluniversum einfügen, das die Marke seit über 50 Jahren gestaltet, indem innerhalb der Kategorie Parfüm „Kuriositäten" entwickelt wurden. Die Gestaltung arbeitet mit Schwerkraft und Kapillarwirkung, damit sich das Parfum über ein Filzstück schließlich im ganzen Zimmer ausbreitet. Das zeitlose Design spielt auf eine Sanduhr an und verweist sofort auf die Funktionsweise: Der Duft breitet sich in dem Tempo aus, das man beim tropfenweisen Fallen des Parfüms beobachten kann. Es besteht komplett aus recyceltem Material und benötigt keine Energiequelle.

La marque de niche du prestigieux parfumeur **Diptyque** souhaitait inventer un nouveau diffuseur d'ambiance en complément de ses célèbres bougies. Le nouveau produit devait également se faire une place dans l'univers narratif raffiné que la marque construit depuis plus de 50 ans, grâce à ses « curiosités » en parfumerie. Le design fait appel à la gravité et à la capillarité pour que le parfum imbibe un morceau de feutre et s'en évapore. Le principe de cette création intemporelle, clin d'œil au sablier, est très intuitif : le parfum se diffuse à la même vitesse que le liquide tombant goutte à goutte. Entièrement fait de matériaux recyclés, il ne requiert aucune énergie.

HERBORIST
LOTUS MEMORY

Design: Cao Jun
Company: Shanghai Jahwa United
Country: China
Category: Perfumes

BRONZE PENTAWARD 2013

SALVATORE FERRAGAMO
THE MINI FRAGRANCE COLLECTION

Design: Fanny Le Bonniec, Oscar Del Cerro
Company: Sotano Studio
Country: Spain
Category: Perfumes

BRONZE PENTAWARD 2014

CACHAREL
CATCH-ME

Design: Patrick Veillet
Company: Patrick Veillet
Country: France
Category: Perfumes

BRONZE PENTAWARD 2013

MARC JACOBS
DOT

Design: Sayuri Shoji in collaboration
with Marc Jacobs
Company: Sayuri Studio
Country: Japan
Category: Perfumes

SILVER PENTAWARD 2013

**IPSA
PREMIER LINE**

Art Direction/Design: Aoshi Kudo
Creative Direction: Shuichi Ikeda
Logo Design: Helmut Schmid
Company: Communication Design Laboratory
Country: Japan
Category: Make-up, body care, beauty products

SILVER PENTAWARD 2014

MARC JACOBS
SEPHORA

Creative Direction: Sam O'Donahue
Design Direction: Felix De Voss
Design: Peter Ash, Nils Siegel
Company: Established
Country: USA
Category: Make-up, body care,
beauty products

GOLD PENTAWARD 2014

LANCÔME DREAMTONE

Creative Direction: Sébastien Servaire
Art Direction/Design: Candido de Barros
Company: R'Pure Studio/Servaire
Country: France
Category: Make-up, body care, beauty products

SILVER PENTAWARD 2014

GUERLAIN
SUPER AQUA

Creative Direction: Sébastien Servaire
Art Direction: Candido De Barros
Company: R'Pure Studio / Servaire
Country: France
Category: Make-up, body care, beauty products

SILVER PENTAWARD 2013

DIVUM TR

Design: Shohei Yagi
Company: Suzhou Menard Cosmetics
Country: China
Category: Make-up, body care, beauty products

GOLD PENTAWARD 2013

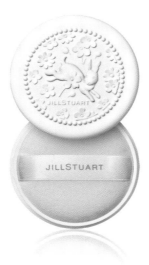

JILL STUART ANGEL

Creative Direction: Jill Stuart
Art Direction: Akemi Masuda
Design: Yoshiaki Koda
Company: Kose
Country: Japan
Category: Make-up, body care, beauty products

BRONZE PENTAWARD 2013

CLÉ DE PEAU BEAUTÉ

Art Direction: Mao Komai
Design: Midori Matsuishi
Company: Shiseido
Country: Japan
Category: Make-up, body care, beauty products

SILVER PENTAWARD 2013

POLA AMU

Creative Direction: Takeshi Usui
Art Direction: Takashi Matsui
Design: Taishi Ono, Yasuha Michikami
Company: Pola
Country: Japan
Category: Make-up, body care, beauty products
BRONZE PENTAWARD 2013

RE: NK
CELL TO CELL ESSENCE

Design: Lee Hee, Kim Ju-Seop, Byun Hee-Youn
Company: Coway
Country: South Korea
Category: Make-up, body care, beauty products

BRONZE PENTAWARD 2014

CMM
MING

Company: Nianxiang Design Consulting
Country: China
Category: Make-up, body care, beauty products

BRONZE PENTAWARD 2014

Made from traditional Chinese plant extracts, this day-and-night cream has been created with the discerning and more mature lady in mind. If the most natural and perfect skincare results derive from the synchronization of time and space, following eastern philosophy, then the key to the best design to translate this miracle is found in a similar eastern aesthetic. The lid and the jar thus resemble a peaceful mountain peak reflecting in a tranquil lake, expressing the eternity and harmony of the universe. Turning to the practical, the spoon is here fitted with a magnet to allow it to be easily and stably replaced on the cap when not in use.

Diese Creme für Tag und Nacht wird aus traditionellen chinesischen Pflanzenextrakten für die anspruchsvolle und reifere Dame hergestellt. Wenn der fernöstlichen Philosophie zufolge die natürlichsten und perfektesten Ergebnisse der Hautpflege mit der Synchronisierung von Raum und Zeit entstehen, vermittelt man dieses Wunder mit dem besten Design in einer entsprechend fernöstlichen Ästhetik. Der Tiegel mit seinem Deckel erinnert an eine friedliche Bergspitze, die sich in einem stillen See spiegelt und so die Ewigkeit und Harmonie des Universums verkörpert. Praktisch auch, dass man das Löffelchen durch seinen Magneten ganz einfach und stabil auf den Verschluss legen kann, wenn es nicht benutzt wird.

À base d'extrait de plantes traditionnelles chinoises, cette crème de jour et de nuit a été conçue pour les femmes matures exigeantes. Si selon la philosophie orientale, le cosmétique naturel parfait tient à une synchronisation espace/temps, le secret d'un design réussi pour exprimer ce miracle réside également dans une esthétique orientale. Le couvercle et le pot rappellent le sommet d'une montagne tranquille se reflétant dans un lac paisible, à l'image de l'éternité et de l'harmonie de l'univers. D'un point de vue pratique, la cuillère est maintenue par un aimant pour être replacée aisément après usage sur le couvercle.

ANESTASIA SENSATIONAL SPIRIT

Design: Karim Rashid
Company: Karim Rashid
Country: USA
Category: Spirits

GOLD PENTAWARD 2013

Anestasia vodka creates a new taste sensation by making the mouth tingle and feel cool, relieving the usual burn of alcoholic spirits. The remarkable bottle design reflects this perfectly with the crystalline and obliquely faceted surface giving it an ultra-futuristic feel. The hard-edged and asymmetrical form also proves to be easy to grip and comfortable for the hand, while the bottle's beauty makes it an ideal tabletop piece, accenting any environment with a look which embodies cutting-edge style.

Anestasia Wodka sorgt für ein neues Geschmacks-erleben, weil er im Mund kribbelt und kühlt. So wird der normalerweise brennende Geschmack bei hochprozen-tigen Getränken gelindert. Dem entspricht perfekt das bemerkenswerte Design mit seiner kristallinen Ober-fläche und den schrägen Facetten, was der Flasche eine ultrafuturistische Note verleiht. Nimmt man die kantige und asymmetrische Form in die Hand, wirkt sie griff-freundlich und angenehm, während die Flasche durch ihre Schönheit zu einem idealen Schmuckstück für den Tisch wird, das jeder Umgebung den Touch hoch-modernen Stils verleiht.

La vodka **Anestasia** offre une nouvelle saveur qui chatouille les papilles et rafraîchit la bouche, loin de la sensation de brûlure des spiritueux. L'impressionnant design de la bouteille évoque parfaitement cette expé-rience, avec une surface cristalline à facettes donnant un air très futuriste. La forme asymétrique permet une agréable prise en mains, et la beauté de la bouteille en fait un objet décoratif apportant une touche avant-gardiste à n'importe quel intérieur.

Commemorating Sir Alexander Walker's epic spirit of adventure and perseverance, the new ultra-premium **Odyssey** is inspired by the original 1932 whisky he brought aboard his voyages on luxury ocean liners. Sensuous and dynamic, the decanter's form captures the emotion of the sea, and with its ability to rock elegantly to and fro when standing, the rolling motion of the waves. When placed in its polyurethane leather-bound cabinet, the bottle is suspended for fluid 360-degree rotation, whilst the design also draws on brass maritime navigational instruments and the precision of highly crafted timepieces. Various elements in the pack nod to an Art Deco past while turning an eye to the future, such as the monogrammed diamond badge and weighty cabinet closure.

Zur Erinnerung an den epischen Abenteuergeist und die Beharrlichkeit von Sir Alexander Walker ließ sich das neue Ultrapremium **Odyssey** vom originalen Whisky des Jahres 1932 inspirieren, den er auf seine Reisen mit Luxuslinern mitnahm. Sinnlich und dynamisch fängt die Form des Dekanters die Stimmung der See ein. Weil er aufgestellt elegant hin- und herzuschaukeln vermag, lässt er an rollende Wogen denken. Wird die Flasche in ihrem mit PU-Leder bespannten Kästchen platziert, verharrt sie auch bei einer 360-Grad-Rotation in aufrechter Position. Das Design spielt auf maritime Navigationsinstrumente und die Präzision von Chronometern höchster Handwerkskunst an. Verschiedene Elemente der Verpackung zollen ihren Tribut der Art-Deco-Vergangenheit, bleiben aber auch zukunftsgerichtet, z. B. das diamantförmige Emblem mit Monogramm oder der gewichtige Verschluss des Kästchens.

En hommage à l'esprit aventurier et persévérant de Sir Alexander Walker, le nouveau **Odyssey** de qualité supérieure s'inspire du whisky de 1932 qu'il emportait lors de ses voyages sur les luxueux paquebots transatlantiques. Sensuelle et dynamique, la forme de la carafe transmet l'émotion de la mer ; avec son léger balancement, elle évoque le mouvement de roulis des vagues. Logée dans son étui en polyuréthane relié en cuir, la bouteille est suspendue pour permettre la rotation à 360 degrés du liquide. Le design rappelle les instruments de navigation en laiton et les mécanismes d'horlogerie de précision. Plusieurs éléments de l'emballage évoquent le passé Art déco tout en jetant un regard vers le futur, comme le losange monogrammé et la solide fermeture du boîtier.

JOHN WALKER & SONS
ODYSSEY

Creative Direction: Laurent Hainaut
Art Direction: Ann Chen
Visual Strategy/Innovation Direction: Nicole Duval
Senior Product Design: Loren Kulesus
Product Design: Marco Leone
Design: Alex Boulware
Production Direction: Linda Tseng
Global Design Direction: Jeremy Lindley
Innovation Direction: Regina Galang (Diageo)
POS & Gifting Direction: Jean-Noel Dollet
Invigoration: Steve Wilson (Diageo)
Company: Raison Pure International
Country: USA
Category: Spirits

SILVER PENTAWARD 2013

LOCK STOCK & BARREL WHISKEY

Art Direction: Kevin Shaw
Design: Cosimo Surace, Guy Pratt
Company: Stranger & Stranger
Country: UK
Category: Spirits
GOLD PENTAWARD 2014

LES ANTIQUAIRES DU COGNAC

Design: Angélique Lecussan,
Morgane Franck de Préaumont
Company: Dragon Rouge
Country: France
Category: Spirits
BRONZE PENTAWARD 2013

TESSERON
COGNAC

TESSERON
COGNAC

TRÉSOR

TRÉSOR

CAMUS
XO ELEGANCE

Creative Direction: Laurent Berriat
Company: Toscara
Country: France
Category: Spirits
BRONZE PENTAWARD 2014

TESSERON
TRÉSOR SIGNATURE COLLECTION

Design: Linea design team
Company: Linea
Country: France
Category: Spirits
SILVER PENTAWARD 2014

CAMUS FAMILY LEGACY

Design: Linea design team
Company: Linea
Country: France
Category: Spirits
BRONZE PENTAWARD 2013

ABSOLUT VODKA
ELYX

Executive Client Direction: Jonas Andersson
Design Direction: Björn Studt, Henrik Billqvist
Client Management: Britt-Marie Möller
Client Direction: Alfred Alfred (No Picnic)
Industrial Design: Urban Ahlgren,
Thomas Schaad (No Picnic)
Design Engineering/Visualization:
Stefan Wennerström (No Picnic)
Client: The Absolut Company
Global Direction Design Strategy: Anna Kamjou
Global Direction Innovation: Lena Danielsson
Global Marketing Direction: Louise de Fautereau
Global Marketing Management: Sébastien Borda
Company: The Brand Union
Country: Sweden
Category: Spirits

SILVER PENTAWARD 2013

CHANGYU

Design: Wu Kuanfu, Tang Sisi
Company: Shenzhen Excel Package Design
Country: China
Category: Spirits

BRONZE PENTAWARD 2014

DEAU COGNAC L.V.O. LA VIE EN OR

Design: Alpha Centauri Design Agency
Gold Decoration: Arthus Bertrand
Company: Distillerie des Moisans
Country: France
Category: Spirits

SILVER PENTAWARD 2014

ERNEST TOLJ

Design: Mary Lewis
Company: Lewis Moberly
Country: UK
Category: Fine wines, champagne

GOLD PENTAWARD 2013

BLEASDALE
THE IRON DUKE

Creative Direction: Matthew Remphrey
Design: Kerina West
Company: Parallax Design
Country: Australia
Category: Fine wines, champagne

SILVER PENTAWARD 2014

SHANGRI-LA
LEGEND. DREAMLAND

Design: Jingkuan Zhou
Company: K2 Creative Design
Country: China
Category: Fine wines, champagne

BRONZE PENTAWARD 2014

CHATEAU RUBAN

Graphic Design: Juraj Vontorcik,
Juraj Demovic, Livia Lorinczova
Illustration: Igor Benca
Company: Pergamen Trnava
Country: Slovakia
Category: Fine wines, champagne

BRONZE PENTAWARD 2014

800 LOVE LETTERS WINE

Design: Wu Shao Nan
Company: Shenzhen Excel Package Design
Country: China
Category: Fine wines, champagne

SILVER PENTAWARD 2013

CROCHET

Design: Rita Rivotti
Company: Rita Rivotti
Wine Branding & Design
Country: Portugal
Category: Fine wines
GOLD PENTAWARD 2014

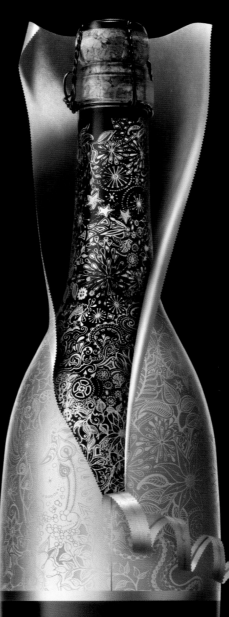

ABSOLUT VODKA
TUNE

Creative Direction: Patrick Gebhardt
Executive Client Direction: Jonas Andersson
Client Management: Camilla Sand, Frida Frisén
Client Direction: Alfred Alfred
Project Management: Jonas Westius (No Picnic)
Industrial Design: Anna-Carin Neale, Thomas Schaad (No Picnic)
Visualization: Stefan Wennerström (No Picnic)
Creative Direction: Urban Ahlgren (No Picnic)
Client: The Absolut Company
Global Marketing Management: Tamara Urukalo
Global Direction Design Strategy: Anna Kamjou
Global Direction Innovation: Nina Gillsvik
Company: The Brand Union
Country: Sweden
Category: Fine wines, champagne

BRONZE PENTAWARD 2013

BITRI
EACH BOTTLE HAS A SECRET

Art Direction: Eduardo Aires
Design: Ana Simões
Company: White Studio
Country: Portugal
Category: Fine wines, champagne

SILVER PENTAWARD 2013

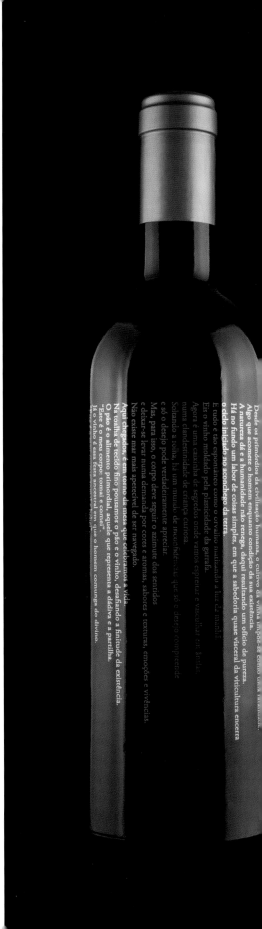

CHATEAU FENHE

Design: Wu Kuanfu
Company: Shenzhen Excel Package Design
Country: China
Category: Fine wines, champagne

BRONZE PENTAWARD 2014

THE CHANGYU FAMILY COLLECTION

Design: Jian Wei Miao, Sun Xiao
Company: Jian Wei Miao
Country: China
Category: Fine wines, champagne

SILVER PENTAWARD 2014

CHAMPAGNE TAITTINGER

Design: Champagne Taittinger design team
Production: Sleever
Country: France
Category: Fine wines, champagne

BRONZE PENTAWARD 2013

HENNESSY
XO EXCLUSIVE COLLECTION

Project Management: Patrick Marrot (Hennessy)
Brand Management: Clément Beloqui (Hennessy)
Design: Tom Dixon
Production: Virojanglor
Country: France
Category: Casks, cases, gift boxes, ice buckets

BRONZE PENTAWARD 2014

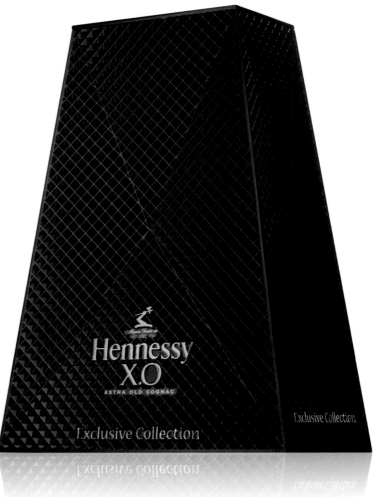

MOËT & CHANDON ROSÉ IMPÉRIAL

Design: François Takounseun, Gérald Galdini, Aurélie Sidot, Gabriel Brouste
Company: Partisan du Sens
Country: France
Category: Casks, cases, gift boxes, ice buckets

SILVER PENTAWARD 2014

JOHNNIE WALKER BLACK LABEL

Creative Direction: Simon Adamson
Design: Andy Wallace
Design Direction: Oli Bedwell
Planning Direction: Edward Hayes
Company: Bloom London
Country: UK
Category: Casks, cases, gift boxes, ice buckets

GOLD PENTAWARD 2013

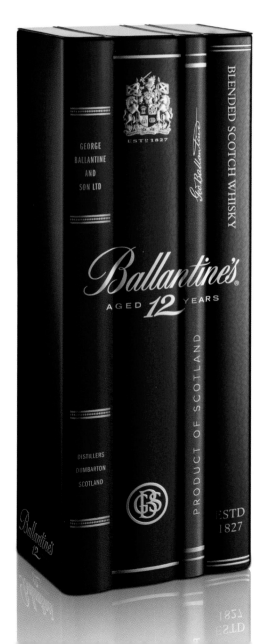

BALLANTINE'S 12 GIFT PACK

Design: Graeme Bridgeford (AirInnovation)
Head of Packaging Development: Kilmalid
(Chivas Brothers)
Production: Virojanglor
Country: France
Category: Casks, cases, gift boxes, ice buckets

BRONZE PENTAWARD 2013

BOMBAY SAPPHIRE

Design: Samantha Wilkes, Guillaume Furminger,
Gary Nettleton, Sabine Merfeld, James McAllister,
Lucy Russell, Asiya Hasan Damen
Company: Webb deVlam
Country: UK
Category: Casks, cases, gift boxes, ice buckets

SILVER PENTAWARD 2013

Keeping **Bombay Sapphire**'s brand philosophy, "Infused with Imagination", central to the packaging design, the winner in the busy travel retail sector is the one that can grab the attention of travelers who are in a hurry and are confronted by a wealth of purchasing options. Technology offers much for design, and although electroluminescent ink is not new this was the first time it was successfully integrated into a packaging design. Electro begs to be picked up off the shelf, and when this happens it activates a hidden mechanical switch which sends a current through the pathways in sequence, creating a mesmerizing cascade for the eyes.

Im rührigen Reiseeinzelhandel gewinnt, wer die Aufmerksamkeit der Travelers erlangt, die in Eile und von den vielen Kaufmöglichkeiten überwältigt sind. So bleibt die Markenphilosophie von **Bombay Sapphire** „Infused with Imagination" Kern des Verpackungsdesigns. Technologie ermöglicht neue Wege in der Gestaltung: Obwohl elektrolumineszierende Druckfarbe nichts Neues ist, wurde sie hier zum ersten Mal erfolgreich ins Verpackungsdesign integriert. Electro drängt sich förmlich auf, vom Regal genommen zu werden: Dann schickt ein versteckter mechanischer Schalter Strom in einer bestimmten Folge durch die Leitung, was zu einer faszinierenden optischen Kaskade führt.

Le leader du « Duty free » est celui capable d'attirer l'attention des voyageurs pressés et exposés à une quantité d'options. La technologie apporte beaucoup au design, et même si l'encre électroluminescente n'est plus une nouveauté, elle l'a été à sa première utilisation pour un design d'emballage. Fidèle à sa philosophie « Infused with Imagination », la marque **Bombay Sapphire** a lancé Electro. Tout dans cet emballage invite à le choisir : un mécanisme caché s'active alors et envoie en séquence une lumière dans les sillons, offrant un hypnotique effet de cascade.

DOM PERIGNON
PULSAR BOX

Design: Dom Perignon
Production: DAPY – DO International
Country: France
Category: Casks, cases, gift boxes, ice buckets

SILVER PENTAWARD 2013

VEUVE CLICQUOT
AMERICAN MAILBOX

Art Direction: Sébastien Servaire
Client: Veuve Clicquot – Chloé Stefani,
Marco De Dionigi, Nicolas Remy
Production: Virojanglor
Company: R'Pure Studio/Servaire
Country: France
Category: Casks, cases, gift boxes,
ice buckets

SILVER PENTAWARD 2014

Champagne packaging is a key factor in each brand's image and identification, and here the design extends beyond the form of the typical case to create an aesthetic object which also has functional use. In keeping faithful to the pop spirit of Carte Jaune brut, the design revisits a fashion idea by taking inspiration from the Marilyn dress. The cylindrical packaging pops out and becomes an ice bucket, at the same time clothing the emblematic bottle in an attractive, pleated dress. The sleeve is reusable and chic, with reasonable costs and simple materials—a smart lifestyle statement!

Die Verpackung von Champagner ist ein wesentlicher Faktor für Image und Erkennbarkeit der Marke. Hier baut das Design die Form des typischen Weinkühlers aus und schafft ein ästhetisches und doch funktionales Objekt. Um dem Pop-Spirit von Carte Jaune Brut treu zu bleiben, ließ man sich fürs Design durch das berühmte Kleid von Marilyn Monroe inspirieren. Die zylindrische Packung springt auf und wird zum Eiskühler. Gleichzeitig kleidet sie die symbolträchtige Flasche in eine attraktive, plissierte Hülle. Sie ist chic, wiederverwendbar und setzt durch vernünftige Kosten und einfache Materialien ein cleveres Lifestyle-Statement.

Les emballages de champagne sont déterminants pour l'image et l'identification de chaque marque. Ici, le design s'éloigne de la forme standard pour créer un objet esthétique et pratique à la fois. Fidèle à l'esprit pop du brut Carte Jaune, il réinterprète une idée de mode en partant de la robe de Marilyn. L'emballage cylindrique se déploie et devient un seau à glace qui gaine la bouteille emblématique d'une superbe robe plissée. Le manchon est réutilisable, son coût de fabrication raisonnable et les matériaux simples : toute une leçon sur l'art de vivre !

VEUVE CLICQUOT
ICE BUCKET

Art Direction: Sébastien Servaire
Creative Direction: Candido Debarros
Graphic Design Direction: Justine Dauchez
Product Development Direction: Erwann Pivert
Account Direction: Amélie Anthome
Account Management: Emeline Piers
Photography: Arnaud Guffon
Company: R'Pure Studio / Servaire
Country: France
Category: Casks, cases, gift boxes, ice buckets

GOLD PENTAWARD 2014

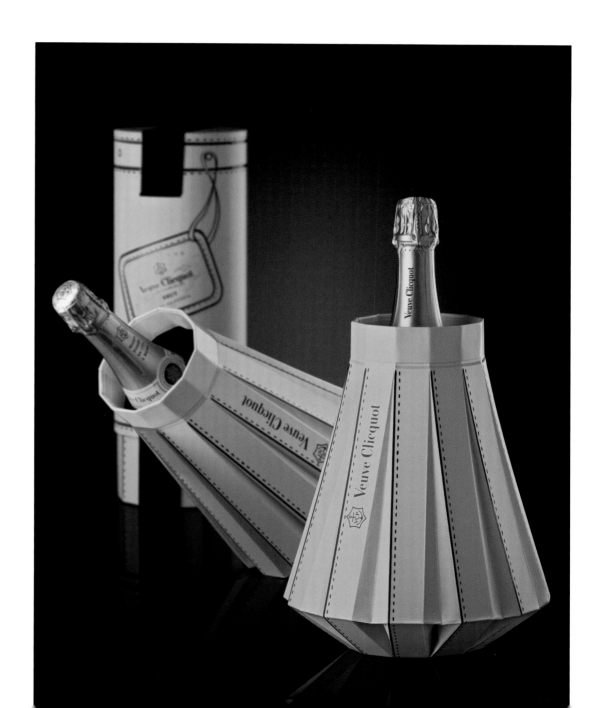

BELVEDERE
UNFILTERED

Creative Direction: Loïc Molina (Le Bihan)
Head of Product Design: Julien Zorzin
Design: Arnaud Toth
Production: Wildcat Packaging
Company: Chic
Country: UK
Category: Casks, cases, gift boxes, ice buckets

BRONZE PENTAWARD 2014

ARMAND BASI

Creative Direction/Art Direction/Design:
Josep María Garrofé (gift box)
Design: Antoni Arola (fragrance bottle),
Raquel Quevedo (fragrance bottle's box)
Company: Garrofé Brand & Pack
Country: Spain
Category: Casks, cases, gift boxes, ice buckets
BRONZE PENTAWARD 2014

JOHNNIE WALKER GIFT RANGE

Creative Direction: Dominic Burke
Senior Design: Damien Fournival
Creative Direction: John Paul Hunter
Senior Design: Lizzy Fisher
Company: Design Bridge
Country: UK
Category: Casks, cases, gift boxes, ice buckets
BRONZE PENTAWARD 2013

To communicate the special quality of **Claramunt**'s olive oil, handwritten lettering was used for the logo just as if it were the signature on a piece of art. Developing this concept, the bottle for each variety was designed independently but with the same conceptual theme, using four illustrations based on great Spanish artists to represent the different feelings and qualities derived from both fruit and oil. The rounded shapes and movement of Arbequina invoke freshness and a touch of beauty, while the autumn warmth and quiet evenings of Frantoio suggest temperance with a passion for taste. Austere Koroneiki breathes an island dryness, with bright sunlight, leaving misty Picual to complete the quartet with impressions of volume and tradition.

Ein handgeschriebenes Lettering im Logo von **Claramunt** vermittelt die besondere Qualität des Olivenöls, als wäre es die Signatur eines Kunstwerks. Zur Entwicklung dieses Konzepts wurde jede Variante des Öls mit einer eigenständigen Flasche, aber dem gleichen konzeptionellen Thema designt. Dazu verwendete man ausgehend von berühmten spanischen Künstlern vier Illustrationen, um die sich aus Frucht und Öl ergebenden Emotionen und Qualitäten zu repräsentieren. Die abgerundete Form und Bewegung der Arbequina beschwört Frische und Noten der Schönheit, während die Frantoio mit ihrer herbstlichen Wärme und den stillen Abenden an Mäßigung mit einer Passion für Geschmack denken lassen. Die nüchterne Koroneiki atmet die Trockenheit der Insel unter strahlendem Sonnenlicht, und die neblige Picual komplettiert das Quartett mit ihren Impressionen von Größe und Tradition.

Pour expliquer la qualité de l'huile d'olive **Claramunt**, le logo est fait de lettres manuscrites, telle la signature d'une œuvre d'art. Dans la même ligne, la bouteille de chaque variété a ses caractéristiques propres tout en suivant la même thématique : quatre illustrations inspirées de célèbres artistes espagnols expriment les sentiments et les qualités dérivées du fruit et de l'huile. La forme ronde de l'Arbequina suggère fraîcheur et beauté, alors que la chaleur de l'automne et les soirées paisibles de Frantoio évoquent tempérance et passion du goût. La variété austère Koroneiki fait penser à la sécheresse d'une île baignée d'un soleil éclatant. Picual vient compléter ce quatuor avec des impressions de volume et de tradition.

CLARAMUNT EXTRA VIRGIN OLIVE OIL

Design: Isabel Cabello Arrabal, Enrique Moreno Porriño
Company: Isabel Cabello Studio
Country: Spain
Category: Gourmet food

GOLD PENTAWARD 2013

VERTO ET GREENO

Design: Global Image
Illustration: Iban Barrenetxea
Company: Verto et Greeno
Country: Spain
Category: Gourmet food
BRONZE PENTAWARD 2013

MALEAS OLIVE OIL

Art Direction: Simos Saltiel
Design/Illustration: Elina Steletari
Company: Red Creative
Country: Greece
Category: Gourmet food
SILVER PENTAWARD 2014

BOUTARY

Creative Direction: Franck Basset
Art Direction: Dimitri Rastorgoueff,
Judith Nguyen Kim
Company: Carré Basset
Country: France
Category: Gourmet food

GOLD PENTAWARD 2014

MIOGEE

Design: Kang Weijie
Company: 12 Degree Branding
Country: China
Category: Gourmet food

SILVER PENTAWARD 2013

LADOLEA

Graphic Design: Leandros Katsouris
Product Design: Spyros Kyzis
Company: Melissi
Country: Greece
Category: Gourmet food

SILVER PENTAWARD 2014

MIGHTY RICE

Creative Direction: Gregory Tsaknakis
Design: Joshua Olsthoorn
Illustration: Ioanna Papaioannou
Company: Mousegraphics
Country: Greece
Category: Gourmet food

BRONZE PENTAWARD 2013

NEWBY TEAS
THE GOURMET COLLECTION

Design: Newby Teas creative team
Company: Newby Teas
Country: UK
Category: Gourmet food

BRONZE PENTAWARD 2014

CHA TZU TANG

Design: Victor Branding Design team
Company: Victor Branding Design
Country: Taiwan
Category: Gourmet food

SILVER PENTAWARD 2013

SONG FENG TSUI

Design: Guiping Nie, Jiao Wang, Yu Zhou
Company: Transmedia Advertising
Country: China
Category: Gourmet food

BRONZE PENTAWARD 2014

HOUSE OF SILLAGE

Design: June Lee (House Of Sillage)
Production: DAPY – DO International
Country: France
Category: Limited editions, limited series,
event creations

SILVER PENTAWARD 2013

Inside the special, limited-edition cap of this perfume bottle a miniature snowglobe scene of New York City can be discovered, decorated with lights and clothed in a coat of snow. The polycarbonate globe protects the delicate zamak figurines and tree, each piece being hand polished and then wrapped in silver or gold ornament by metalliztion. The central Christmas tree is decorated with 72 Swarovski stones, each carefully positioned and placed by hand. When the cap is turned upside down the magic happens and the small city comes to life under a fresh fall of snow.

Im Verschluss dieser Parfümflasche in Limited Edition befindet sich eine besondere Miniatur von New York City als Schneekugel, mit Lichtern geschmückt und von Schnee bedeckt. Die Kuppel aus Polykarbonat schützt die filigranen Zamakfiguren und den Baum. Jedes Stück wurde von Hand poliert und durch Metallisierung in silbernes oder goldenes Ornament gehüllt. Den zentralen Weihnachtsbaum dekorieren 72 Swarovski-Steine, alle sorgfältig per Hand positioniert. Wird die Flasche umgedreht, geschieht das Wunder, und die winzige Stadt wird unter den fallenden Flocken lebendig.

Le bouchon de ce parfum d'édition limitée est une boule à neige renfermant une miniature de la ville de New York, qui est décorée de lumières et recouverte d'un manteau de neige. Le globe en polycarbonate protège les fragiles figurines et l'arbre en zamak, chaque élément ayant été poli à la main et recouvert d'argent ou d'or par métallisation. Le sapin de Noël au milieu est décoré de 72 pierres Swarovski placées à la main. Quand le bouchon est retourné, la magie se produit et la petite ville prend vie sous la neige.

LANCÔME
BLACK CRYSTAL LIGHT EDITION

Design: Gérald Galdini, François Takounseun,
Aurélie Sidot, Emilie Etchelecou
Company: Partisan du Sens
Country: France
Category: Limited editions, limited series,
event creations

GOLD PENTAWARD 2013
SLEEVER INT. PRIZE

In order to mark itself out from other cognacs, **Hardy** commissioned crystal-maker Lalique to design something rather special for its latest carafe. "Le Printemps" (Spring) takes the form of a scent bottle with feminine lines, and a spectacular, sculpted stopper with subtle green tints reminiscent of some of the creations by René Lalique himself from the early 20th century. This limited-edition design is the first in a series of four outstanding carafes, all by Lalique, with the other seasonal varieties of "Eté", "Automne" and "Hiver" following at two-year intervals. The colors and designs are being kept a close secret.

Um sich von anderen Cognacsorten abzuheben, beauftragte **Hardy** den Kristallhersteller Lalique damit, als aktuelle Karaffe etwas ganz Besonderes zu designen. „Le Printemps" (Der Frühling) greift in seiner Flakonform feminine Linien auf. Der spektakuläre, skulpturale Verschluss in dezent grüner Färbung erinnert an Schöpfungen von René Lalique selbst aus dem Anfang des 20. Jahrhunderts. Dieses Design in Limited Edition gehört zu einer Serie mit vier auffälligen Karaffen, die alle von Lalique gestaltet und in den jahreszeitlichen Varianten „Eté", „Automne" und „Hiver" in zweijährigem Abstand folgen werden. Farben und Designs werden streng geheim gehalten.

Afin de se démarquer des autres cognacs, **Hardy** a commandé à la célèbre Maison Lalique le design d'un modèle spécial pour sa dernière carafe. « Le Printemps » prend la forme d'un flacon de parfum aux lignes féminines ; dans les tons verts, son bouchon sculpté des plus spectaculaires n'est pas sans rappeler certaines créations de René Lalique du début du XXᵉ siècle. Ce design en édition limitée est le premier d'une série de quatre carafes uniques lancées à 2 ans d'intervalle, toutes signées Lalique, et répondant aux noms des saisons « Eté », « Automne » et « Hiver ». Les couleurs et les designs sont un secret bien gardé.

HARDY COGNAC LE PRINTEMPS

Design: Bénédicte Hardy
Crystal-maker: Lalique
Company: Hardy Cognac
Country: France
Category: Limited editions, limited series, event creations

GOLD PENTAWARD 2014

KENZO PARFUMS
KENZO AMOUR

Design: Karim Rashid
Company: Karim Rashid
Country: USA
Category: Limited editions,
limited series, event creations
BRONZE PENTAWARD 2014

GLENROTHES 40 YEAR OLD

Design: Bronwen Edwards, David Beard
Company: Brandhouse
Country: UK
Category: Limited editions, limited series,
event creations
BRONZE PENTAWARD 2013

JEAN-PAUL GAULTIER "CLASSIQUE" X COLLECTION

Design: Stéphanie Turan
Company: R'Pure Studio/Servaire
Country: France
Category: Limited editions,
limited series, event creations

BRONZE PENTAWARD 2013

PENHALIGON'S CHRISTMAS GIFT COLLECTION

Design: jkr design team
Company: jkr
Country: UK
Category: Limited editions,
limited series, event creations

SILVER PENTAWARD 2014

JADE DE JARDIN

Design: Jennifer Tsai
Company: Proad Identity
Country: Taiwan
Category: Limited editions,
limited series, event creations

BRONZE PENTAWARD 2014

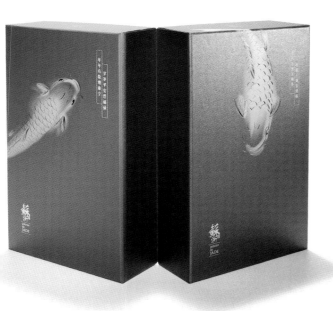
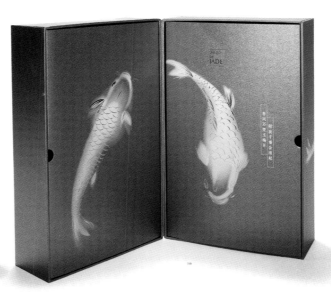

Creative Direction: Tsuneki Maeda
Art Direction/Design: Satoshi Ito
Design: Kotobuki Seihan Printing Design Center
Company: Suntory Business Expert
Country: Japan
Category: Limited editions, limited series, event creations

SILVER PENTAWARD 2013

This whisky was produced by **Suntory** to commemorate the 50th anniversary of the world's best-known rock 'n' roll band, the Rolling Stones. Only malts distilled and barreled in 1971, 1972, 1981 and 1990 — special years for the Stones — were used for the blend. The bottle features a low-relief molding of the band's instantly recognizable lips and tongue logo on the front, which really comes to life when viewed from an angle. This element recurs up the neck of the bottle, to the stately silver stopper, while the containing box, looking not unlike an amplifier, is lined with black leather to create a unified design that embodies the rock 'n' roll lifestyle synonymous with the Rolling Stones.

Dieser Whisky wurde von **Suntory** zur Feier des 50. Geburtstags der Rolling Stones produziert, der bekanntesten Rock-'n'-Roll-Band der Welt. Nur Malts, die 1971, 1972, 1981 und 1990 – besondere Jahre für die Stones – gebrannt und in Fässer gefüllt wurden, waren in diesem Blend erlaubt. Die Flasche zeigt auf der Vorderseite das berühmte Logo der Band. Die ausgestreckte Zunge mit ihren Lippen fällt sofort ins Auge und wird lebendig, wenn sie von der Seite betrachtet wird. Dieses Element erscheint auch am Flaschenhals und dem prächtigen silbernen Verschluss. Der Flaschenkasten ähnelt einem Verstärker und wurde mit schwarzem Leder ausgekleidet. Dieses einheitliche Design verkörpert den mit den Stones gleichgesetzten Rock-'n'-Roll-Lifestyle.

Ce whisky a été produit par **Suntory** pour commémorer le 50e anniversaire du groupe de rock n' roll le plus connu au monde : les Rolling Stones. Seuls des malts distillés et mis en fûts en 1971, 1972, 1981 et 1990, années spéciales pour le groupe, ont été utilisés pour le mélange. Le bas de la bouteille a été moulé dans la forme emblématique des lèvres et de la langue, qui s'animent en fonction de l'angle de vue. Cet élément se retrouve en haut du goulot, sur le majestueux bouchon en argent. Semblable à un amplificateur, la boîte est tapissée de cuir noir pour donner un design propre au style rock n' roll rimant avec Rolling Stones.

BACARDI
DEWAR'S LEGACY COLLECTION

Creative Direction: Glenn Tutssel
Design: Olly Rudd, Glenn Tutssel
Production Direction: Andrew Smith
Company: Brand Union
Country: UK
Category: Limited editions,
limited series, event creations

SILVER PENTAWARD 2014

COMPASS BOX
THE ENTERTAINER

Creative Direction: Kevin Shaw
Design: Guy Pratt
Company: Stranger & Stranger
Country: UK
Category: Distributors'/Retailers' own brands

GOLD PENTAWARD 2013

The Entertainer is a special-edition whisky blend for London's world-famous Selfridges department store. Stylistically, this blended Scotch harks back to the early years of the 20th century, when blends contained higher proportions of malt to grain whisky, and had a more peaty taste after being aged in more active casks. All of this yielded whiskies with a greater concentration of flavor. The Entertainer is a raucous, full-blown extravaganza of a whisky, it's rich, it's decadent, smoky and surprising, and so is the design of the label and box. Only 1,000 bottles were produced.

The Entertainer ist ein Whisky-Verschnitt in Sonderauflage für das weltberühmte Londoner Warenhaus Selfridges. Stilistisch greift dieser Blended Scotch auf die ersten Jahre des 20. Jahrhunderts zurück, als Blends im Vergleich zum Grain-Whisky größere Anteile Malz enthielten. Nach der Reifung in aktiveren Fässern schmeckten sie torfiger. All dies führte zu Whiskysorten mit größerer geschmacklicher Konzentration. The Entertainer ist ein raues, ausgereiftes Whisky-Feuerwerk: Er ist reichhaltig, er ist dekadent, rauchig und erstaunlich – was man auch vom Design des Etiketts und der Verpackung sagen kann. Hiervon wurden nur 1000 Flaschen produziert.

The Entertainer est l'édition spéciale d'un mélange de whisky pour le célèbre grand magasin londonien Selfridges. Ce Scotch rappelle le début du XXᵉ siècle, quand les mélanges contenaient plus de malt que de whisky de grain et avaient un goût plus tourbeux après avoir vieilli en fûts. Résultat : des whiskys avec une saveur plus concentrée. The Entertainer est une création décapante et authentique, riche et décadente, fumée et surprenante, tout comme le design de l'étiquette et de la boîte. Seules 1 000 bouteilles ont été produites.

DAY BIRGER ET MIKKELSEN SCENTED LINE

Creative Direction/Copywriting: Marie Wollbeck
Art Direction/Design: Erik Dolk
Art Direction: Martin Gylje
Client Management: Marianne Brandi
Company: BAS
Country: Sweden
Category: Distributors'/Retailers' own brands

SILVER PENTAWARD 2013

Jherocushion
Handmade by Fatboy

Jheronimus Bosch lives as never before. The atmosphere, themes and symbolism of his work is timeless. From this perspective, Jheronimus is created. The brand focuses on the development of contemporary products inspired by the work of the artist.

Jheronimus

Best of the category
Household maintenance
Home improvement & decoration
Electronic & non-electronic
Brand identity programs
Distributors'/Retailers' own brands

other markets

Pet products
Entertainment
Tobacco products
Self-promotion
Packaging concept

JHERONIMUS

Creative Direction: Paul Roeters
Design: Roger Huskens
Company: Studio Kluif
Country: Netherlands
Category: Best of the category other markets

PLATINUM PENTAWARD 2013

The **Jheronimus** brand is inspired by the works of the early Dutch painter Hieronymus Bosch, using the form of his first name in its old orthography. Bosch's work is characterized by the use of imaginative, illustrative and what would today be called surrealistic imagery, and for the packaging for this line of household products these distinctive aspects of his work were translated into a new context with a contemporary photographic style. The packaging is thus intended to evoke a perfect combination between a rich past and a bright future.

Die Marke **Jheronimus** ist inspiriert vom niederländischen Renaissancemaler Hieronymus Bosch, dessen Vorname in seiner alten Orthografieform verwendet wird. Charakteristisch für dessen Schaffen ist eine phantasievolle, illustrative und – heute würde man sagen – surrealistische Bildgestaltung. Dieses Haushaltssortiment setzt in seiner Verpackung die markanten Aspekte aus Boschs Werk durch den modernen fotografischen Stil in einen neuen Kontext. So kombiniert die Packungshülle die reichhaltige Vergangenheit mit einer vielversprechenden Zukunft.

La marque **Jheronimus** est inspirée des œuvres du peintre hollandais Hieronymus Bosch et correspond à l'ancienne orthographe de son prénom. Le travail de Bosch se caractérise par une imagerie imaginative et illustrative, que l'on qualifierait de nos jours de surréaliste. Pour l'emballage de cette ligne de produits pour la maison, trois aspects de ses œuvres ont été adaptés avec un style photographique contemporain. L'emballage vise à évoquer le mariage parfait entre passé riche et avenir prometteur.

Everybody recognizes the portraits people make when they're playing around with a copying machine or a scanner. It's a simple idea and made a great design for the packaging for this small independent Spanish company's copying/printing paper. No professional models or photographer were involved, just the 'agency family' and a scanner! The resulting images are used randomly, and customers can choose from nine different faces. The next portrait series will be made by the customers themselves, through a Facebook-scanner contest in the near future.

Jeder kennt Porträts von Leuten, die am Kopierer oder Scanner herumspielen. Diese simple Idee sorgt hier für ein tolles Design der Verpackung des Drucker-/Kopierpapiers dieser kleinen, unabhängigen spanischen Firma. Profimodels oder Fotografen waren hier nicht involviert, die „Agenturfamilie" kümmerte sich mit einem Scanner selbst darum! Die resultierenden Bilder wurden durch Zufallsprinzip ausgewählt, Käufer können unter neun verschiedenen Gesichtern wählen. Die nächste Porträtserie soll von den Kunden stammen, und zwar demnächst über einen Scanner-Wettbewerb auf Facebook.

Tout le monde a déjà vu les portraits que des personnes font pour s'amuser avec une photocopieuse ou un scanner. L'idée est simple et a donné lieu à un design réussi pour cette petite entreprise espagnole de papier à copier et à imprimer. Il n'a pas été utile de faire appel à un photographe et à des modèles professionnels : les collègues de l'agence et un scanner ont suffi. Les images obtenues sont utilisées de façon aléatoire et les clients ont le choix entre neuf visages. Par le biais d'un concours lancé sur Facebook, les propres clients réaliseront bientôt la prochaine série de portraits.

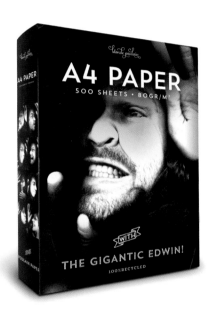

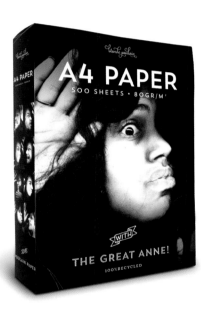

BLONDE POULAIN
A4 PAPER

Design: Paul Roeters, Pablo Nicolás Botía
Company: Studio Kluif
Country: Netherlands
Category: Best of the category other markets

PLATINUM PENTAWARD 2014

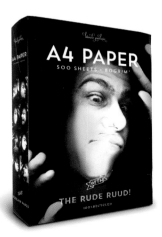

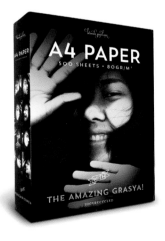

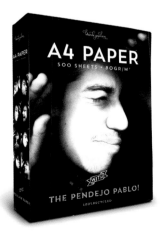

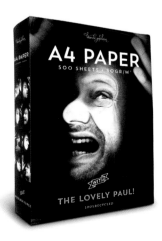

true GLOVE

**TWO HANDS —
TWO DIFFERENT
TATTOOS**
*a unique design for
each hand*

Dutch Tulip
pattern grip

Contoured
for a perfect fit

Comfy cotton
flock lining

Velvety surface

FINE NITRILE GLOVES *tattooed*
One pair

**LATEX FREE
ALLERGY FREE**

L

**LARGE
SIZE**

USAGE AND CARE:
After use, wash outside of gloves
with soap and water and let air dry.
Do not put in dish washer. Store in a
cool, dry place away from direct
heat and sunlight.

TRUEGLOVE B.V.
Teleportboulevard 110, 1043 EJ
Amsterdam, the Netherlands (EU)
www.trueglove.com

Gloves made in Malaysia by
 SUMITOMO RUBBER GROUP, Japan
www.dhp-dunlop.co.jp

0 736983 002860

TRUEGLOVE

Art Direction: Nadie Parshina
Copywriting: Svetlana Chugunova
Tattoo: Dmitry Hendrikson
Photography: Polina Tverdaya
Company: Ohmybrand
Country: Russia
Category: Household maintenance

GOLD PENTAWARD 2014

These household gloves, with their bold tattoo prints, different on each hand, will make you want to put them on right away. They create a playful mood, stylishly exaggerated by the special packaging, so that the less glamorous chores around the house will no longer be boring or monotonous: with a little imagination, perhaps you're at a fashion show or in front of a mass of photographers, in your beautiful shoes and fancy gloves. The pack design is made up like a magazine cover, with tips and gossipy headlines, but as well as being informative it also links up through the QR code to the manufacturer's site where other designs can be found.

Diese Haushaltshandschuhe mit ihren auffälligen Tattoos (für jede Hand anders) möchte man am liebsten sofort anziehen. Sie versetzen einen in eine spielerische Stimmung, stylish betont durch die besondere Verpackung. So bleiben die weniger glamourösen Haushaltspflichten nicht länger langweilig oder monoton: Mit ein wenig Fantasie versetzt man sich z.B. in eine Modeshow oder vor eine Gruppe Fotografen und trägt schöne Schuhe und schicke Handschuhe. Die Packung mit ihren Tipps und Klatsch-Überschriften ist wie die Titelseite eines Magazins gestaltet, doch auch informativ, da sie über den QR-Code zur Website des Herstellers verlinkt, wo man weitere Designs finden kann.

Ces gants de ménage imprimés de tatouages différents pour chaque main sont totalement irrésistibles. Ils donnent un ton ludique que l'emballage original vient encore renforcer, afin que les tâches domestiques même les moins « glamour » ne soient plus ennuyeuses et monotones. Avec un peu d'imagination, vous êtes sur un cat-walk de mode ou face à une foule de photographes, dans vos superbes chaussures et vos gants sophistiqués. L'emballage est pensé comme une couverture de magazine, avec des conseils et des titres aguicheurs. En plus des informations qu'il apporte, il comporte aussi un code QR lié au site du fabricant, où d'autres modèles sont disponibles.

UP
PLAYFUL LIFE

Creative Direction: Paul, Huang You-Sheng
Art Direction: Rose, Lee Yuan-Chun
Company: Tsukito Design
Country: Taiwan
Category: Household maintenance

SILVER PENTAWARD 2013

To celebrate **Daz**'s 60th anniversary in a way that would put a smile on UK consumers' faces and let them look back on the past, this special pack takes a trip down memory lane to look at the clothes that would have been washed using Daz down the decades. Inspired by all facets of life, the simple illustration style leaves the brand's signature red intact by using only hand-drawn sketches in white, as clean as when they're freshly washed. The whole pack is thus playfully covered in garments grouped into loose clusters of fashion trends from the 1950s up to the present day.

Zur Feier des 60. Geburtstags von **Daz** lädt diese Sonderverpackung auf eine Reise in die Vergangenheit ein. Sie lässt den britischen Verbraucher lächeln, wenn er einen Blick auf all die Kleidung wirft, die im Laufe der Jahrzehnte mit Daz gereinigt wurde. Inspiriert von allen Facetten des Lebens, lässt der einfache Illustrationsstil die Signaturfarbe Rot der Marke unberührt und verwendet nur handgezeichnete Skizzen in Weiß, als wäre alles frisch gewaschen. Die gesamte Verpackung wird somit spielerisch von Kleidungsstücken bedeckt, die lose in den Modetrends der 1950er bis zum heutigen Tag gruppiert sind.

Pour célébrer le 60e anniversaire de **Daz**, tout en faisant sourire les consommateurs britanniques et leur rappelant des souvenirs, cet emballage montre des vêtements qui auraient été lavés avec Daz pendant plusieurs décennies. S'inspirant de divers aspects de la vie, le design respecte le rouge si caractéristique de la marque et l'assortit de croquis dessinés à la main, aussi blancs que du linge propre. L'emballage est joyeusement décoré de vêtements regroupés par tendances de mode des années 50 à nos jours.

P&G
DAZ

Design: Joseph Robinson, Marianne Madsen
Company: Design Board
Country: Belgium
Category: Household maintenance

SILVER PENTAWARD 2013

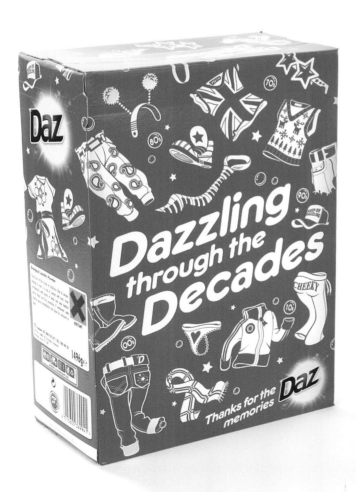

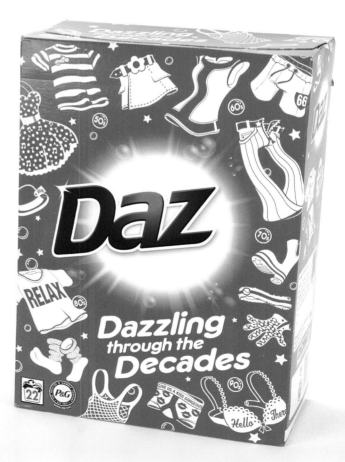

ECOFLORA

Design: Carolina Alzate, David Freyre,
Francisco Hernandez, Lina Uribe, Daniel Mojica
Production: RB Plasticos
Client: Claudio Pereda, Juan Fernando Botero
Company: imasD Branding + Packaging
Country: Colombia
Category: Household maintenance

BRONZE PENTAWARD 2014

ECOVER
OCEAN BOTTLE

Design: Logoplaste Innovation Lab
Creative Direction/Biomimicry: Carlos Rego
Process Management: Tom Domen,
Kirsten Vangenechten (Ecover)
Company: Logoplaste Innovation Lab
Country: Portugal
Category: Household maintenance

BRONZE PENTAWARD 2014

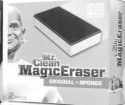

P&G
MR. CLEAN

Creative Direction: Clark Goolsby
Design: Steph Goralnick, David San Miguel
Illustration: Derek Rillo
Company: Chase Design Group
Country: USA
Category: Household maintenance

GOLD PENTAWARD 2013

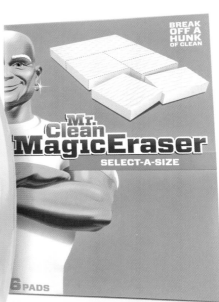

AM

Design: Johan Liden, Rinat Aruh,
Rogerio Lionzo, Erik Jarlsson, Boliang Chen
Company: Aruliden
Country: USA
Category: Household maintenance

SILVER PENTAWARD 2014

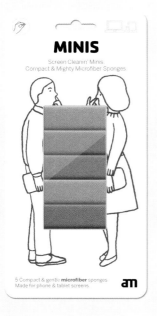

MINIS

Screen Cleanin' Minis.
Compact & Mighty Microfiber Sponges.

5 Compact & gentle **microfiber** sponges.
Made for phone & tablet screens.

MIST

Screen Cleanin' Mist.
All-In-One Spray & Cloth.

Antibacterial all-in-one spray & microfiber
cloth. Made for laptops & tablet screens.

SPRAY

Screen Cleanin' Spray.
All-In-One Spray & Cloth.

Antibacterial all-in-one spray & microfiber
cloth. Made for laptops & desktop screens.

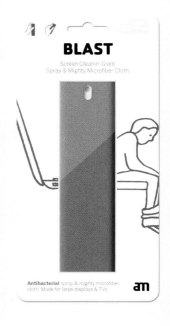

BLAST

Screen Cleanin' Giant.
Spray & Mighty Microfiber Cloth.

Antibacterial spray & mighty microfiber
cloth. Made for large displays & TVs.

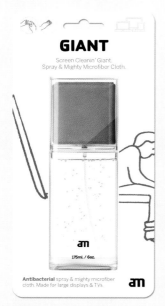

GIANT

Screen Cleanin' Giant.
Spray & Mighty Microfiber Cloth.

175ml. / 6oz.

Antibacterial spray & mighty microfiber
cloth. Made for large displays & TVs.

WIPES

Screen Cleanin' Wet Wipes.
On-The-Go Resealable Packets.

18 **Antibacterial** wet wipes in compact
resealable packets. Made for all screens.

PUMP

Screen Cleanin' Pump.
All-In-One Spray & Sponge.

Antibacterial all-in-one cleaning pump.
Made for large displays, keyboards & TVs.

CLOTHS

Screen Cleanin' Cloths.
Gentle & Mighty Microfiber Fabric.

3 Mighty & gentle **microfiber** cloths.
Made for all screens & displays.

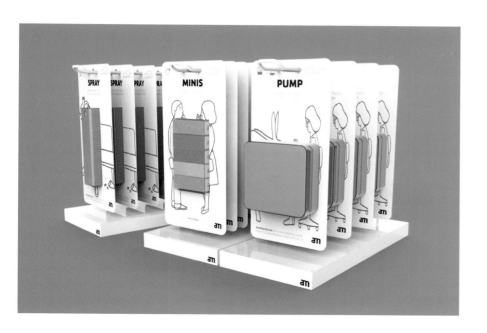

GAUSS ELEMENTARY

Design: Marina Zhilicheva,
Denis Frolov
Company: Varton
Country: Russia
Category: Household maintenance

BRONZE PENTAWARD 2013

PAINT BY CONRAN

Creative Direction: Massimo Acanfora
Illustration: Holly-Anne Rolfe
Design: Katie Alger
Company: Conran & Partners
Country: UK
Category: Home improvement & decoration

GOLD PENTAWARD 2014

DE NASTIA

Creative Direction: Ildar Shale
Design: Anjelica Ufimskaya
Company: Punk You Brands
Country: Russia
Category: Home improvement & decoration
BRONZE PENTAWARD 2013

VILMORIN
1743

Creative Direction: Sylvia Vitale Rotta,
Camille Riboud, Guy Ringelstein
Senior Design: Christelle Dauteur
Company: Team Créatif
Country: France
Category: Home improvement & decoration
BRONZE PENTAWARD 2013

ANOR

Design: Jennifer Tsai
Company: Proad Identity
Country: Taiwan
Category: Home improvement & decoration

GOLD PENTAWARD 2013

H4U

Executive Creative Direction: Somchana Kangwarnjit
Art Direction: Orawan
Company: Prompt Design
Country: Thailand
Category: Home improvement & decoration

SILVER PENTAWARD 2013

**ANDERS PETTER
BACKARYD**

Project Management: Ulf Berlin
Brand/Concept Direction: Jacob Bergström
Art Direction: Niclas Öster
Design: Sara Modigh
Production Management: Maja Wetterberg
Production Design: Monica Holm
Company: Designkontoret Silver
Country: Sweden
Category: Home improvement & decoration

SILVER PENTAWARD 2013

OBH NORDICA

Brand/Creative Direction: Jacob Bergström
Insight Direction: Niklas Dahl
Planning: Malin Edvardsen
Design: Jonas Berg, Sofia Frank Öberg
Design Assistant: Adam Ahlström
Copywriting: Johannes Rosenborg, Eva Jönsson
Production Design: Monica Holm
Production Management: Christine Schönborg
Client Management: André Hindersson
Company: Designkontoret Silver
Country: Sweden
Category: Home improvement & decoration

SILVER PENTAWARD 2014

INTRATUIN

Design: Paul Roeters,
Jeroen Hoedjes, Edwin Degenhart
Company: Studio Kluif
Country: Netherlands
Category: Home improvement & decoration

SILVER PENTAWARD 2014

ORGANIC
STARO CHIVE
SEEDS
Allium schoenoprasum

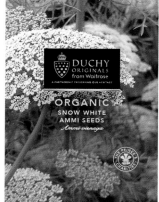

ORGANIC
SNOW WHITE
AMMI SEEDS
Ammi visnaga

ORGANIC
GOLDY DOUBLE
SUNFLOWER SEEDS
Helianthus annuus

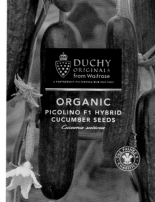

ORGANIC
PICOLINO F1 HYBRID
CUCUMBER SEEDS
Cucumis sativus

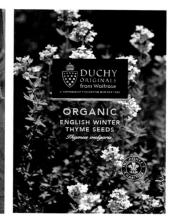

ORGANIC
ENGLISH WINTER
THYME SEEDS
Thymus vulgaris

ORGANIC
NASTURTIUM
SEEDS
Tropaeolum majus

ORGANIC
DUNDOO F1 HYBRID
COURGETTE SEEDS
Cucurbita pepo

ORGANIC
RED BEAUTY
ZINNIA SEEDS
Zinnia elegans

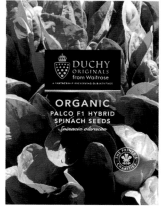

ORGANIC
PALCO F1 HYBRID
SPINACH SEEDS
Spinacia oleracea

ORGANIC
WHITE PINNACLE
CANDYTUFT SEEDS
Iberis amara

ORGANIC
DUCHY F1 HYBRID
CABBAGE SEEDS
Brassica oleracea

ORGANIC
DWARF YELLOW SPRAY
SUNFLOWER SEEDS
Helianthus annuus

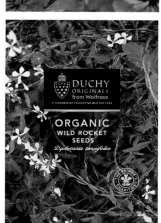

ORGANIC
WILD ROCKET
SEEDS
Diplotaxis tenuifolia

ORGANIC
OLD SPICE MIX
SWEET PEA SEEDS
Lathyrus odoratus

ORGANIC
VIT LAMB'S LETTUCE
Valerianella locusta

ORGANIC
BLACK BEAUTY
AUBERGINE SEEDS
Solanum melongena

ORGANIC
CLASSICO
BASIL SEEDS
Ocimum basilicum

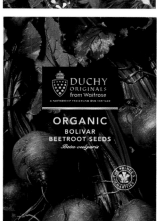

ORGANIC
BOLIVAR
BEETROOT SEEDS
Beta vulgaris

DUCHY ORIGINAL WAITROSE SEEDS

Creative Direction: Mary Lewis
Company: Lewis Moberly
Country: UK
Category: Home improvement & decoration

BRONZE PENTAWARD 2014

This new personal wireless-lighting system allows people to create and control their home lighting from their personal smart device, changing colors or setting different shades of white according to choice. It can be used anywhere, and to create light settings based on favorite photos or by using expert light recipes or timers. The device of the color wheel attracts consumers and strongly conveys the possibilities of playful interactivity in a wordless manner, also adding value on an informative level — after opening the box, the reverse of the color wheel becomes a step-by-step installation guide.

Dieses neuartige funkgesteuerte Beleuchtungssystem erlaubt, dass Nutzer ihre Haushaltsbeleuchtung mit dem eigenen Smartphone bedienen und Farben beliebig ändern oder unterschiedliche Weißtöne einstellen. Es kann überall verwendet werden, es lassen sich Lieblingsfotos integrieren, Expertenlichtlösungen oder Timingfunktionen einsetzen. Das Farbrad des Systems spricht den Nutzer an. Es vermittelt eindrücklich die Möglichkeiten spielerischer Interaktivität ohne Worte und wertet somit auch die informative Ebene auf: Nach Öffnen der Verpackung wird die Rückseite des Farbrads zur schrittweisen Installationsanleitung.

Ce nouveau système d'éclairage sans fil personnalisé permet de contrôler l'illumination de la maison depuis un dispositif intelligent, de changer de couleur et de choisir différentes intensités de lumière blanche. Il peut être utilisé partout, permet d'utiliser vos photos préférées pour faire des réglages, et inclut des minuteries. La roue de couleurs est attrayante et illustre à elle seule les possibilités d'interactivité ludique. Elle a aussi une valeur informative : une fois la boîte ouverte, le dos de cette roue présente un guide détaillé d'installation.

PHILIPS LIGHTING
HUE

Structural Packaging Design: Flex/the Innovationlab
Communication Design: Iris Worldwide
Client: Philips Lighting
Company: Flex/the Innovationlab
Country: Netherlands
Category: Electronic & non-electronic

GOLD PENTAWARD 2013

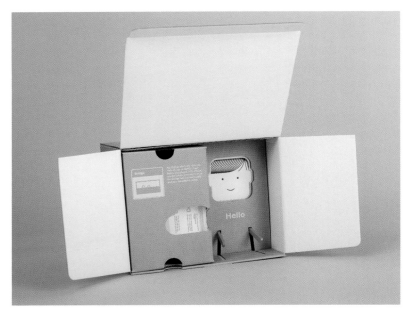

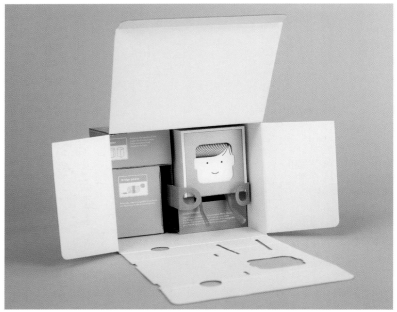

BERG
LITTLE PRINTER

Creative Direction: Dane Whitehurst
Design: Nick Dungan; Hadley Baker (Design BERG)
Company: Burgopak
Country: UK
Category: Electronic & non-electronic

BRONZE PENTAWARD 2013

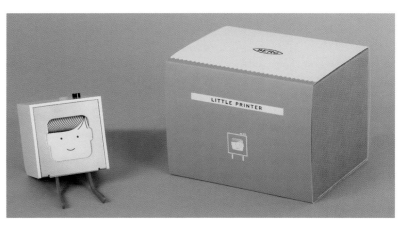

NABI HEADPHONES

Creative Direction: Daniel Miyahara
Design Direction: Joy Chartsiriwattana
Creative Management: Antony Pai
Design: Daniel Miyahara, Antony Pai,
Armer Amante, Sonia Gonzalez
Production Artist: Armer Amante
Product Design: Justin Nishiki
Packaging Engineering: River Rodibaugh
Company: Fuhu
Country: USA
Category: Electronic & non-electronic

SILVER PENTAWARD 2013

Nicolas-Jacques Conté invented the graphite lead and the Carré pastel, which in 1795 led to the establishment of the **Conté à Paris** brand, specializing in sketching pencils and pastels. Instead of the usual uninspiring packaging, with sketches of still-lifes drawn using the contents of the particular set, these packs show scenes of Paris to inspire people to want to draw, tied to each set of colors. A set of black-only Conté pastilles features a black cat on a dark night walking on a Parisian cobbled street; a set of white shows the famous dome of Sacré Cœur cathedral: and the putty rubber sits in front of a Parisian rubbish cart. The logo is a redesign based on an old trademark Conté à Paris used in the 1800s.

Nicolas-Jacques Conté erfand den modernen Graphitbleistift und die Carré-Pastellkreide. Das führte 1795 zur Gründung der Marke **Conté à Paris**, spezialisiert auf Zeichenbleistifte und Pastellkreiden. Man verzichtet auf die übliche, wenig inspirative Verpackung mit Stilllebenskizzen, wie man sie mit dem jeweiligen Inhalt zeichnen kann. Vielmehr zeigen diese Packungen je nach enthaltener Farbgruppe Pariser Momente, um Menschen zum Zeichnen zu inspirieren. Auf einer Packung mit schwarzer Zeichenkreide huscht eine schwarze Katze bei dunkler Nacht über Pariser Kopfsteinpflaster, die weiße Zeichenkreide krönt die berühmte Kuppel der Kathedrale Sacré Cœur, und das Radiergummi sitzt vor einem Pariser Kehrwagen. Das Logo wurde anhand eines alten, im 19. Jahrhundert von Conté à Paris verwendeten Warenzeichens neu designt.

Avec l'invention par Nicolas-Jacques Conté de la mine graphite et des pastels Carré, la marque **Conté à Paris** a vu le jour à Paris en 1795, se spécialisant en crayons et pastels. Au lieu de l'habituel emballage montrant des croquis de natures mortes faits avec le contenu du kit, ces boîtes présentent des scènes de Paris encourageant au dessin. Les scènes apparaissent dans plusieurs gammes de couleurs : un jeu de pastilles Conté noires représente un chat noir marchant la nuit dans une rue pavée parisienne, un jeu de blancs montre le célèbre dôme du Sacré Cœur, et une gomme mie de pain est placée devant un conteneur de poubelles de la ville. Le design du logo a été repensé à partir d'une ancienne marque Conté à Paris utilisée dans les années 1800.

CONTÉ À PARIS

Creative Direction: David Turner, Bruce Duckworth
Design Direction: Jamie McCathie
Design: David Blakemore, Jamie McCathie
Photography: Craig Easton
Typography: Nick Cooke
Illustration: Geoffrey Appleton
Artwork: James Norris
Retouching: Peter Ruane
Company: Turner Duckworth: London & San Francisco
Country: UK, USA
Category: Electronic & non-electronic

SILVER PENTAWARD 2013

Not For Sale is a non-profit organization working to stop human trafficking, and to provide dignified work for women vulnerable to exploitation in Amsterdam and abroad — in Amsterdam alone, over 25,000 women work as prostitutes. With this series of products the aim was to create a story that was as powerful as the brand name and mission, to support the launch of Not For Sale Soup. In Amsterdam's red-light district, Not For Sale offers culinary training to people in need, helping them prepare soups that are sold to help women working in the brothels. Not For Sale transforms the exploited into the empowered, and with every jar of soup the women are promised a new future. This soup is Not for Sale. We are Not For Sale.

Die Non-Profit-Organisation **Not For Sale** setzt sich gegen Menschenhandel und Zwangsprostitution in Amsterdam und anderswo ein. Allein in Amsterdam arbeiten 25.000 Frauen als Prostituierte. Diese Produktserie setzt sich das Ziel, eine Story zu schaffen, die ebenso kraftvoll ist wie der Markenname und seine Mission, den Start der Not For Sale Soup. Im Rotlichtbezirk von Amsterdam bietet Not For Sale Kochkurse für Hilfsbedürftige an. Sie lernen Suppen zuzubereiten, deren Verkauf in Bordellen beschäftigten Frauen helfen soll. Not For Sale bringt ausgebeuteten Menschen ein Gefühl der Handlungsmacht zurück, und jeder Teller Suppe verspricht den Frauen eine neue Zukunft. Diese Suppe ist Not For Sale. Wir sind Not For Sale.

Not For Sale est une association à but non lucratif qui lutte contre la traite de personnes et pour offrir un travail digne aux femmes en risque d'exploitation à Amsterdam et dans le monde. Seulement à Amsterdam, plus de 25 000 femmes exercent la prostitution. Avec cette série de produits, l'objectif était d'inventer une histoire aussi puissante que le nom et la mission de l'association pour lancer Not For Sale Soup. Dans le quartier rouge d'Amsterdam, Not For Sale propose des formations culinaires aux personnes dans le besoin pour qu'elles préparent des soupes, lesquelles sont vendues pour aider les femmes travaillant dans les maisons closes. Not For Sale rend aux personnes exploitées leur autonomie et chaque pot de soupe donne à ces femmes l'espoir d'un avenir meilleur. Cette soup est Not for Sale. Nous sommes Not For Sale.

NOT FOR SALE

Creative Direction/Design: Tosh Hall
Design: Jessica Minn
Company: Hall
Country: USA
Category: Brand identity programs
SILVER PENTAWARD 2013

DRIPP COFFEE SHOP

Creative Direction: David Turner, Bruce Duckworth, Sarah Moffat
Design: Chris Garvey, Rebecca Au Williams
Design Direction: Chris Garvey
Illustration: Chris Garvey
Company: Turner Duckworth: London & San Francisco
Country: UK, USA
Category: Brand identity programs

GOLD PENTAWARD 2013

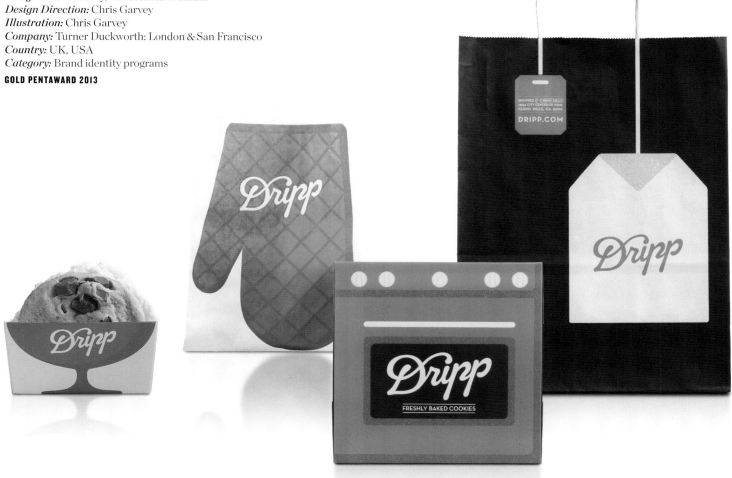

BLACK DOG

Creative Direction: Jef Wong
Design: Damien Alexander, Matt Hammond
Creative Strategy: Michael Crampin
Company: Designworks
Country: New Zealand
Category: Brand identity programs

SILVER PENTAWARD 2013

SILVER FERN FARMS
BRAND BOOK

Creative Direction: Jef Wong
Design: Matt Hammond
Strategy: Noel Blackwell
Copywriting: David Lyall
Company: Designworks
Country: New Zealand
Category: Brand identity programs

BRONZE PENTAWARD 2013

AMERICAN RED CROSS
VISUAL IDENTITY

Creative Direction: David Turner, Bruce Duckworth, Sarah Moffat
Design: Britt Hull, Robert Williams
Lead Production: Craig Snelgrove
Photography: ARC staff, Turner Duckworth staff
Company: Turner Duckworth: London & San Francisco
Country: UK, USA
Category: Brand identity programs

BRONZE PENTAWARD 2013

PLUS PRIVATE LABEL
Design: Sara Jones
Company: Anthem Worldwide
Country: UK
Category: Distributors'/Retailers' own brands
BRONZE PENTAWARD 2013

SPAR
WASHING DETERGENTS
Design: Michelle Wiegman, Barbara van den Hoorn
Company: Yellow Dress Retail
Couvntry: Netherlands
Category: Distributors'/Retailers' own brands

GOLD PENTAWARD 2014

SUNDAY

Company: Sadowsky Berlin
Country: Israel
Category: Distributors'/Retailers' own brands

SILVER PENTAWARD 2014

MAMIE & CO

Design: Séverine Smieszkol, Manuella Mary
Company: Nouveau Monde DDB
Country: France
Category: Distributors'/Retailers' own brands

BRONZE PENTAWARD 2013

LOVING HOME
CUTTING BOARDS

Creative Direction: Hyunjoo Choi
Design: Seungje Choi, Eunjin Oh
Company: Emart
Country: South Korea
Category: Distributors'/Retailers' own brands

SILVER PENTAWARD 2013

WAITROSE MID-TIER PET FOOD

Creative Direction: David Turner, Bruce Duckworth
Design Direction: Mark Waters
Design: Jennie Spiller
Photography: Steve Hoskins
Artwork: James Norris, Sebastian Archer-Cox
Company: Turner Duckworth: London & San Francisco
Country: UK, USA
Category: Distributors'/Retailers' own brands

SILVER PENTAWARD 2013

GAMMA KLEURID

Creative Direction: Thea Bakker
Photography: Sharon Montrose
Model: Zebra 'Widow Maker'
Client: Intergamma/GAMMA
Company: VBAT
Country: Netherlands
Category: Distributors'/Retailers' own brands

GOLD PENTAWARD 2013

GRANVILLE ISLAND PET TREATERY

Creative Direction/Design: Margherita Porra
Company: Arithmetic Creative
Country: Canada
Category: Pet products

SILVER PENTAWARD 2014

SAVOUR LIFE

Creative Direction: Ben Croft
Design: Evan Papageorgiou
Company: Channelzero
Country: Australia
Category: Pet products

SILVER PENTAWARD 2014

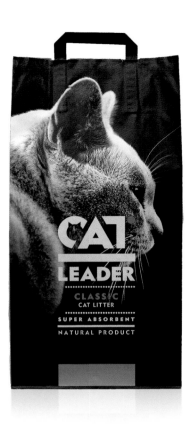
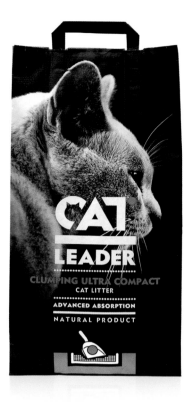

CAT LEADER

Creative Direction: Dimitris Gkazis
Design: Vicky Nitsopoulou
Copywriting: Nikos Paleologos
Company: Busybuilding
Country: Greece
Category: Pet products

SILVER PENTAWARD 2013

WHO CARES

Creative Direction: Dimitris Gkazis
Design: Vicky Nitsopoulou,
Kostis Sotirakos, Maria Kefala
Company: Busybuilding
Country: Greece
Category: Pet products

GOLD PENTAWARD 2013

PLUME & COMPAGNIE

Project Management: Hadrien Lecca
Design Direction: Marie-Pierre Fricou
Design: Marie Schockweiller
Company: Brand Union
Country: France
Category: Pet products

GOLD PENTAWARD 2014

WHISKAS
CATS PLAY HOUSE

Design: Guillermo Acevedo Beltran
Company: Vaya! Agency
Country: Colombia
Category: Pet products

BRONZE PENTAWARD 2013

AGRI RETAIL
BOERENBOND WELKOOP

Design: Tahir Idouri,
Jobert van de Bovenkamp
Company: Millford
Country: Netherlands
Category: Pet products

SILVER PENTAWARD 2013

PLUSMATE EARPHONE SERIES

Creative Direction: Hyunjoo Choi
Design: Kayoung Lee
Company: Emart
Country: South Korea
Category: Entertainment

GOLD PENTAWARD 2013

Plusmate, a private-label brand owned by South Korea's Emart hypermarket chain, developed this earphone series to express the differences between the characteristic tones of various genres of music, such as jazz, classical, country or rock. Consumers can then choose the earphones best suited to their taste, with musicians playing stringed instruments being used to represent the four musical genres. The cable is wound up neatly and positioned on the pack to replace the strings of the different instruments, while the heads of the earphones become the eyes of the musicians, adding a humorous note to the overall design.

Plusmate ist eine Eigenmarke, der südkoreanischen Hypermarktkette Emart. Für sie wurde diese Kopfhörer-serie entwickelt, um die Unterschiede zwischen den typischen Klängen der verschiedenen Musikgenres wie Jazz, Klassik, Country oder Rock auszudrücken. Die Käufer wählen jene Kopfhörer, die am besten zu ihrer Lieblingsmusik passen. Die Musiker darauf repräsentie-ren mit ihren Saiteninstrumenten die vier musikalischen Genres. Das Kabel wurde so auf die Verpackung gewi-ckelt, dass daraus die Saiten der verschiedenen Instru-mente entstehen, während die Ohrknöpfe zu den Augen der Musiker werden. Das verleiht dem Design insgesamt seine humorvolle Note.

Plusmate, marque maison de la chaîne de super-marchés Emart en Corée du Sud, a conçu cette gamme d'écouteurs pour illustrer les différents tons de genres musicaux, comme le jazz, la musique classique, le country ou le rock. Les consommateurs peuvent choisir les écouteurs adaptés à leur goût, avec des musiciens jouant des instruments à cordes et illustrant les quatre genres musicaux. Le câble est savamment enroulé de façon à imiter les cordes des instruments, alors que les écouteurs forment les yeux des musiciens pour ajouter une note humoristique au design.

Lingua Simplex is a language-learning aid that works as an educational game presented in high-visibility boxes. The Pairs Games contain cards with explanatory symbols, and text cards concerning verbs to be read aloud to the other players. Each game pack represents a character based on a national stereotype and when the box is opened, and the lid moved up and down, the illustrations become partly animated in line with the character traits depicted. Promotional testing involved distributing the games in schools and on university language courses, while later market success has led to plans to add five further languages.

Die Sprachlernhilfe **Lingua Simplex** funktioniert wie ein Lernspiel und wird in einem auffälligen Karton angeboten. Ähnlich wie bei einem Memory-Spiel finden sich auf den Karten erklärende Symbole sowie Text, der den Mitspielern laut vorgelesen werden soll. Jede Spielepackung zeigt eine Person, die auf einem nationalen Stereotyp basiert. Wird die Packung geöffnet und der Deckel nach oben oder unten verschoben, erwachen die Illustrationen entsprechend der dargestellten Charakterzüge zum Leben. Um das Marketing zu testen, wurden die Spiele an Schulen und Sprachkursen in Unis verteilt – so erfolgreich, dass fünf weitere Sprachen ins Sortiment aufgenommen wurden.

Lingua Simplex est une méthode d'apprentissage linguistique présentée dans des emballages attrayants. Les jeux de paires incluent des cartes aux symboles pertinents, et d'autres avec des verbes qu'il faut lire à voix haute aux autres joueurs. Chaque boîte représente un personnage type d'un pays ; à son ouverture, le couvercle se déplace verticalement et les illustrations prennent vie en accord avec les attributs du personnage. Des tests promotionnels ont été réalisés en distribuant les jeux dans des écoles et dans des cours de langues en faculté. Le succès commercial remporté a motivé l'idée d'ajouter cinq autres langues.

LINGUA SIMPLEX PAIRS GAMES

Executive Creative Direction/ Design: Jonathan Sven Amelung
Editing: Alicia Maritza Amelung
Illustration: Angela Wittchen
Company: Amelung Design
Country: Germany
Category: Entertainment

GOLD PENTAWARD 2014

SAMSUNG

Design: Zheng Ming Wang (SDC),
Yulan Zhang, Yuan Liang (KHT)
Company: Samsung Design China, KHT Brand
Consulting & Management
Country: China
Category: Entertainment

BRONZE PENTAWARD 2014

PANTECH VEGA IRON
SMARTPHONE PACKAGING

Design: Duhan, Kim
Company: Pantech
Country: South Korea
Category: Entertainment

BRONZE PENTAWARD 2013

SONY
CYBER-SHOT DSC-QX100/QX10

Design: Kazunori Nozawa
Company: Sony
Country: Japan
Category: Entertainment

BRONZE PENTAWARD 2014

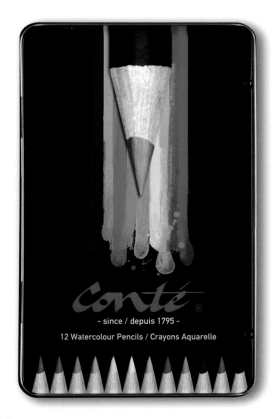

BIC
CONTÉ

Executive Creative Direction: Tristan Macherel
Design: Aurélie Lacues
Company: Landor Associates
Country: France
Category: Electronic & non-electronic

SILVER PENTAWARD 2014

ROYAL MAIL

Creative Direction: Richard Scholey
Design: Harry Heptonstall, Mika Shephard
Illustration: Graeme Jenner
Company: The Chase
Country: UK
Category: Entertainment

SILVER PENTAWARD 2013

KEY
PLEASURE TOYS

Creative Direction: José García Eguiguren,
Mateo Flandoli
Company: Gworkshop Design
Country: Ecuador
Category: Entertainment

SILVER PENTAWARD 2013

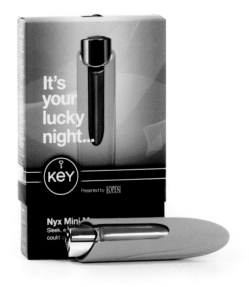

HAPPY PLUGS
CHARGE CABLES AND EARBUDS

Design: Andreas Vural
Company: Happy Plugs
Country: Sweden
Category: Entertainment

SILVER PENTAWARD 2014

suivez
votre
inspiration

GITANES
L'ESPRIT

Design: Gildas Boissier
Company: Enjoy Design
Country: France
Category: Tobacco products

GOLD PENTAWARD 2013

Q ELECTRONIC CIGARETTE

Design: Leanne Balen
Art Direction: Tracy Kenworthy
Company: Dessein
Country: Australia
Category: Tobacco products

SILVER PENTAWARD 2013

CAMEL

Design: Matt Thompson,
Christian Bird, Gokce Sahbaz,
Ajit Aghera
Illustration: Vault 49
Company: Design Bridge
Country: UK
Category: Tobacco products

SILVER PENTAWARD 2013

PRIDE

Design: Li Jianghui
Company: Jinjia
Country: China
Category: Tobacco products

GOLD PENTAWARD 2014

TAHWA CHUANMO

Design: Tiger Pan
Company: Tigerpan packaging design studio
Country: China
Category: Tobacco products

BRONZE PENTAWARD 2014

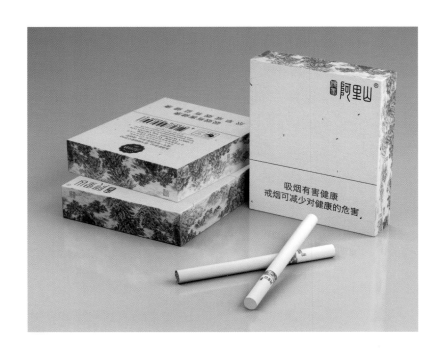

**JT PIANISSIMO
JAPANESE FLOWER EDITION**

Art Direction: Aya Takei, Akira Miyazawa (JT);
Katsunori Nishi, Miho Kariatsumari,
Haruka Takeuchi (Honolulu)
Company: Honolulu
Country: Japan
Category: Tobacco products

BRONZE PENTAWARD 2013

CHINA TOBACCO HUNAN

Design: Cheng Lin, Hung Jen Lin
Company: Khan A+D
Country: Taiwan
Category: Tobacco products

BRONZE PENTAWARD 2014

TAHWA
BRUCE LI

Design: Tiger Pan
Company: Tigerpan packaging
design studio
Country: China
Category: Tobacco products

SILVER PENTAWARD 2014

TAHWA ALISHAN

Design: Tiger Pan
Company: Tigerpan packaging
design studio
Country: China
Category: Tobacco products
BRONZE PENTAWARD 2013

PHOENIX
V12

Design: Tiger Pan
Company: Tigerpan packaging
design studio
Country: China
Category: Tobacco products
SILVER PENTAWARD 2014

STRANGER & STRANGER ULTIMATE DECK

Creative Direction: Kevin Shaw
Design: Cosimo Surace, Ewa Oliver,
Francesco Graziani
Company: Stranger & Stranger
Country: UK
Category: Self-promotion

GOLD PENTAWARD 2013

Every year Stranger & Stranger creates a limited-edition product to mark the festive season and celebrate success with the people who make it happen. Taking a decisive break from the customary Christmas bottle, on this occasion the agency elected to give out the **Ultimate Deck**, a pack of 54 picture cards from Dan and Dave. This departure commemorated the breaking-out from their comfort zone in 2012 to dabbling in fine foods, cosmetics and luxury luggage. For the first year, the agency also had a second limited batch produced, of just 100, and offered to the public for sale.

Jedes Jahr schaffen Stranger & Stranger als Sonderauflage ein Produkt, um die Feiertage am Jahresende zu betonen und mit jenen Menschen den Erfolg zu feiern, die ihn verdient haben. Man beschloss, sich deutlich von der üblichen Geschenkflasche zu Weihnachten abzusetzen: Die Agentur wählte für diese Gelegenheit das **Ultimate Deck**, ein Kartenspiel mit 54 Karten von Dan and Dave. Dieses Ausscheren feierte auch den Ausbruch von 2012 aus der Komfortzone: Seitdem versucht man sich in Feinkost, Kosmetik und luxuriösem Reisegepäck. Die Agentur hat in diesem Jahr auch zum ersten Mal eine zweite Auflage von insgesamt nur 100 Stück produzieren lassen, die in den öffentlichen Handel ging.

Chaque année, Stranger & Stranger sort un produit en édition limitée pour marquer le début des fêtes de fin d'année et célébrer les réussites avec les personnes y ayant contribué. Pour rompre avec la coutume de la typique bouteille pour Noël, l'agence a pour cette occasion choisi d'offrir **Ultimate Deck**, un jeu de 54 cartes illustrées par Dan et Dave. Ce choix est venu marquer leur sortie de leur zone de confort en 2012 pour se lancer dans les produits gourmets, les cosmétiques et les bagages de luxe. La première année, l'agence a produit une seconde édition limitée de 100 unités seulement qu'elle a mises en vente.

2013 THANKSGIVING WINE
FEATHER LEAF

Creative Direction: Stan Church
Design: Ithinand Tubkam
Company: Wallace Church
Country: USA
Category: Self-promotion

BRONZE PENTAWARD 2014

EQUATOR BEER

Design: Mark Grey and Equator design team
Company: Equator Design Consultants
Country: UK
Category: Self-promotion

SILVER PENTAWARD 2013

STB
EVEN BETTER WITH AGE

Design: Neil P. Watts (senior), Holly Littlejohn
Creative Direction: Glenn W. Taylor
Creative Direction Assistant: Lois Blackhurst
Company: Stocks Taylor Benson
Country: UK
Category: Self-promotion

SILVER PENTAWARD 2014

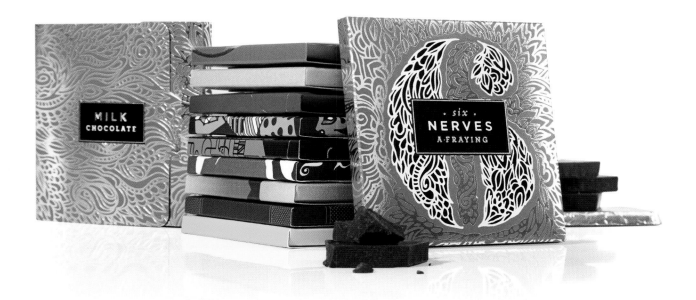

12 DAYS OF CHOCOLATE

Concept/Design: Chase Design Group
Production: Clear Image Printing
Outer Box, Logo and Insert: Jinny Bae
One Delicious Holiday: Jon Arriaza
Two Perfect Proofs: Clark Goolsby
Three French Curves: Stephanie Goralnick
Four Misspelled Words: David San Miguel
Five Golden Rules: Paula Hansanugrum
Six Nerves a-Fraying: Margo Chase
Seven Interns Trimming: Evangeline Joo
Eight Clients Calling: Beverly Hartono
Nine Blind Embossings: Stephanie Kuga
Ten Nights Not Sleeping: Margo Chase
Eleven Projects Printing: Hea Kim
Twelve Servers Humming: Clark Goolsby
Company: Chase Design Group
Country: USA
Category: Self-promotion
GOLD PENTAWARD 2014

KIWI EGGS FOR GENTLE SEX

Design: Polaris Team
Company: Polaris
Country: Ukraine
Category: Self-promotion
BRONZE PENTAWARD 2013

MERRY CHRISTMAS

Creative Direction: Isabelle Dahlborg Lidström
Design: Jin Fujiwara, Johan Lagervall,
Andreas Lewandowski
Production Management: Judith Socha
Company: Nine
Country: Sweden
Category: Self-promotion

SILVER PENTAWARD 2014

DESSEIN
CELEBRATING 25 YEARS OF DESIGN

Design: Tracy Kenwortthy,
Leanne Balen, Geoff Bickford
Company: Dessein
Country: Australia
Category: Self-promotion

BRONZE PENTAWARD 2013

BUDDY
MULLED WINE CHARADE

Design: David Jones
Creative Direction: David Jones, Mark Girvan
Illustration: Jamie Nash
Company: Buddy Creative
Country: UK
Category: Self-promotion

BRONZE PENTAWARD 2014

WC 2012 GIFT VODKA

Creative Direction/Design: Stan Church
Company: Wallace Church
Country: USA
Category: Self-promotion

SILVER PENTAWARD 2013

POILU

Design: Simon Laliberté (student)
Supervisor: Sylvain Allard
School: École de Design, Université du Québec à Montréal (UQAM)
Country: Canada
Category: Packaging concept (other markets)
GOLD PENTAWARD 2013
BIC STUDENT PRIZE

981 FOR HOT EMERGENCY

Creative Direction: Irinel Ionescu
Project Management: Ana Poiana
Company: Ampro Design Consultants
Country: Romania
Category: Packaging concept (other markets)
BRONZE PENTAWARD 2013

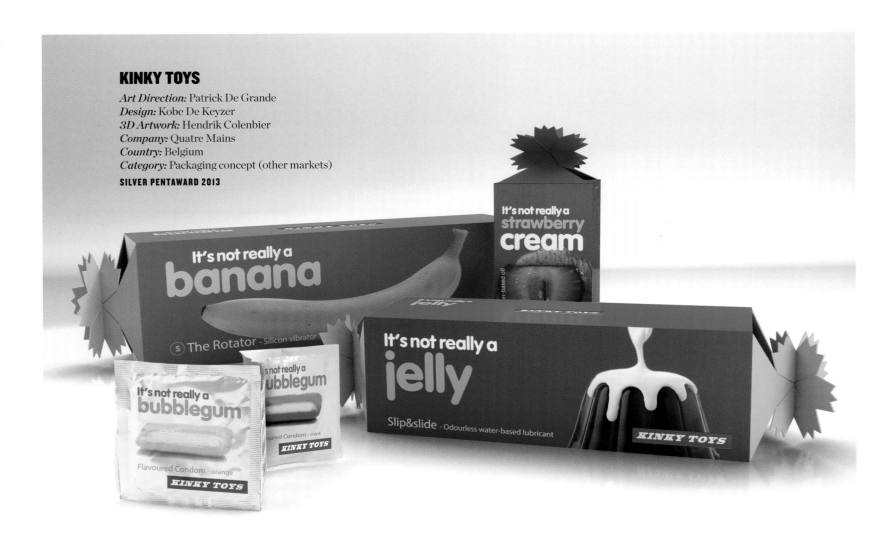

KINKY TOYS

Art Direction: Patrick De Grande
Design: Kobe De Keyzer
3D Artwork: Hendrik Colenbier
Company: Quatre Mains
Country: Belgium
Category: Packaging concept (other markets)

SILVER PENTAWARD 2013

Even today, buying sex toys can still be a bit of a private activity. To avoid any sense of embarrassment this design builds on familiar comparisons between food and certain body parts, but in a playful way without being vulgar. The packaging looks like a special treat, with the bright colors and twisted ends combining sex and food like they were made for each other — see them as forbidden fruits, or an innocent but naughty snack. The "what" and "how" is covered on the reverse of the packaging, with the teasing image and "not really..." tagline left to do the work on the front. The inoffensive packaging is intended to appeal to the curious novice, as well as perhaps interesting non-specialized retailers and in turn reaching new consumers.

Auch heutzutage gehört der Kauf von Sexspielzeug eher zu den privaten Aktivitäten. Um jegliche Peinlichkeit zu vermeiden, spielt dieses Design auf die bekannten Vergleiche zwischen Essen und bestimmten Körperteilen an – aber spielerisch, ohne vulgär zu sein. Die Verpackung wirkt mit ihren leuchtenden Farben und den zusammengedrehten Enden wie ein besonderes Bonbon. Hier werden Sex und Lebensmittel kombiniert, als wären sie füreinander gemacht – man betrachte beide als verbotene Früchte oder als unschuldigen, aber unanständigen Snack. Das „Was" und „Wie" erscheint verdeckt auf der Packungsrückseite, um alles andere kümmern sich das verlockende Bild und der Slogan „Not really ..." der Vorderseite. Die unaufdringliche Verpackung spricht den neugierigen Neuling ebenso an wie vielleicht interessierte, nichtspezialisierte Einzelhändler, und so erreicht man wiederum neue Kunden.

Aujourd'hui encore, acheter des gadgets sexuels relève du domaine du privé. Pour éviter tout possible embarras, ce design repose sur des comparaisons courantes entre la nourriture et certaines parties du corps, d'une façon amusante et sans tomber dans le vulgaire. L'emballage fait penser à une collation, avec des couleurs vives et une forme de papillote. Il associe sexe et nourriture comme s'ils avaient été faits l'un pour l'autre, tels des fruits défendus ou un en-cas innocent mais osé. Le « quoi » et le « comment » figurent au dos de l'emballage, avec l'image taquine et le slogan « not really ... » à l'avant qui fait passer le message. L'emballage inoffensif a été conçu pour attirer le novice curieux, mais aussi intéresser les commerces non spécialisés visant à capter de nouveaux clients.

CEO DISH SOAP

Design: Masha Solyankina, Vi Kaplina,
Nikita Petrov, Roman Vlasov (students)
Teacher: Leonid Slavin
School: British Higher School of Art and Design, Moscow
Country: Russia
Category: Packaging concept (other markets)

BRONZE PENTAWARD 2013

KAPUT
ANTI-NUISIBLES

Design: Anne Douat (student)
Teacher: Jackie Stewart
School: ECV Paris
Country: France
Category: Packaging concept (other markets)

SILVER PENTAWARD 2013

NOM D'UN CHIEN

Design: Marina Bacot (student)
Teacher: Pascal Caudret
School: ECV Paris
Country: France
Category: Packaging concept (other markets)

SILVER PENTAWARD 2014

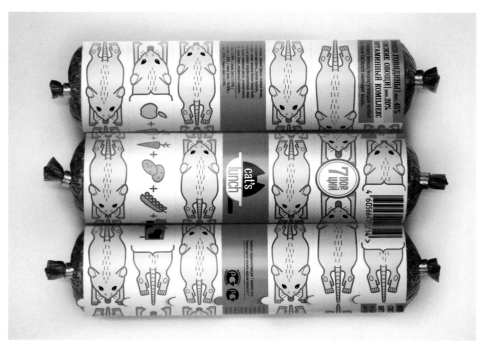

CAT'S LUNCH

Design: Alexandra Istratova
Company: Alexandra Istratova
Country: Russia
Category: Packaging concept (other markets)

BRONZE PENTAWARD 2014

A range of chilled 'ready meals' for dogs based on recipes their owners might enjoy and share with their pets, pre-cooked, so they can be served hot or cold in the tray. Healthy ingredients and a range of flavors are presented in a mashed-up mix, just like the leftovers from a meal: in fact, a bit of a 'dog's dinner'. The slipper design – something a dog can't resist getting its teeth into – comes in different styles to match the recipes in a playful, engaging way. The 'Dog's Breakfast' is a range of dried food packaged in 'rolled newspaper'-style pillow packs, another favorite 'snack' for dogs as it falls through the letterbox in the morning.

Die Rezepturen für diese gekühlten „Hunde-Fertig-gerichte" könnten auch Herrchen und Frauchen schmecken und sie die Mahlzeiten mit ihren Haustieren teilen lassen. Schon vorgekocht wird dieses Sortiment aus der Packung heraus warm oder kalt serviert. Wie ein feines Essen ähneln die Gerichte aus gesunden Zutaten mit verschiedenem Geschmack wohl dem, was bei Tisch übrig bleibt. Das Hausschuh-Design erinnert an etwas, in das zu beißen ein Hund kaum widerstehen kann. Die je nach Rezeptur verschieden gestaltete Verpackung setzt den Inhalt spielerisch-unterhaltsam um. Das Trockenfutter „Dog's Breakfast" ist in Pillow Packs verpackt, die einer zusammengerollten Zeitung ähneln – einem weiteren beliebten Hunde-„Snack", der morgens durch den Briefschlitz fällt.

Cette gamme de repas réfrigérés pour chiens se base sur des recettes que leurs maîtres aimeraient partager avec eux. Précuisinés, ils peuvent être servis chauds ou froids, directement dans leur emballage-plateau. Dignes de restes d'un repas qui finiraient dans la gamelle du chien, les mélanges incluent des ingrédients sains et tout un éventail de saveurs. Le design de la pantoufle, avec laquelle tout chien aime jouer, est décliné dans plusieurs styles attrayants en accord avec les recettes. « Dog's Breakfast » est une gamme d'aliments secs enroulés dans un emballage qui imite un journal, autre objet que les chiens aiment attraper.

DOG'S DINNER

Design: Chris MacDonald, Kelly Bennett, Moyra Casey
Company: Afterhours
Country: UK
Category: Packaging concept (other markets)

GOLD PENTAWARD 2014

TINY FEATHER

Design: In-young Bae, Shang-lun Yang (students)
Instructor: Barry Berger
School: Pratt Institute
Country: USA
Category: Packaging concept (other markets)

BRONZE PENTAWARD 2014

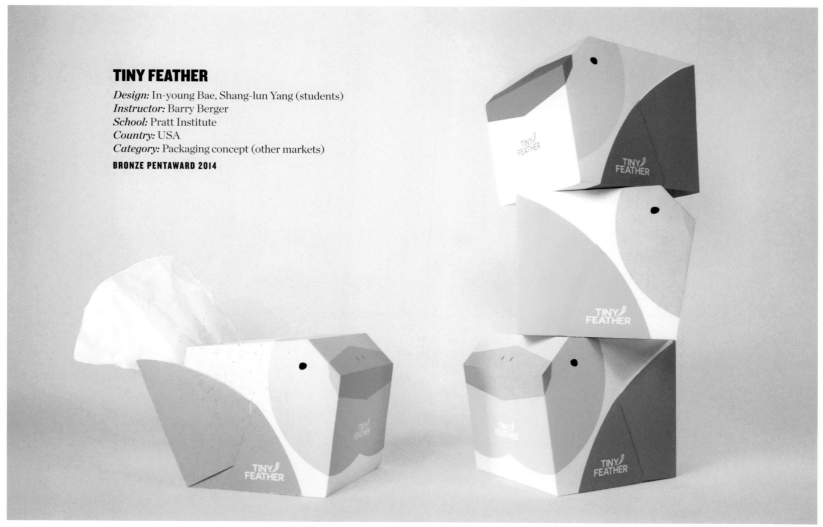

ROTTEN' FRUIT

Design: Manon Fauvel (student)
Teacher: Jackie Stewart
School: ECV Paris
Country: France
Category: Packaging concept (other markets)

SILVER PENTAWARD 2014

This conceptual project for bin bags takes an everyday item but one lacking in originality, and with **Rotten' Fruit** we can say goodbye to bad smells in the kitchen. These new-style bin bags have the texture and natural scent of different fruits, and by using the same system as a tissue box they can easily be removed one at a time. The packaging is made mostly of transparent plastic, letting the image of the fruit show through, which makes the brand stand out on the shelf and attracts shoppers with the different-sized varieties of pineapple, strawberry or watermelon. A touch of class for one of life's basic chores!

Dieses neue Konzept für Mülltüten greift ein alltägliches Produkt auf, dem es leider an Originalität mangelt. Bei **Rotten' Fruit** ist endlich Schluss mit schlechten Gerüchen in der Küche. Diese neuartigen Müllsäcke riechen wie Früchte und sehen auch so aus. Wie bei einem Taschentuchspender werden die Tüten einfach einzeln entnommen. Die Verpackung besteht vor allem aus transparentem Plastik, durch die das Bild der Frucht sichtbar ist. So fällt die Marke im Regal auf und zieht mit ihren verschieden großen Packungen als Ananas, Erdbeere oder Wassermelone die Aufmerksamkeit der Käufer auf sich. Das veredelt eine ganz normale Haushaltsaufgabe ein wenig!

Ce concept de sacs-poubelles réinvente un objet quotidien dénué d'originalité. Grâce à **Rotten' Fruit**, fini les mauvaises odeurs dans la cuisine, avec de nouveaux sacs qui possèdent la texture et le parfum naturel de différents fruits. Leur emballage identique à celui de mouchoirs en papier facilite leur extraction ; composé principalement de plastique transparent pour laisser voir l'image du fruit, il permet à la marque de se distinguer dans les rayons et d'attirer les regards avec des modèles d'ananas, de fraise et de pastèque dans plusieurs tailles. De quoi doter cette corvée domestique d'une certaine classe !

PENTAWARDS JURY

GÉRARD CARON
France, Chairman of the Pentawards International Jury
+ Regarded as the founder of marketing design in France and Europe. + Set up Carré Noir in 1973 (today a member of the Publicis group). + Co-founder and former president of PDA (Pan-European Brand Design Association). + Author of many publications, organizer of conferences and seminars. + Conceived and designed the website *www.admirabledesign.com*. + Has created no fewer than 1,200 brand identities and 13,000 package designs.

MOYRA CASSEY
UK, Creative Partner, Afterhours
+ Graduated in 1997 from the Glasgow School of Art and started her career at Springetts (UK). + Specialized in brand identity and packaging. + Clients include: Twinings, AkzoNobel, Noble Foods, Mondelēz International and P&G.+ Awards include: Silver, three Golds and a Platinum Pentaward, several Fab Awards (including a Fabulous) and also Fresh, Dieline and Mobius awards (including a best in show).

ISABELLE DAHLBORG LIDSTRÖM
Sweden, Creative Director and Managing Partner at NINE
+ Graduated from Berghs School of Communication and Beckmans Designhögskola in Sweden. + More than 20 years' experience in the international design industry in NYC, Copenhagen and Stockholm. + A passion for solving business challenges by using structural and graphic design, form and function, paired with a deep understanding of the challenges of business and industry. + Awards include: Pentawards, Diamond: Best of Show and several Silver awards, Green Good Design Award, Red Dot Design Award, IF Award, the Water Innovation Awards,

three times Bronze at Guldägget design award, IDEA silver. + Clients include: Sony Ericsson, Astra Tech, Tetra Pak, BillerudKorsnäs, SCA and Carlsberg. + Member of the Berghs School of Communication Advisory Board, the Design Committee of the Swedish Association of Communication Agencies, Spice jury for three years, Eurobest design jury, Guldägget, Core 77 and Kolla.

DAN DITTMAR
USA, Director of Brand Design, BIC USA
+ BS Graphic Design, University of Maryland. + MS Organizational Leadership, Quinnipiac University. + Previous experience leading brand design and packaging identity for the Campbell Soup Company across multiple product categories. + Currently leading brand and packaging identity for all BIC branded categories (BIC Stationery, BIC Lighter and BIC Shaver portfolio segments). + Previous Presenter at Design Management Institute International Conference. + Presenter at Destination Design Management Conference AIGA Metro-North Speaker Panelist.

RAF DE GEYTER
Belgium, Principal Design Manager, P&G
+ Master's in Industrial Design, Artesis Hogeschool Antwerp. + Master's in Marketing Management, Vlerick Leuven Gent Management School, Ghent. + Joined Procter & Gamble in 1998, gaining 15 years' experience in leading package and product design for brands such as Ariel, Lenor, Dreft, Tide, Swiffer and Mr. Clean. + Currently responsible for upstream design innovation programs in fabric care.

DAYTON HENDERSON
USA, Senior Director, Global Design for Kimberly-Clark
+ As design leader, he and his team support Kimberly-Clark's Consumer, Professional and Health Care

businesses in supplying health and hygiene products across the globe. + Began his career as a graphic designer before joining Kimberly-Clark in 1984. + Held varied and progressive design leadership roles for the company while gaining experiences across its businesses. + K-C Design is responsible for design strategies, resources, deployment and training to help build Kimberly-Clark brands. + Awards include: Diamond Pentaward in 2009.

SOMCHANA KANGWARNJIT
Thailand, Executive Creative Director of Prompt Design, Bangkok
+ Graduated from King Mongkut's Institute of Technology Ladkrabang with a degree in industrial design. + Founded Prompt Design in 2009. + Clients include: Nestlé, Pfizer, CP, Kimberly-Clark, L'Oréal, Yuasa. + Jury member for various design competitions. + Guest columnist for different publishers as well as professor at top universities. + Awards include: Gold, Silver and Bronze Pentawards, Asian Young Designer of the Year from Designnet, Dieline, Communicator Awards, ASIA Star Packaging Award.

YOSHIO KATO
Japan, Creative Director and Senior Specialist, Brand Marketing Department, Beverage & Food Business Division, Suntory Beverage & Food
+ Graduated from Aichi Prefectural University of Fine Arts and Music (major in Design) in 1979. + Joined Suntory Design Department in 1979. + 1997: Creative Director and General Manager, Suntory's Design Department. + 2011: Senior Specialist and Creative Director, Suntory Design Department. + 1997: Vice-chairman of the Board, Japan Package Design Association. + 2014: President of the Japan Package Design Association; member of Japan Graphic Designers Association. + 2003–2014: Part-time lecturer at Tokyo-Art University of Fine Art and Music. + 1997–2014: Part-time lecturer at Aichi University of Fine Arts and Music. + 2008–2014: Part-time lecturer at Tama Art University Department of Graphics.

KYU-WOO KU
South Korea, Managing Director of the Aekyung Design Centre, Seoul
+ Graduated from Dankook University in 1983. + Joined Aekyung Industrial Design Department in 1991. + External positions: President of Korea Package Design Association, Vice-president of Korea Design Management Association. + Design Organization Member of the Asian Games Organizing Committee for 2014.

SARAH MOFFAT
USA, Creative Director at Turner Duckworth: London & San Francisco
+ Born and raised in the North of England, she has been with Turner Duckworth since graduating from Kingston University with a graphic design degree. + After eight years in the London studio, she joined the San Francisco team. + Responsible for the strategic and creative output of the US studio, as well as the constant exchange of ideas and design critiques for the London studio. + Clients include: Coca-Cola, Waitrose, Mondelēz, Kraft and Levi's. + Awards include: a Cannes Lions Grand Prix, a Grammy and a D&AD Pencil and several Pentawards.

CHRIS PLEWES
Canada, Vice-president and Creative Director at Davis Design
+ Creative Director at Davis Design with over 30 years of branding and package design experience. – Having resided in Singapore and Toronto, he has extensive experience in global and regional brands. + With Davis he is active on large and small branding assignments in US, Canadian, European and Asian markets.

CHRISTOPHE PRADÈRE
France, CEO and Founder of BETC Design Paris
+ Master's in design from Domus Academy in Milan in 1992. + Euro RSCG Design 1995–2000: responsible for the retail and corporate design divisions of clients such as Air France, Peugeot and also luxury brands such as Lancôme and Christofle. + Founded BETC Design in 2001. + Focus on global design and design management approaches in the creative industry markets for customers including: Orange, Air France, Peugeot, Louis Vuitton, Rémy Martin, Louis XIII, Chivas, Jean-Paul Gaultier, L'Oréal and Piper Heidsieck. + He develops his brand experience through a holistic approach combining social sciences, marketing and global creative strategy. + Lecturer posts: Parsons School for Design, IFM, ESSEC, École Nationale Supérieure des Arts Décoratifs and SKEMA Business School.

JONATHAN SANDS
UK, Chairman of Elmwood
+ Jonathan Sands led a management buyout of Elmwood in 1989, aged 27. + With offices in Asia, North America and Europe, Elmwood is an ideas-based branding business and Jonathan in particular always has the courage of his convictions. + Clients include: ASDA, BBC, Durex, The COI, Glasgow 2014, McCain, Royal Mail, Nestlé and Nike.

GRAHAM SHEARSBY
UK, Group Creative Director of Design Bridge
+ Graham Shearsby is Executive Group Creative Director and, with the help of his team of creative directors, he oversees the three studios in London, Amsterdam and Singapore. + Born in East London, Graham entered the creative world in 1979, straight from school. + Joined the John Blackburn Partnership as a studio junior and won a D&AD Yellow Pencil for Typography for Cockburn's Ports in 1985. + Joining Allied International Designers in 1986, he met his future partners in what would, later that year, become

the fledgling Design Bridge. + Graham has spearheaded the company's creative growth and seen it acquire a wealth of international awards.

JAMIE STONE
Singapore, Global Head of Design / Nutrition, GSK
A UK-born graduate of Northumbria University, Design for Industry Degree in the class of 2001. + He went on to work as an in-house designer for P&G for five years, before leaving to set up Stone | Product Design, as a start-up design agency offering 3D and 2D design services to the multitude of P&G brand teams. Stone | Product Design merged into NewEdge in early 2008. + Partner and Head of Design for NewEdge, a UK/USA- based Design / Strategy / Research agency with a primary focus on creating, sizing and delivering NDP pipelines for FMCG clients including P&G, Kellogg's and Kraft. + Based in Singapore, with a seat on the Nutrition Leadership team, he has overall responsibility for all creative strategy and output in 3D Structural Design, Technical Design, Branded Package Design, BTL and In-Store Activation for the full Nutrition portfolio.

GREGORY TSAKNAKIS
Greece, Creative Director and Manager of Mousegraphics, Athens
+ Born in Thessaloniki in 1963, he studied Graphic Design at the Technological Institute in Athens and almost simultaneously started Mousegraphics. + With some luck, attitude and of course, great love for design, he started working on packaging design. + Over the past 25 years, Mousegraphics has grown and today employs 11 people working on projects in all fields of visual branding. + Awards include: Pentawards, Epica Award, Red Dot Communication Design Award, German Design Award, the Dieline, European Design Award, Ermis Award and the Greek Graphic Design & Illustration Award.

INDEX

INDEX

IMPRINT

**EACH AND EVERY TASCHEN BOOK
PLANTS A SEED!**
TASCHEN is a carbon neutral publisher. Each year,
we offset our annual carbon emissions with carbon credits
at the Instituto Terra, a reforestation program in Minas
Gerais, Brazil. To find out more about this ecological
partnership, please check: www.taschen.com/zerocarbon
Inspiration: unlimited. Carbon footprint: zero.

To stay informed about TASCHEN and our upcoming
titles, please subscribe to our free magazine at
www.taschen.com/magazine, download our magazine
app for iPad, follow us on Twitter and Facebook,
or e-mail your questions to contact@taschen.com.

© 2014 TASCHEN GmbH
Hohenzollernring 53, D-50672 Köln
www.taschen.com

Editor
Julius Wiedemann
Editorial Coordination
Daniel Siciliano Bretas and Nora Dohrmann

Design
Sense/Net, Andy Disl and Birgit Eichwede, Cologne
Layout
Peter Frommann and Daniel Siciliano Bretas
Production
Stefan Klatte and Ute Wachendorf

English Revision
Chris Allen
German Translation
Jürgen Dubau
French Translation
Valérie Lavoyer for Delivering iBooks & Design, Barcelona

Printed in Germany
ISBN 978-3-8365-5382-7